MY FAMILY
AND OTHER
DISASTERS

MY FAMILY AND OTHER DISASTERS

LUCY MANGAN

guardianbooks

Published by Guardian Books 2009

2 4 6 8 10 9 7 5 3 1

First published in Great Britain in 2009 by
Guardian Books
Kings Place, 90 York Way
London N1 9GU

www.guardianbooks.co.uk

A CIP catalogue record for this book
is available from the British Library

ISBN 978-0-85265-124-7

Typeset by Palimpsest Book Production Limited,
Grangemouth, Stirlingshire

Printed and bound in Great Britain by CPI Bookmarque,
Croydon, Surrey

CONTENTS

INTRODUCTION

The purest thrill experienced by any editor comes when he or she trips over a seam of raw, undiscovered talent. It happens very rarely, perhaps a handful of times in any career. And on the face of it there wasn't much about the painfully diffident young woman doing work experience on the *Guardian*'s G2 section to suggest one of those delicious moments was in the offing.

Unusually, among the stream of wannabe journalists offering their labour for free in exchange for a taste of newspaper life and line on their CV, Lucy had qualified as a lawyer and I remember being mildly intrigued by the speed with which she had thought better of the career she had spent years training for. To the best of my recollection, she barely uttered a word during her first week in the office. But then came the hamster piece.

It was one of those assignments every features journalist dreads. Some headline-courting designer or other had successfully courted outraged headlines by announcing that they were going to produce a coat from 100 hamster pelts. But what would happen if you tried to produce your own? How would pet suppliers react to a bulk rodent order – and the gradual realisation of what it was for?

It required industrial quantities of chutzpah simply to walk into several London pet shops and make the outlandish enquiry, but as soon as Lucy filed we knew we had stumbled over much more than that. Rereading it five years on I still find myself crying with laughter at her account of calling the Worshipful Company of Skinners in search of advice: 'Let me ask the beadle,' says the man who answers the phone. I hear a muffled shout. "Ted – I've got someone here who wants to skin a hamster." It sounds bad when he says it.' Or her attempt to procure the requisite number of pelts from Harrods: 'A man in green overalls opens the pet house door. Customers aren't allowed inside in case they distress the animals. This does not bode well. Still, I ask brightly, how many hamsters could I buy today? There is yet another pause. My afternoon is becoming distinctly Pinteresque.'

It was clear that Lucy was blessed with comic timing and a deliciously arch prose style but it took a while longer to discover that she even came preloaded with a wealth of material that made her a natural columnist. First, there were the assorted prejudices and idiosyncrasies. Her intense dislike of children – 'the bane of my life ever since I first turned up at primary school and found myself surrounded by the little buggers.' Or her even more intense dislike of foreign countries: 'Nowadays, to spend your summer holiday in Britain is to make people suspect that you are either secretly destitute or still on limited licence after a recent parole.' Or her obsessive parsimony: 'I spent the formative years of my life chronically dehydrated by a household rule that stipulated that you couldn't have a drink with soup.' Or her famously absent – congenitally missing rather than just deficient – sense of smell.

Then there was the sitcom-ready cast of characters who soon became familiar from her weekly columns. Chief among them of course is Lucy's mother, the rather ferocious, gin-swilling displaced northerner (she hasn't left Lewisham in 30 years except to go 'home') who 'believes that the rules of grammar are semi-divine and wholly immutable' and 'darns everything, including leftovers and the paper napkins we all steal from cafes.' Then there is Mr Mangan bumbling amiably along in the background of this terrifying matriarchy. 'We lost track of him somewhere around Boxing Day, but Dad is believed to be still alive and happy somewhere in the house.'

Unsurprisingly, a favourite topic of Mangan enthusiasts is the extent to which the characters so acidly drawn in her columns bear any relation to the real members of her family. One of my favourites was one in which she relates the conversation when she calls her parents to tell them that she is to marry. 'What's that noise? [She asks after sharing the good news with her father.] Well, if she's actually kicked the stool away, you should probably go and get her down. You know – just hold her legs and unhook it, like you did when I got that B at A-level.'

Meeting Lucy's parents for the first time at her wedding I asked whether they minded their cartoonish depiction. It did grate very occasionally, allowed Mrs M, but the account of the engagement phone call was by no means unrepresentative.

Although Lucy – or Manganese as she is known at the *Guardian* for reasons I can no longer remember or perhaps never existed – has only written for the paper for five years, she has established a following every bit as large and devoted as some of the title's most celebrated contributors. The moment I realised that she was on the way to becoming a fully-fledged star was when, in the space of a week, I was asked about her by both a famous novelist and my (somewhat exacting) mother-in-law. My mother-in-law, who bears a passing resemblance to the maternal character in Lucy's columns (except that she makes Mrs M look profligate), is not a woman who is easily impressed. As long as I have known her she has been studiedly underwhelmed by accounts of encounters (strictly in the line of business) with top politicians or even A-list movie types. But when the subject of Lucy came up her eyes widened and she couldn't resist: 'Have you actually *met* Lucy Mangan?'

Ian Katz, deputy editor of the *Guardian*

CHAPTER ONE

I, WEIRDO

'I'd like to buy 100 hamsters, please'

When the news broke that hamster-skin coats had gone on sale in the super-posh House of Bruar in Perthshire, the only question in my mind was – how quickly could I fling myself on a Caledonian-bound train and purchase one? Then a friend pointed out that someone of my limited means should not be splashing out £1,750 on anything she can't live in or drive away. Only one avenue therefore remained open – I would have to make a coat of many epidermises myself. But who would sell me the necessary 100 rodents? And what would I do with them once I had got them.

The Worshipful Company of Skinners turns out to be no help at all. 'I'm sorry,' says a kindly man on the other end of the phone, 'I'm afraid we've had nothing to do with the fur trade for 300 years now. We do charity work with the endowments old fur traders have given us, though.'

That is very bad news, I tell him sorrowfully. How am I going to find someone who can teach me how to skin a hamster? There is a pause. 'I've no idea, madam,' he says, still kindly. 'We wouldn't have skinned hamsters anyway. We worked with ermines, mostly – "for people of exalted rank", as we used to say.' But we live in a democracy now. Surely it's time for a less elitist approach to flaying small animals. Another pause. 'Let me ask the beadle,' he says. I hear a muffled shout. 'Ted – I've got someone here who wants to skin a hamster.' It sounds bad when he says it. He comes back. 'I'm sorry, we're drawing blanks here,' he says. A taxidermist is the only thing I can think of.'

Never mind. After all, as Mrs Beeton once almost said, first you must catch your hamster. After several abortive attempts to contact the National Hamster Council and the British Hamster Association, I decide to try another tack. The Bruar coat is made from special Russian hamsters, after all, so why not tap into the top end of the market? If Harrods will open after hours for Skeletal Spice's shopping trips, surely it will be willing to accommodate my request during normal working hours? I tuck a copy of the *Daily Mail*'s article about what they accurately term 'the hamster coat' under my arm and set off.

A man in green overalls opens the pet house door. Customers aren't allowed inside in case they distress the animals. This does not bode well. Still, I ask brightly, how many hamsters could I buy today? There is yet another pause. My afternoon is becoming distinctly Pinteresque. 'How many do you want?' Mr Overalls replies. About 100. His face takes on a guarded look. I become momentarily hopeful that I have stumbled across a gatekeeper to the hamster-trading netherworld, but instead of inviting me into the pet house for further discussion and the exchange of untraceable small bills, he asks what I want them for. 'There's a business opportunity I saw in the paper today,' I say. 'I thought I'd get a piece of this action.' He looks at me. This is not a bonding moment. Figuring I have nothing to lose, I show him the article. It negates the need for further explanation. 'We would only sell them as pets,' he says sternly. 'We're fully accredited by the Pet Care Trust, and so will anyone else be if you try them.'

Is there a hamster wholesaler he could put me in touch with? 'We have our sources but they would only sell them as pets too.' I give up. Honestly, no wonder Britain's losing its primacy in the world order when entrepreneurship is thwarted at every turn.

Hurlingham Pet Shop on the New King's Road is markedly less salubrious than Harrods. Inside, I find a scene of almost Dickensian charm. Three children (sisters Stacey, 14, Martina, 11 and Stevie, eight) are perched precariously on various bundles of bedding and bags of cat litter, hugging animals to their chests and discussing in impassioned voices which one they should buy. One of the potential pets is a hamster. This could be tricky.

I feel like Cruella de Vil. I point to a hamster still in its cage. Could I have 100 of those? 'No,' explains a young man, who is called Lee. 'Those sort of fight together.' That wouldn't be a problem, I say, pushing the article towards him. He does not notice. 'You want Chinese or Russian hamsters?' he asks. Indeed I do! I wave the paper in front of him – he has read my mind! At last Lee takes the article and begins an admirably thorough perusal. Meanwhile, the child with the hamster invites me to stroke it. I decline graciously. 'I'm not very keen on hamsters,' I say, with one eye fixed meaningfully on Lee. 'That's a nice colour, though.'

Eventually Lee looks up. I've never seen naked horror on a human face before. 'So,' I say optimistically, 'How about it?' 'This is what you want them for?' he says.

'Yes!' I exclaim delightedly.

'We couldn't . . . We wouldn't . . .' he croaks. 'You really want to make a coat out of hamsters? That's – that's not nice.'

Hearing the words 'coat' and 'hamster' the three children are drawn to us like iron filings to a magnet. 'What does she want?' asks the middle one. I flinch from her accusing eyes. I want to make a coat. What's wrong with that? 'Animals,' says the smallest one, struggling for expression, 'deserve to live.'

But I want a coat. They are unmoved by my passion for fashion. 'If anyone killed my hamster, I'd get a machete and kill them so they'd know what it was like,' says the middle one. The oldest one sums up the general sentiment in the room. 'You are so cruel. Get out of this shop,' she demands and the rest, including Lee, wholeheartedly concur. The smaller one is shaking her head. 'Killing hamsters – that's deep, man. That is deep.'

Confronted with this appalled quartet, I crack. I'm not really a hamster killer, I'm a journalist trying to find out if anyone would indulge my depraved desires. And, I am delighted to tell them, nobody would. Eventually, after some confusion ('What was you going to do with all the hamsters when you got them, then?'), matters are settled to everyone's satisfaction, and I am allowed to leave the shop with my own skin intact.

3 MARCH 2004

I do not smell

I am not a fully sentient being. To those who have seen me first thing in the morning, this will come as no surprise. But in this case I am referring to the fact that I am congenitally anosmic; or, as I more helpfully put it when people thrust perfumed articles under my nose and invite an opinion on the aroma, I was born without a sense of smell.

It took until I was seven to convince my mother. She reluctantly acknowledged the truth of my claim ('Air! It's just air, Mummy!') after making me sniff the fumes from her bottle of nail varnish remover until I looked up hopefully and said: 'My eyes are burning – is that what you mean?'

Although I would still privilege that experience over the time I was persuaded by well-meaning school friends that, as I couldn't smell Emma Webster's perfume, I should drink it. This was, I recall, on the grounds that taste and smell are so closely linked that it would give me at least some idea of the delicious scent I was missing. Alas, all it taught me was that perfume is not a viable beverage, and all it taught the rest was that White Musk-laced vomit still smells, ineluctably, like vomit.

Max Christian, a fellow congenital anosmic, whose website (maxuk.net) has several pages devoted to the subject, had similar difficulties. 'My first girlfriend's parents were industrial chemists,' he says. 'They didn't believe me either, so they gave me a bottle of concentrated hydrochloric acid, just to be sure. What they hadn't realised is that I would hold it right under my nose before trying to smell it.

'Apparently that's not something [normal] people would actually be capable of. Before anyone could stop me, I had inhaled enough fumes to keep all past, present and future members of the Grateful Dead happy for a week.'

Naturally, the problems of being olfactorily challenged don't compare to those that attend blindness or deafness, but certain accommodations do have to be made, which you only fully appreciate when you start living alone. I had enough sense to buy a smoke alarm, but it wasn't until my sister called round and nearly collapsed from the smell of a hob burner I had accidentally switched on that I realised I needed something that would alert me aurally to gas leaks before I blew up the street. The good people of Corgi eventually put me in touch with www.besltd.uk, which sells such detectors. A few bouts of food poisoning alerted me to the fact that I can eat, unperturbed, food which would cause those with functioning nasal passages to don hazmat suits and call in the public health authorities. I now shop every two days, check best-before dates assiduously and treat three-day-old milk with the respect it deserves.

I have also learned to stock my shelves with visitors as well as myself in mind. So I have fruit teas in the house even though they appear to be nothing more than an expensive way of colouring a mug of hot water, wine (variants on a vinegar theme to my useless palate, but people look bewildered when you offer them hot chocolate with everything) and herbs, even though they are a matter of supreme indifference to me. When I cook for other people and a recipe says 'season to taste', I consult my written list of what green bits are supposed to complement what, add them until the dish looks decorated enough and hope for the best. I'm still mastering garlic.

My mother – possibly in an attempt to make up for earlier acetone abuse – used to smell all my clothes for me, but now I have to operate a strict rota and wash everything after I've worn it once. Occasionally, of course, the system breaks down, and for those who have had to sit next to me at work or on the tube at those times, I can only apologise.

On the other hand, I am a very good babysitter. I can't smell nappies or any of the preliminary gases that tell you something spectacular is on its way, so I have to watch my charges like a hawk for the brief cessations of activity and that faraway look in their eyes that tells me they are about to excrete something delightful. No kid is going to fall into a pond or lynch itself from a bunk bed on my watch. Although we may burn to a crisp if a fire starts out of eyeshot, of course.

I subscribe to the 'what you've never had, you never miss' school of thought, as does Christian and many of the visitors to his site, but for those who lose their sense of smell later in life – through viral infections, nasal surgery or head trauma – the effect on their quality of life can be enormous. 'I see a great number of people who are seriously depressed after losing their sense of smell,' says David Roberts, ear, nose and throat consultant at Guy's and St Thomas's hospital in London. 'It's a very emotive sense, ingrained in us, in our pleasures – like mating and sexual desire – and in our warning systems. The nerves stimulated by smell send messages to one of the oldest, most primitive parts of our brain, which is why it's so integral to our lives.'

Professor Tim Jacob at Cardiff University, who researches olfaction and had to start a second website when anosmics read about his work on the first one and started inundating him with requests for information, agrees. 'You will have found other ways of adapting, using texture and consistency to get information about food. But other people get very disturbed [by the loss],' he says.

'The tongue can only distinguish the four basic tastes: bitter, sweet, salty, sour. Smell detects flavour and nuance, so they lose all significant sense of taste. About 17 per cent become clinically depressed – they become oversensitive about having body odour and frightened of going out.'

And those are just the obvious things. As Jacob also notes: 'You lose lots of subliminal information and links with the emotional centre of the brain. Smells are inextricably linked with memories and form the backdrop to your sensory experience. They are tremendously evocative. The smell of your first girlfriend's perfume or boyfriend's aftershave, anything associated with strong emotion, will always trigger a rush of memory.'

I am beginning to feel quite intrigued by this unknown world, but this quickly deepens into concern about what else I am missing. 'And, of course, you are attracted to people who smell different from you because it suggests they have a different immunotype,' says Jacob. 'It's the evolutionary system trying to get you to pass on two sets of immunity advantages to your offspring.'

Galvanised by the thought of spawning only sickly, wizened mites, I ask about treatment. For those who have lost their sense of smell through infection or damage, the news is relatively good. 'They usually regain some ability because the olfactory nerve, unlike the rest of the dozen cranial nerves, is capable of regeneration,' says Roberts. Steroid-based drug treatments can help further. Nasal polyps causing blockages to olfactory passageways can be treated medically and surgically. But, as one might expect, less can be done to rectify congenital causes.

I will have to soldier on, and draw what comfort I can from a recent exchange with an ex-boyfriend who, as we reminisced about our relationship, said wistfully: 'You were the best girlfriend in the world. You let me bring curry home from the pub every night and I could fart as much as I liked.' I'm putting it in my next personal ad.

20 JULY 2004

Suffer, little children

I hate children. I hate animals too, but I thought admitting the former would bring me fewer death threats. Plus, animals are relatively easily avoided if you live in London and remember to check people for cat hair and Pedigree Chum smears before you make friends with them.

Children, on the other hand, have been the bane of my life ever since I first turned up at primary school and found myself surrounded by the little buggers. And as American writer Florence King so rightly points out in her autobiography, *Confessions of a Failed Southern Lady*: 'The worst thing was, it appeared that I was one of them. I hadn't known that before. I thought I was just short.'

She was lucky. I was short as well, which left me prey to enormous older girls with ra-ra skirts and nascent maternal longings who would pick me up and cart me round the playground long after I had volubly expressed my lack of zeal for this proceeding ('I'm going to kill you. And all your pets'). I didn't much like boys either, but at least their investigations into the vexed question of how far one can throw a midget across asphalt had a dispassionate, scientific aspect about them that I admired. The answer, for those of you unable to avail yourselves of an 18th-century travelling freak show to conduct your own scientific inquiry, is about three yards, the length of a hopscotch grid. It was also empirically proven that a protective parka is aerodynamically unsound and should therefore be wrenched from the protesting midget's feeble grasp before the project is undertaken.

I thought I'd be free of their malevolent ways by now, but in fact they're still having a decidedly negative effect on my quality of life. If they're not being rolled in bubble wrap and driven the 37 yards between their front door and school in a Sherman tank in front of my bus, they're disturbing my morning reverie with their lively demonstrations of ringtones, bullying and, in one memorable instance, self-piercing.

As an additional disturbance to my equilibrium, their juvenile sociopathy forces me, via the National Code of Dissatisfied English People (head-shaking, lip-pursing, the otherwise lost art of tut-tutting), into unwilling coalition with dead-eyed women wearing 'I love Jim Davidson' badges and men who are clearly on their way home to polish their Nazi memorabilia collections before a hard evening's masturbating over pictures of Princess Michael of Kent.

Now my friends are having babies. The last one I visited gave me an unsolicited 20-minute peroration on pureed peas, while leaking from orifices I barely knew existed. And while I am grateful to another for my induction into a hitherto unsuspected world of cloacal knowledge, I fear this information will aid me little in my quest to make enough new friends to replace the ones crushed by infant tyrants.

But kids aren't content with wreaking havoc on individual lives. They like to work on a broader canvas, too. For example, it is their inability to distinguish between a supersize Mars bar and a long and healthy life that is forcing the makers of such snacks to withdraw them from sale. Why are they letting themselves be dictated to in this way? Why are adults being denied the opportunity to eat their own bodyweight in one handy bar of pleasure if they so choose? A king-size Twix is not a toy. It's designed to get people through the kind of problems that only grown-ups suffer, such as divorce, redundancy, or the eighteenth series of *Where the Heart Is*.

Newsagents should simply be banned from selling the big stuff to the small fry. The hunt to find rogue traders willing to breach the regulations will fill the void left since selling cigarettes to minors became punishable by death rather than a gentle ticking-off from a kindly bobby as it was in my (admittedly emphysemic) youth, and no longer worth the 300 per cent mark-up it occasioned. And all that scouting around will help the little blobs lose weight, too. Although we need to be careful – if they start slimming down and getting more energetic, they'll need somewhere to work it off and start asking what happened to all the playing fields.

I know it's not all their fault, of course. Their unformed atavistic souls know no better, and if there are no parents around to peel their fat fingers off whatever fabulous confections of hydrogenated vegetable fat and sucrose take their fancy, then I suppose Mr Cadbury et al have to do it for them. And now, if you will excuse me, I have some memorabilia to polish.

29 SEPTEMBER 2004

Why, Miss Mangan, you're beautiful

As with sex, so with makeup. There exists in a girl's life a brief window of opportunity (roughly between the ages of 14 and 17) for experimentation and honing technique, for discovering what works for you and what doesn't, and deciding what's an essential weapon in the armoury and what's an only-to-be-deployed-when-aiming-to-make-a-truly-irresistible-assault howitzer. If, as I did, you miss that opportunity (in my case through parental disapproval of cosmetics as a risible misdirection of energies that could be more usefully applied to GCSEs and piano practice), then you are liable to remain woefully ignorant of and intimidated by the subject, until some kindly, more experienced soul happens along to show you the ropes. Thus when a vision of loveliness detached herself from the fashion desk and wandered over to mine to ask, in impressively diplomatic terms, whether I would like to avail myself of the chance to write about getting a makeover at the hands of skilled professionals, I leapt at it.

Thus came I to find myself in a cold studio in Hackney, east London, surrounded by a veritable phalanx of people preparing to teach me the rudiments of the cosmetic arts. Hair first. 'Who cuts it usually?' says the lovely Hamilton – who is far more charming than I expected of someone used to dealing with the lustrous locks of celebrities rather than skanky journalists, and who does much to arrest my spiralling fear of impending humiliation. 'I think she's called Val,' I whisper, thinking of the bored woman who occasionally passes blood-flecked scissors over my head in the local high-street salon while dropping fag ash down my neck. It's enough to give Hamilton the measure of the problem and he takes matters into his own swift and sure hands, cuts for a few minutes and removes my resemblance to a 1950s schoolgirl. I gain courage and ask if there is any way I could have a fringe without looking like Milly-Molly-Mandy.

'We must be psychic!' he grins. 'I was hoping I could give you a sweeping fringe.' I have no idea what he means but by this stage I would lie down in front of oncoming traffic if he asked me to, so I nod wordless but fervent agreement. He flashes his (unflecked) scissors again and hands me over to Ruby Hammer (co-creator of Ruby & Millie cosmetics) who will do my makeup.

'What do you normally wear?' she asks, briskly but kindly.

'Nothing.'

'If you're going out?'

'Mascara, lipstick and a two-in-one powdery foundation thing.' Which I've had for three years, I neglect to add, having decided during the preceding sleepless night that minimal information provision is a wise course of self-protective action.

'In that case,' she says, 'I'm going to keep it fairly simple, so that you'll feel you can try recreating it at home. I'm not interested in showing people things they'll be scared to try themselves – what's the point of that?'

Ruby is positive and practical. My skin's not bad at all, she tells me, though the dark circles under my eyes need help, and I should start using eyelash curlers because my eyes (while a good colour) slope downwards. This pragmatic approach is very soothing, as is the certainty with which she plucks, moisturises, eyeshadows, blends, mascaras, and glosses and conceals as necessary, all the while dispensing advice and reassurance.

I can't tell you how strange it feels to abdicate responsibility and have someone look after me like this. It's like being a child again, and I am enchanted with both the process and the results. This temporary regression is the only reason I can give for the sudden and otherwise inexplicable desire to cry that occurs as Ruby finishes. Fortunately, it passes before I do anything embarrassing – and, more importantly, before I ruin my lovely makeup, which (once I am out of the unforgiving fluorescent lights) makes me look . . . well, how I've always wanted to look: feminine, not frightening; different, not desperate. As the old song has it – 'I like it, I love it, I want some more of it'. So, if you will excuse me, I'm off to brave a cosmetics counter. And to hell with piano practice.

19 FEBRUARY 2005

Do you believe in yetis?

In a week where the American courts are playing God with Terri Schiavo, ministers ecclesiastical and political here are joining together to make moral issues into election issues, and Jamie Oliver is being hailed as the new messiah, you can only admire the *Journal of Psychology* for further muddying the secular versus religious waters by publishing a study from the University of Minnesota supporting the idea that there is, as the tabloids put it, a 'God gene'. Or, to quote the slightly more sober terms of the report: 'These findings support the hypothesis that the heritability of religiousness increases from adolescence to adulthood'. This seems to be the sociological way of saying that being born into religious families is the most powerful determinant of the degree of belief held by children (and presumably of the likelihood that they will end up telekinetic and doused in pig's blood during that rocky adolescent period), but that a genetic predisposition plays a significant part in whether they continue to believe into adulthood.

As I sit here at my parents' kitchen table, looking out of the window at my mother zigzagging between flowerbeds like some kind of post-menopausal pinball as she plants out 50 triffid seedlings in the lashing wind and rain because this is the day she has earmarked for gardening and because she is not a woman to amend a self-imposed timetable due to a footling matter like adverse weather conditions, I can only hope there is nothing in heredity. Given that she also has a 36DD bust, thighs like an Indian brave and I look like – well, uncannily like one of the triffid seedlings – my hopes are reasonably high.

As far as belief goes – well, that's trickier. For starters, the only reason I am here enjoying a brief sojourn at the Ministry of Love is because a childhood dream could be about to come true. A short walk (or, in days of yore, a heavily supervised bike ride) away is Sydenham Park, where, early on Tuesday morning, a man putting his pet moggy out was attacked by a rather larger member of the feline family that was later described by a police officer (who belied all accepted stereotypes of his breed by arriving on the scene within minutes) as 'about the size of a labrador'.

Confusing species-conflation notwithstanding, I was delighted. I have always had a soft spot for Beast of Bodminesque sightings, Loch Ness monster rumours, the yeti legend, and so on. They appeal to the small streak of irrationality that runs through me despite my best efforts to scrub it out, in much the same way that my love of country music indulges an equally stubborn vein of sentimentality, which might otherwise result in having babies or Athena posters around the place.

But it's an irrational streak that is not quite strong enough to allow me to believe in God, although I'm not sure whether this is because I do not have the VMAT2 gene or because I lack the need to believe that there is an ultimate explanation for everything, deeply obscured by the broiling chaos of humanity and inhumanity though it may be. This seems to demand a degree of control freakery which is missing from my makeup, although – glancing out of the window again at a woman who is now snipping ivy shoots above windowsill level as a raging storm gathers – I can hardly see how.

The Loch Ness monster et al appeal because they are implausible but are just – just – within the realms of possibility. I don't believe Nessie exists but I hope – I hope, I hope, I hope – that there is in the loch a surviving relic or unique offshoot of prehistoric times that has simply escaped full sighting and identification for aeons, such as the coelacanth, but with extra humps. The yeti likewise, but with extra fur and lung capacity. I'd like the Beast of Bodmin eventually to be revealed as a sabre-toothed tiger but I'll happily settle for a panther.

Such legends indulge the need for mystery in life, but they require hope rather than faith, and as we have somehow arrived at a state when it seems to be the former that is in shorter supply, particularly in politics (which should be enough to scare anyone witless), I'm going to sit here at the table and keep my fingers crossed that a labrador-sized cat will at some point today pad his sinewy way across the garden.

Either that, or I'll start praying to God that I am not now looking at my rain-soaked mother on her hands and knees tidying the compost heap.

23 MARCH 2005

Hell is other countries

I think I was, as those much-neglected philosophers the Pony-Tails once put it, born too late. A generation ago, I understand, people were happy if they got to load themselves and the kids on to a train bound for Brighton and spend a week washing away their cares and rickets by the freezing sea. Two generations back and the masses were content to sniff the bustle of one of their betters who had just taken a bracing walk around the entailed estate.

Nowadays, however, to spend your summer holiday in Britain is to make people suspect that you are either secretly destitute or still on limited licence after parole. And you can't even dispel their fears any more with a quick trip across the channel. Mainland Europe has been drained of its exoticism. Where we were once content to explore, according to age and taste, the sophistications of France, the charms of Italy or the numberless attractions of Spanish islands willing to host scenes of Caligulan debauchery every summer, this will no longer do. Now if you don't go kayaking on the Limpopo, carve pogo sticks with a lost Patagonian tribe or teach the River Cafe cookbook to the ape creatures of the Indus, you can consider it an annual leave wasted.

I don't. Now that the choice of where to go and what to do is entirely my own, I stay at home. I read, watch television, have friends round – everything I enjoy doing in my leisure hours, but for longer stretches. It's free, easy and enjoyable, though I do occasionally need someone to come in and turn me on the sofa to avoid pressure sores. The only real downside is that over the years, as the perception of foreign holidays has shifted from novel luxury to something akin to a statutory right, is that from June until August I find myself too frequently embroiled in conversations that start: 'So, where are you going on holiday this year?'

'Nowhere,' I reply. 'You must be,' insists the already appalled interlocutor. To which, of course, I can only reply – why must I?

I have left these shores twice in my lifetime, and I fully hope and expect never to do so again. Being fair-skinned and yet liberally spattered with moles just begging to turn melanomic, lying in the sun holds few attractions and anything that promises a more acceptable climate usually involves exercise – skiing, snowboarding, climbing, hiking – which to a woman of my negligible co-ordination and fitness levels would render the fortnight more akin to a heavily punitive regime than a fun furlough. It has been empirically proven that weekend breaks with partners are the most common cause of axe murder among 24-to-35-year-olds and anyone who deems flying to New York for a shopping trip fun is a certifiable fool with an over-extended credit card where their brain should be.

I'd like to claim that my untravelled history is the result of a principled stand against the destructive tourist industry. I dare say I could keep a speech up my sleeve about the air industry being a major polluter of the planet and indirectly and unwittingly subsidised by the taxpayer in the form of fuel tax concessions. Or one about the number of peaceful hamlets which were one minute happily playing host to the odd traveller who had stumbled across it, the next, watching in horror as thousands descend like locusts in leisurewear, nibbling every stalk of 'authenticity' and character down to the nub. Or about the tiresome smugness of gap-year types who think that a couple of months trekking through Nepal gives them all the insight into life's great questions they will ever need and a bout of amoebic dysentery in a developing country somehow pre-emptively purges them of all the sins they're going to commit in order to make sure of that job at McKinsey in three years' time.

Such a justification would be at best the partial truth. A larger portion of my domestic inclinations can be explained as a reaction to this creeping concept of compulsory holidaying in order to become a fully paid-up member of an unnamed club. People's insistence on finding ever-more fabulous vacations is an adult form of peer pressure that I had hoped to leave behind once I emerged from my school days. Just as I could never understand why I should drag myself out clubbing when I had no sense of rhythm, or shag some clueless, pustular boy-shaped bag of sweat when I had no real desire to contract chlamydia, I cannot understand why I should be expected to go on holiday when I have not the slightest scintilla of an urge to do so.

Such an explanation, however, only goes so far. It is fairly easy, after all, to resist peer pressure if you don't see the inherent attraction of the club's *raison d'être*. So why do I not have the urge to jet off to distant lands? I'd like to state up front that it's not xenophobia. I have no detectable distaste for foreign culture, people or languages and I speak semi-fluent French and Spanish.

Undoubtedly what keeps me at home is partly genetic. I take after my mother in more ways than I care to enumerate, and she hasn't left Lewisham in 30 years except to go 'home', as she still refers to Preston half a lifetime after she left it. Thus my formative holiday experiences were all, of maternal necessity, domestic. Easter meant a week up north with grandma, who would encourage me and my sister to eat our own bodyweight in Bakewell slices and wine gums, then walk it off along the riverbank while she peeled a sack of potatoes for the next meal. Summer meant two weeks with grandma flirting with Type 2 diabetes and death by drowning.

It's also partly experience. It is not difficult to distinguish between either of my trips abroad and a riotous success. The first time I set out for distant lands I was 16 on a disastrous student exchange trip to France, a week I still cannot recall without curling into a foetal knot, which makes it hard to type any further details.

My second expedition abroad was ten years later, when an extremely well-travelled friend became so exasperated with my insularity that she renewed my passport, booked me a plane ticket and took me with her and eight friends to a villa in Tuscany. It was actually quite a nice week. I hosted a series of fresh meat conferences for mosquitoes and I wouldn't leave the villa until someone bought me factor 40 suncream (essentially a cardigan in a bottle), but after that I saw Sienna, Florence, Pisa and innumerable duomos, all of which were marvellous.

Then I came home to the news that grandma was dying and I had to hightail it up there just in time to say goodbye, thank her for all the wine gums and force her tiny wizened hand to sign a codicil that ensured I got her enamel bread bin when she breathed her last 20 minutes later. Still, valuable additions to my collection of late-40s homeware notwithstanding, it took the edge off the Tuscan furlough and did little to lessen my antipathy towards leaving the country.

Simple slothfulness has a lot to answer for, too. Given that some days it's all I can do to muster the energy for a bowel movement, arranging a holiday was always going to be an unlikely undertaking, especially now that it would also require dispelling so many years' accrued ignorance. I have no idea how to book a flight, hire a car, recognise a good hotel, convert currencies and, oh, how little I care. Not convinced? Add up the number of holiday disasters – flight cancellations, mildewed hotels, multitudinous forms of diarrhoea, stolen bags, lost luggage, relationship breakdowns, blah-di-endless-blah – and the number of resounding successes. The bad will very comfortably outweigh the good.

Ultimately, though, my travel-phobia is as much to do with how much I like staying at home. For a start, this is the only circumstance in which my control freakery and selfishness can be fully accommodated to nobody's detriment. No hotel is going to be run entirely to my specifications and with solely my convenience in mind in the way that my flat is. No travelling companion is going to let me spend my time off exactly as I like best – reading books, watching television, reading more books and going to bed at 2am with a packet of chocolate digestives and another book. One or other of us is quickly going to go demented. Sharing a house with friends is bad enough on native soil – throw in the

stresses of an unfamiliar locale, the necessity of finding a compromise among people crushed under the pressure to relax, have
a good time and get value for money, and you can consign relationships that have brought you hours of love, support and happiness
to the dustbin of history before you've finished the first communal
risotto.

The central importance holidays have assumed in our cultural life
is at least as much a monument to the level of pressure the vast
majority of people labour under, domestically, professionally, or both.
We live on a crowded isle with the longest working hours in Europe
and in an increasingly 24-hour society. Unless you can find some
means to protect your mental and physical space from constant
invasion then a couple of weeks away functions as an escape valve,
the one thing that keeps your hands off the Prozac bottle. But if
you are lucky enough, as I am, to be what I call self-confident and
others call bloody-minded, have a home and a job that you like and
require nothing more for contentment in your life than to be left
alone to live it your way, then why in the name of Thomas Cook
would you want to leave it?

27 JULY 2005

Who'd be a child?

George Eliot was wrong when she said that childhood has no fore-
bodings. Most have far too many. When I was six, I frequently
convulsed in fear at innumerable things – dirt, crowds, shops, strange
food, snakes, going barefoot, visitors, burglars, you name it, I thought
it was either poisonous (the soles of the feet I considered prime
entry points for germs, to explain the barefoot thing) or going to
take me away from my mum. I worried about everything, until the
all-consuming problem of how I was going to run home in under
four minutes if the nuclear war was declared while I was at school
pushed all smaller concerns from my mind.

Today, as concerns rise over childhood anxiety, I would presumably be labelled obsessive compulsive, but in the early 80s the phrase was not yet in use, so we knew it by the more informal title 'Lucy's going mental'.

So my ever-patient mother spent much of my childhood braving the stares and questions of curious shoppers keen to know why her child was edging round shops, arms pressed to her sides like a miniature, hyperventilating guardsman. Every evening she got me off to sleep, and how we laugh now at how I crouched in mortal terror on the pillow while she checked under the bed (for fluff), within the bed (for snakes), and while she delivered hundreds of reassurances I required that none of us was going to die of cancer in the night. Then the having to get out of bed (slippers ON) to check between every single thing hanging in two wardrobes to make sure there were no (very thin) bad men hiding between the clothes. I knew there could be no one in there but I couldn't stop, so I would sob apologies while my mother kept repeating that it didn't matter, staying with me until I fell asleep from sheer exhaustion. Then she'd creep into her room, cry on Dad's shoulder and fall asleep 20 minutes before the alarm went off. Dad, it must be observed, never woke up, but this was probably only marginally less comforting than having him conscious as he was wont to make suggestions such as leaving me on a hillside while they concentrated their energies on raising my sister. Oh, happy golden days of childhood.

Research by psychiatrists at the Duke University Medical Centre in North Carolina have found that 9.5 per cent of young children could be suffering anxiety disorders, and the only surprising thing about that for me is that it's so low. I was basically a happy and secure child from a stable family who still managed to fall (temporarily) into an abyss of anxiety and fear. And, apart from the nuclear war thing, I only had to deal with age-old childhood fears. If you'd added endemic fear among adults of paedophiles, terrorists, crime, Aids, global warming trickling down to the infant populace,

I'd have tried to run in four directions at once until I tore the limbs loose from my body. I was consumed with guilt and worry about schoolwork – if I'd been subjected to government quality control tests every 10 minutes, or given homework as soon as they'd clamped the umbilical cord (as I believe the latest white paper recommends), you'd have had to scrape me off the ceiling. It's a wonder any kids make it to 18 any more.

30 NOVEMBER 2005

Grooming tips for the bone idle

I know you are probably reading this after a morning's paralysing indecision in front of the wardrobe. Do you follow Victoria Beckham's recently published 10 fashion commandments, or do you instead adhere to Coleen McLoughlin's rival recommendations, as published in this week's *Closer* magazine? The problem is that both ladies cruise around in the tinted-windowed celebrity limousine of life – admittedly one in lower gear than the other – leaving their advice less immediately applicable to us mere mortals. So for those still very much push-biking their ordinary carcasses through life, I would like to share an alternative sartorial decameron based on my own personal experience:

1. Don't buy clothes. It's boring and pointless if you haven't got a body like a pipe cleaner. I believe that if you've got enough in the wardrobe simply to cover your disgusting flesh, you have done your duty by God and society.

2. Live in one pair of jeans until they rot. Then buy another and stay in for six weeks until you manage to take them to one of those places that charges half as much again as the purchase price to lop eight inches off the ends and hem them in such a way as to make you suspect that a cohort of disabled howler monkeys is being exploited in a sweatshop out the back.

3. Make sure that all your tights are laddered.

4. Keep all your jewellery in a tangled and unreachable mass under the bed. Remember – trying to accessorise what we're wearing is like gilding a turd.

5. Examine yourself in a full-length mirror before going out. I find it a very useful aide-memoire as to why it's not worth bothering. And at a time of growing water shortages, tears can be saved in a bucket and used for washing up.

6. Do believe the hype. Unless you have been born with taste, style, flair and originality you need money – pots of it, to buy lovely clothes from gorgeous shops. You cannot shop at Primark and look good without an innate talent for it. So if you ain't rich, you're staying ugly.

7. No one ever sees socks, so they don't have to match or be entirely free of holes. People will tell you that attending to unseen details is a mark of discipline and self-esteem. They are wrong. It is the first sign of madness.

8. Don't ever try to haul yourself out of the sartorial doldrums, either by yourself or by taking up the offers of various kind and increasingly distressed friends who want to help you help yourself. You might feel happier and start going out more, and then you will have to find out about picture houses, music and teddy boys and stuff, and an endless pursuit of gaiety and fun will begin, which will be exhausting.

9. A good haircut can transform your whole look. But growing it over your face is a lot simpler and just as effective.

10. You won't get anything right, so don't bother

16 MARCH 2006

How to dump a TV show

Given that America has supplied the bulk of my most meaningful relationships over the years – the educational jingles of *Sesame Street*, the valuable lessons imparted by *Little House On the Prairie* (total blindness need be no barrier to making your own weight in poke bonnets every evening), the inspirational heroism of Buck Rogers, the subtle historical revisionism of *The A-Team*, the bittersweet viewings of *Joe 90* and the dying art of puppeteering, and of course the glorious decade that belonged to *Friends* and *Frasier* – it is only right that from there should also emerge the answer to the question of what to do when these relationships fail.

The website of the US television magazine *Entertainment Weekly* has started a blog on which viewers can break up with their formerly favourite TV shows. Now, I may not know much, particularly as my spiritual and emotional development was largely left to bespectacled puppets, soldiers of fortune and Big Bird, but I know the birth of a perfect modern ritual when I see one. My involvement with at least one soap, three sitcoms and seven crime series long ago outstripped my connection with so-called 'real people', and my boyfriend has had to dress up as Vic Mackey from *The Shield* for months now in order to get me to evince any interest in him whatsoever.

So it is only right that those of us who count the little people inside the television as part of our inner circle should be granted a means of dumping them when they betray us. I've only drafted three letters so far, but with each I feel the deep psychological peace of closure.

Dear *CSI*,

I loved you once, despite your hideous disfigurement from the beginning in the form of Gil 'Get me, I'm sooo gnomic' Grissom. Perhaps it was the slow but satisfying march towards resolution and justice at the end of every hour that gave me a feeling of stability in an ever-changing world. Perhaps I was curious to see how Catherine would complete her apparently inexorable metamorphosis into a paperknife. Maybe it was just the fascination occasioned by Nick Stokes's pointy head. Whatever. It's over. You have pushed me too far. Gil shags Sara? There's a word for that. And that word is: nooooo! Or, possibly, yeeucch! But we're done.

Dear *Lost*,

Looking back, we were never right for each other. I was always trying to make you into something you're not – *Buffy*, *The X-Files*, even *Angel* – and you were always total crap. Maybe another place, another time, it could have worked. A nineteenth-century mental asylum, perhaps, where I'd never seen television before and my mind was so perforated that your attempts at narrative structure would make sense, instead of driving me to bite the cat in fury.

Dear *Two and a Half Men*,

I don't know what I was thinking. I know our liaison was brief, but I still feel dirty. And not in a good way.

Now if we can just temper the extravagant formalities that surround the breakdown of 'real' relationships (postcards to replace decrees nisi, shoulders shrugged instead of proffered for crying on, carrot cake instead of proper cake) then the balance of ceremonies should be suitably redressed to suit the modern age.

13 SEPTEMBER 2006

Not using your gadgets? Send them to me!

Stashed in cupboards across the country, so it has been claimed this week, lie a total of 1.75bn gadgets that are not being allowed to fulfil their convenience-and-leisure-maximising destinies by people who buy them, lose interest and/or the accompanying instructions and then leave them to moulder away in their boxes instead of putting them to good use. Well, not in my house.

Most of the gadgets named and shamed as a waste of money in the survey by insurers Esure are out, proud and in service in the kitchen at Mangan Towers. How do I love them? Let me count the ways:

The George Foreman lean mean grilling machine

This tops the list of unused appliances – 9.8m countrywide, apparently, worth about £431m – but I cannot understand why. It's bloody brilliant. Heats up in less time than a normal grill, halves the cooking time by searing both sides of your meat-slab-of-choice at once, and just needs a quick wipe afterwards. Goodbye grill fires, goodbye having to take three days off work to clean the frigging pan with a steel brush and hydrochloric acid; hello George Foreman, my new god.

The sandwich toaster

It makes toasted sandwiches. Hot, buttery, cheesy, sardiney, tomatoey, anything-you-likey sandwiches. What more do I have to say to convince the 8.5 million people who are ignoring theirs to embrace the Breville and its lesser branded cousins? That it transforms a quotidian dry, cold- bread-and-filling experience into something almost dangerously decadent without costing you any more in the way of time, effort or calories? That it alone can make lunch worth living for? Think for a moment. That's right. Dig it out. Get toasting. Get toasting now.

The slow cooker

For anyone who hates cooking but likes food, the slow cooker should come before the wheel in your list of top inventions. Do you know what I call the 5.4 million people who let theirs go unused? Crock-Pot crackpots, that's what! And why? Because all you have to do is lob into one of these babies (whose running costs, incidentally, are about a billionth of an oven) any cheap cut of meat, whatever veg you've got lying around, stock, wine and a bay leaf if you're feeling posh or adventurous, salt and pepper, turn it on, get on with your life, come back eight hours later and dish up a dinner that I promise you will taste as if it were devised by a committee of Nigellas, cooked by a team of Gordons and blessed by Jamie. It is not a gadget. It is a miracle.

The breadmaker

Five minutes to put the flour, yeast, water, milk powder, sugar and butter in, two hours for the machine to turn out a perfect, warm, golden, fragrant loaf free of artificial ingredients but replete with folk memories of merrie England, thatched cottages and the Famous Five on picnics. And if you get a clever one with a special dispenser (ideally one that doesn't break after you've used it twice, thank you so much Panasonic, what a well-spent £99 that was), you can do all sorts of things with seeds, nuts and raisins, and take the virtuous results round to any of your friends who are in need of a decent bowel movement. Yes, that means you, the 5.4 million who haven't yet touched yours.

29 SEPTEMBER 2006

Let's sterilise the celebs

When I am president of the world, there will be questions applicants will have to answer so I can determine who will be allowed to breed and who will be given the snip before they're even allowed out of the licensing office. For men, these will largely comprise queries as to whether they intend to stick around for the child's formative years or prefer simply to wipe their genitalia on the curtains and disappear into the horizon. For women, they will centre round whether she's likely to choose to become pregnant or simply let the barman have a go because it's easier than going to the cashpoint to pay for the next round.

But in light of the news that Michael Jackson's ex Debbie Rowe has relinquished visitation rights to their two children in return for £395,000 a year ('It was hard for her,' a friend of hers assures us, 'but she's broke'), I thought I'd take this opportunity to press forward a plan that could be executed by today's governments even before I bring off my worldwide coup and establish an impregnable power base in Catford. For it is this: ban celebrities from having children.

Obviously the legislation would have to be drafted quite widely to ensure that a generation of children raised in blankets by suspected paedophiles, viewed as saleable commodities by their mothers and otherwise royally messed up, does not come into existence. The definition of 'having children' would have to encompass not only the traditional methods of screwing one's husband, wife, partner, personal trainer, a variety of eager fans, passing acquaintances, backing dancers or fellow fame-whore-come-island-contestant, but also adoption, surrogacy, stealing, bartering and whatever idiosyncratic means are ultimately discovered to have brought about Wacko's offspring. Or Suri Cruise. There's no point in outlawing international baby-mongering if all the determined celebrity has to do is become a seventh grade Operating Thetan and call on the Zorgistas to do the nasty and beam down the results to the happy earth couple and Annie Leibovitz.

An adoption ban would put the kibosh on the likes of Brangelina and Madonna trolling round the world, requiring suffering nations to spread their motherless infants before them so they can pick the choicest morsels from a baby buffet. It would stop the revolting sight of Madonna donating money to Malawi in order to push her Kabbalah cack into impressionable minds and, it seems, to encourage the African government to waive its usual prohibitions against intercontinental babynapping. No more untimely ripping of children from their national wombs to build, in Jolie's nauseating phrase, 'a rainbow family'. They will just have to find another way to attest to their limitless compassion, cultural tolerance and unimpeachable anti-prejudice credentials. Maybe one that translates into donating money without strings or controlled publicity photos.

Once external means of baby-getting have been made illegal, it only remains for all celebrities of fertile age to be forcibly contracepted. This is easy enough – you simply inject Depo-Provera along with Botox into the girls and commission a crack team of surgeon-starlets who can perform one-handed vasectomies while servicing the boys. They won't complain: given the choice between losing its looks or the opportunity to get blown in a restaurant booth and losing its gametes, the celebrity will lose the gametes every time.

21 OCTOBER 2006

I'm alphabetising my books — oh no!

I have spent the last few days giving in to what I had hitherto condemned as a thoroughly unnatural urge. After a lifetime spent fighting against those who would seek to alphabetise, chronologise or otherwise formally compartmentalise my 1,500 babies, I have started to sort out my books.

Previously, my ideological position has always been that books should be left to find their own order. The frequently referenced will rise to the top; the comfort reads and the ones that you just like to see and know are there will find their way naturally to appropriately prominent shelves. Those you have read only once and know you never will again, drift quietly down to less accessible areas between chairs, behind the computer and under the stairs. Thus, your books will eventually end up arranged in strata that best serve your needs without feeling injured by deliberate relegation or smug thanks to premeditated elevation. This, to me, is the mark of a civilised household, in which cordial relations between books and owner can be maintained at all times.

But times change and we change with them. And so, gradually – almost imperceptibly – I have begun to catalogue and re-shelve. The practice soothes, frustrates and unnerves in roughly equal measure. It soothes because, of course, I get to re-acquaint myself with every beloved volume and even discover a long-lost friend or two I thought had disappeared to borrowers (NB Must undo curses heaped on various innocent heads).

It frustrates because the process frequently raises more questions than it answers. To go from allowing an artless sifting process to ruthless alphabetisation has proved too much of a leap, so I have fallen to grouping them according to read and unread, classics and non-classics, passionately loved and not-quite-so-passionately loved, precious books I need to hand so that I can grab them and extol their virtues to guests at length (*Private – Keep Out!* by Gwen Grant, now republished by Barn Owl Books, buy eight copies for yourself, your children and your children's children), and so on. These, as sensitive readers among you can no doubt imagine, are not categories that permit the simplicity efficient cataloguing requires.

Finally, it is unnerving because if there's one thing I frigging hate, it's change. External change is bad enough, but the sudden advent of altered instincts is far more unsettling. And I can't be sure where this has come from. Toryboy hovers hopefully, insisting that it is a perverse but significant form of nesting instinct and means I am getting ready to let him impregnate me. How this squares with my plan to throw him out so that I can turn his study into a library, I don't know, but it's easier just to let him ramble on until I have a chance to change the locks, so I say nothing about my plans for radical interior design.

Me, I think it's less a harbinger of new life than it is an intimation of mortality. For the first time in my life I have many more books in my house than I have read. My reading used to be able to keep pace with my purchasing. This, I realise now, allowed me to believe that all my desires and ambitions could be fulfilled within my allotted span on earth. Now I know that there will for ever be more books I want to read than I can possibly manage in a lifetime. So as I try to make manageable the chaos I once used to embrace, and impose efficiency on the reading I used to let be governed by chance and mood, I must admit to myself that what I am doing is fighting uselessly against entropy, decay and death. You see what I mean about unnerving?

10 FEBRUARY 2007

Bums and tums among the terminally dumb

One of the perils of venturing into the bowels of the local community-cum-leisure centre is that it takes only a momentary lapse of concentration to end up in the strange nether world of half-forgotten dingy back rooms that had been – in more publicly funded days – intended for use by various members of the local neighbourhood's citizenship intent on self-improvement and/or esoteric forms of craftwork.

My sister, who had come to stay with me for a few days in order to put more shelves up in my house, lay some floor tiles and run through with me once again the difference between my arse and my elbow, dragged me there so that I could demonstrate the physical subset of my failings in an aerobics class. The only one available was Bums and Tums: Ladies Only, so we set off down the rabbit warren in the direction indicated by the hung-over teen at reception. As my sister tried to explain once again what she does for a living (something to do with computers – I honestly don't understand any more than that. For all I know she works for SPECTRE and is entirely responsible for building the Megatron Nimbus 2000 that is inducing global warming), we took a wrong turning or two. Instead of ending up at the women-only aerobics class, we found ourselves in a women-only discussion group which, according to the piece of A4 paper stuck to the wall above the nominated group leader's head, was going to answer the question of why men still rule the world. I was delighted – I'll take a little light feminist debate among a surprising number of spider plants and cushions (indispensable tools with which to fight patriarchal oppression) over jumping about and sweating any time. My sister was less certain.

We joined just as the women were taking it in turns to stand up and introduce themselves. 'Hello,' says the first one. 'My name is Sue, spelled S-O-O, because I felt it was more special.'

Hmm. '"Special" spelled "S-T-U-P-I-D,"' muttered the voice at my side. Already filled with a broader sisterly spirit, I not only hushed my relative but fought the urge myself to point out that rather than distinguishing herself from all the other Sues, what Soo had actually done was align herself with Matthew Corbett's glove puppet.

The next one stood up. 'Hello, my name is Clare, which means 'light', which is appropriate because I do a lot of healing with light.' I was slightly afraid that I was going to have to call her over to heal the blood that was starting to trickle from my sister's ears. Then it was our turn. I started to rise, but my sister put her foot quickly on my throat and made the introductions for both of us. 'My name,' she said, glancing regally around the room, 'is Princess Consuela D'Angostura Bitteres, daughter of King Quattro Formaggi and this is my maid, Margherita Caffenero, and I am afraid we are in the wrong place. Please, do excuse us.' Her exit was graceful yet decisive.

'Soo!' she snarled as she strode down the corridor, me trotting after her as – although I had been more than a little uplifted by the knowledge that consciousness-raising was still taking place in hidden corners of the country and would have liked to stay and hear more – she had grabbed me by the head as she left and so far forgotten to let go. 'Clare! Light! Spider plants! And they want to know why men still rule the world!' I suppose, in the end, I could see her point, if not, for the moment, where we were going.

17 FEBRUARY 2007

Thou shalt not surf

Only a few more hours to go now. Like most of my irreligious friends, I still give up something for Lent, even though (as I have yet to confess to the still-practising Catholic members of my family) it has less to do with a specific desire to commemorate Christ

wandering in the wilderness than a vague sense that I should occasionally remind myself, in this age of plenty, what a spot of deprivation
feels like.

As I cast around for a suitable candidate for rejection, my boyfriend
said: 'Why don't you give up nosing around other people's homes
on property websites for eight hours a day, and I can give up wiping
the saliva off your chin every time you see an original-tiled hallway
and working fireplaces.'

Giving up certain websites for the duration may feel to some like
diluting the original concept of Lent past all that is useful or effective,
but if homeopaths can get away with it in medicine, I can get away
with it in matters spiritual.

And in fact it has been revelatory. It is indeed good for the soul
not to devote large chunks of the day to looking at pictures of
terraced brickery and working out how many people in my family
I would have to kill to live there. (The answer is all of them and
then some. I have 852,647 living relatives without a single eccentric,
extravagantly wealthy aunt among them. I suspect it's something
to do with the Catholicism again. Probably that bit in the Catechism
that says it's better to have 22 babies a month than lay up treasures
that will enable future nieces to live in the Palladian comfort they
deserve.)

I have resisted the online lure despite the temptations posed by
my 435,981 northern cousins, who spent the run-up to Easter buying
new houses and saying: 'I've bought t'cloistered mansion on still-
notapropertyhotspotwhatevert'paperstellyou.com for three and six.
They wanted five shillin' but I said, 'Tha can whistle for it. Yon
helicopter pad wants resurfacing and that Fabergé egg store room's
no better than a coddler's privy.' Tek a look.'

This is because I have realised that what begins as a simple, natural
act of curiosity – my neighbours are putting pictures of the insides
of their homes on the web? Let's go see! – quickly mutates into
something much darker. Mockery of desperate bathrooms, not
inquisitiveness, becomes my driving force, soon followed by all-

consuming lust for others' unerringly perfect taste and miserable dissatisfaction with my own perfectly adequate dwelling. 'How come their house is a vision in sage green paint and polished floorboards, and mine looks like a disused piggery?' I wail. 'Where are my artfully strewn gewgaws and where is, above all, my tangible yet indefinable sense of grace and comfort?'

I look only at normal, terraced houses that were intended for normal, terraced people – I have no interest in million-pound, magazine-spread houses, the people behind them being clearly as diseased as those freaks in *Grand Designs* whose lifetime ambition is to build a home in Pyrex and Tudor oak while a balding man wipes metaphorical snot all over them – and the fact that these are real homes nearby convulses me with envy, hatred and despair. Factor in how much they are worth now to the people who bought them 30 years ago without guile or smug foresight of a property boom, and you can add the further sins of greed and wrath as well. Plotting inheritance-based murder probably mops up the rest.

Next year I think I shall go back to the relatively simple and pleasingly unrevelatory act of drinking unsugared tea. Unless, of course, a distant aunt wins the lottery. Then I shall be busy with other plans.

7 April 2007

What's style worth? Five pounds, tops

I have a confession to make. I did actually want one of those Anya Hindmarch 'I am not a plastic bag' bags. At first I was perturbed by this desire, not least because my regular visit to the local Savacentre is already the highlight of my week (the acres of aisle space! The freedom to roam after being cooped up in the house staring at a computer screen all week! The anonymous crowds offering company without the effort of interaction! The likelihood of a diverting tussle between security guard and teenage shoplifter and the opportunity to add some more recherché expletives to my vocabulary!), and I don't know that my delicate constitution could bear further excitement adhering to the event. Then, of course, there was the fact that you must be at least 30 per cent lemming and 60 per cent fricking bumcrack to allow yourself to be influenced by the madness, made deaf to all sense and reason by the collective throbbing of a million greedily acquisitive hearts, and caught up in the hype around the purchase of a £5 piece of canvas and a couple of rope handles.

So to be possessed by a yearning for the dumbass bag was disconcerting. And yet. And yet – it was indeed not just a plastic bag to me. It was the repository of hopes and dreams, long dormant but which now woke and strained to rise. For if I know one thing about myself, it is this: I am never going to own a designer handbag. Even if my bank manager would allow it, my temperament and the giant hologram head of my mother that looms above me whenever I contemplate making any purchase that breaches the £2 barrier, would not. If I ever spent, say, £320 on a bag (the minimum price for one of what I believe should be termed 'pieces' in official Hindmarch emporia), I think my entire system would shut down. But a fiver for a jumped-up carrier bag I could use again and again and fool myself into thinking I was doing some minor good for the environment as well? That I could probably manage. And if it imparted to me some small measure of the happy glow that designer-clad-and-accessorised celebrities and those very clean, confident – nay, borderline insouciant – people in town seem to have, if it disguises in any way that I found a dried up chip in the pocket of my jacket yesterday, then so be it.

Alas, it turns out that I have much to learn in the ways of the fashionista. I did envisage making an effort to nip down to Sainsbury's an hour or two earlier than usual. I did envisage having to stand in a bit of a queue to receive the coveted canvas vessel. I did not envisage that the western world would camp outside the stores the night before, buy the entire stock eight minutes after opening and be accepting closing bids on eBay by the time I got up in the morning. Clearly I have much work to do on my yearning levels and am still a long way from developing what I now know to be a mild yen for a product into the rabid, obsessive lust required to secure a desirable object in today's competitive market.

I am now in training, ready for whatever next piques my interest and am writing this at 2am in the car park outside the Savacentre, which in six hours is due to start giving away for free its own 'bags for life'. I will be first in line. Baby steps, I know, but I have promised myself that by the time the limited edition This Is Not a Tattered Bus Ticket by Stella McCartney in textured hemp comes out, or These Are Not Your House Keys in reclaimed steel from Dolce & Gabbana, I will be ready. Now the seed of designer desire has been planted, I will not be thwarted again.

5 MAY 2007

A fool and her money

Largely, I think, because I was raised by a mother who treated any display of independent thought by her offspring as a profound personal betrayal, I am essentially a passive person. As a rule, you can prod me and prod me, and I will just sit there, waiting for someone older, wiser and/or smelling of gin to tell me when I can react and how. But no longer. This week, over the course of the phone calls laid out below, I made an evolutionary leap into almost fully sentient humanity. All thanks to the purchase of a second-hand sofa, whose delivery price was quoted as £60. Now that I have thrillingly set the scene, let the drama unfold:

Monday
Sofaman: 'So I'll drop it off Friday. Pay the delivery charge then – £75.'
Me: 'Oh. Oh, well, yes, OK.'

Tuesday

Me: 'Hi, sorry to bother you, it's just something you said yesterday, about a £75 delivery charge . . .'

Sofaman: 'Yes?'

Me: 'It's just that, well, you originally quoted £60.'

Sofaman: 'It's £75 now.'

Me: 'Right. Right. Can I ask why, exactly?'

Sofaman: 'Congestion charge.'

Me: 'Oh, fine. Thanks. See you Friday!'

Wednesday

Me: 'Hello, sorry, me again. I was just looking on a map, and then I had a squint at the congestion charge website, then I called a few people at Transport for London, Capita Group and the AA – and then I strapped a satnav to my head and walked the route just to check – and it seems you can get from your shop to my house without going through the charging zone. In fact, you'd have to go to quite some effort to go anywhere near it.'

Sofaman: 'I've got other deliveries to make that day.'

Me: 'Oh, yes, of course, sorry to bother you. See you Friday.'

Thursday

Me: 'Guess who!? It just occurred to me that if you're making other deliveries, then perhaps those other people could pay the charge – which is actually only £8 – or it could be shared out equally among all of us. Otherwise, it – forgive me – might seem as if you are cannily, one might almost say unfairly, or possibly fraudulently, adding on to the delivery charge exactly the amount of money you knocked off the price of the sofa originally.'

Sofaman: 'It's only 15 quid. Do you want this sofa or not?'

Me: 'I do want this sofa, especially seeing as you've already cashed the cheque that I somewhat, it dawns on me now, misguidedly gave you. But do you see that it is not so much the sum involved that I am objecting to, but the principle of the thing?'

Sofaman: 'No. Will you have the money ready on Friday?'

Me: 'Yes. Cash or cheque?'

Sofaman: 'Cash'

Me: 'All righty.'

Friday

Sofaman: 'There's only 60 quid here.'

Me: 'Yes. I have the rest in this safety deposit box. I'll give it to you when you admit that you have effectively reneged on a contract and forced me to hand over a sum of money that, while nugatory in the grand scheme of things, nevertheless represents unethical business practice, unchristian conduct and the fact that you are one giant, lying sack of shite.'

Sofaman: 'Sure. Hand it over.'

Me: 'Thank you.'

Some will claim this a pyrrhic victory, what with him walking away entirely untouched by events and with the full fee, while I collapsed in a gibbering heap and had to spend two days in a sanatorium, but I prefer to think of it as the acorn from which a mighty oak of assertiveness will grow. I feel a power uncoiling, my friends. Prod me and see.

27 OCTOBER 2007

A shed of one's own

I have always liked Australia. By which I mean, of course, I have always liked the idea of Australia. Having left this country twice (both for brief and ill-advised sojourns to the continent), my direct experience of the country is nil.

But I have watched *Neighbours* and *The Thorn Birds*, and really: who could not warm to the notion of a permanently sunny country studded with tidy suburbs full of embryonic pop stars, interspersed with vast tracts of dusty land where people devote their lives to raising sheep, shagging priests and fighting bushfires – which trinity of pastimes, it seems to me, would provide ample entertainment and a sense of purpose sadly lacking in Catford as long as you could avoid being the maid at Drogheda who, as men descended to help stamp out the flames rapidly encircling the ranch, was abruptly ordered to 'make stew for a hundred!'.

If all this were not enough to make it a veritable Eden, I discovered this week that it also provides state-sponsored sheds. Mensheds Australia has been given a government grant to set up more sheds (200 exist across the country so far) to give the menfolk somewhere to hang out together, whittling, scratching each other's balls and talking about building more sheds, a respite from the strains of work and stresses of home.

Obviously this is one of the most brilliant ideas ever, save for the fact that it is directed, as a result of historical misfortune, at the wrong gender. Somehow over the years, men managed to persuade themselves and us that although they were the ones with the jobs, money, power and the right, as revered head of the household, to burn their children in the fireplace if they clinked their porridge spoons too noisily in the nursery, they still required special retreats in which to collect their thoughts and prepare for another hard day of ruling.

Obviously times have changed. For a start, there is now plastic cutlery for children that I understand has reduced infanticide rates enormously. But otherwise, less than you might hope. During my three long years of cohabiting with Toryboy, I have learned that, no matter how liberal a household is, it is still the female half who is the less likely to be able to call her time her own.

We must attribute this partly to women's genetic predisposition to sabotage their chances of peace and happiness by keeping up a running internal commentary on all the domestic tasks left undone – my own sounds like a Morse ticker machine, others I imagine can liken theirs to the whine of race cars going round an endless track – and partly to the fact that men (yes, I generalise unforgivably) are genetically programmed to have a thought, break into another person's valuable reading/sitting/daydreaming time to express it, then hover until the remark has been given due weight and consideration by its unwilling recipient and he can retire to his own cogitations once more.

So it is that, even though I am a lady, I spend half my waking life dreaming of a house with a garden, with a large shed at the bottom of that garden, obscured from prying eyes by swags and hanks of carefully trained clematis and other assorted foliage, and secured at all points by padlocks the size of a baby's head. I want some grant money. We, in short, who know that we are still at risk of being required to make stew for a hundred at a moment's notice, need that money. And soon, please. I need to get the clematis in before spring.

3 NOVEMBER 2007

To the graveyard!

The first time I watched *Papillon*, I couldn't understand it at all. This, it turned out during prolonged discussion with my parents later, was because I hadn't appreciated that solitary confinement was supposed to be a punishment. I thought he was a favoured prisoner in receipt of special privileges. That's the misanthropic mindset for you, in a nutshell.

My parents, recognising there was little they could do now to make the necessary genetic changes to their pathologically antisocial child, advised me to look for information that would enable me to do a passable imitation of a normal member of society, and hope for the best.

Thus I have been poring over the latest research by the good doctors at our very own Warwick University and Dartmouth College in the US, who have discovered, after careful questioning of two million people and what I can only assume was the greatest mass deployment of clipboards in sociological history, that human happiness is U-shaped. It peaks at 20, then goes into a decline as we head towards middle age, with the average person collapsing face-first into their 44th birthday cake in a dribbling heap of misery and despair before beginning the re-ascent to happiness and emerging at their most content at the ripe old age of 70.

There are those who would say that two million people can't be wrong. There are others of us, of course, who will point these people in the direction of the viewing figures for *EastEnders* and, wordlessly, empirically demonstrate the truth of the matter, which is that well over that number can be wrong, wholly wrong and repeatedly, many times a week and for many years at a time. And there are certainly plenty of people around who would take issue with the notion of happiness first topping out at 20, instead of this being the age at which you find yourself no sooner having sloughed off the worst of the damage done to you by teenage friends and overactive sebaceous glands than you are pitched into the world of work, rent and sexually transmitted diseases that actually matter. But a large number of people – including one of the survey leaders, Professor Andrew Oswald – have found the results heartening because they contradict most people's intuitive sense that happiness declines the older (ie closer to death) you become.

Well, bully for them. The U-shaped model is a definite come-down from my own conceptualisation of happiness, which has always been that it runs in a straight slope upwards towards the grave.

I don't offer this in a preening, 'Look at me, I'm so very cleverly different!' kind of way. I am, after all, basically admitting that not only I have been looking forward to death since birth, but living under the kind of gross misapprehension (by assuming that everyone else has been doing likewise) that can be born only of profound idiocy, which would be, I think we can all agree, an odd boast.

In my defence, however, and after studying the three models I now realise are available to me, I do think mine offers certain advantages. First, it means that all the time your worst years are behind you. Second, if you have children, you will not gaze at their soft, unlined faces with jealousy in your heart, nor long to crush their youthful exuberance with tumbling fists in recompense for your own lost youth. And, third, you will always be looking forward to the next, best thing instead of the next best thing until they carry you out in a box. It's a twisted, insane kind of optimism, but I still think it beats 50 years of gloom sandwiched between a few fleeting years of glory. Onwards and upwards!

9 FEBRUARY 2008

Catford: a tribute (yes, really)

I may move to Leicester. Not only because it is the birthplace of Showaddawaddy and Michael Kitchen, without whose contributions English cultural life would have been the poorer, but also because I learned this week that the city's motto is 'Semper eadem' – always the same – which it has kept (well, naturally, duh) since Queen Elizabeth I granted its royal charter way back when.

I am someone who has always heard phrases such as 'We must have change!' as synonymous with 'We must alter, wreck, destroy, remove! And incur needless expense doing so!' So Leicester is like a mothership calling me home. Particularly because it is putting some of its public money where its maxim is and running a project (go to sempereadem.org) that records places in the city which have remained unchanged for the past 25 years.

In so doing, it is paying photographic homage to the Alfred Lenton bookshop, the Knighton & District Social Club, the Modino Espresso coffee bar and other pockets of the recent past, a period that sometimes seems more distant than any other. Have you not, for example – especially if you have just taken your children on a forced Easter holiday march around sites of historical interest – seen more ancient monuments and stately homes than perfectly preserved espresso coffee bars from the days of your youth? Twenty-five years of preservation may not seem much of an achievement, but a journey of 1,000 years begins with a single quarter century . . .

Anyway, I am now moved to begin my own project here in Catford. It's not a city, so it doesn't have a motto, but if it did, it would probably be: 'Where hope comes to die. Or at least have a bit of a lie-down and think about its next move.' Or, 'Blackheath's just down the road, you know. Keep going if you can.'

But it has been my home for more than 30 years and it's time to give something back. So where to begin? With the cat, of course – the giant, black and white, fibreglass moggie that hangs over the entrance to the shopping centre. I remember it going up before I started secondary school, so it must be 25 by now. Alas, I have lost my diary of Misguided Urban Focal Points from those years, so I cannot check.

Then there's Tesco. Ah, Tescos, Tescos, where Sally gets her best clothes! What is it about those childhood playground rhymes that lodge them so deeply in the mind? Well, in this case, it was the punctuation afforded by Sally's hacking sobs every lunchtime as 100 primary schoolers took up the amusingly ceaseless refrain. Halcyon days. The shop itself is worthy of attention as, hemmed in by high-rises, it may be the only branch of that retail empire which will be forever unable to expand. Three decades from now, it will be the closest thing to a corner shop in the country.

And the chestnut trees, once so thickly planted round these parts that it was said Edwardian inhabitants could walk from Lewisham to Catford in the rain without getting wet. There are only a few left, but around them a great tradition has emerged among local children to look disdainfully at the glossy conkers that fall every autumn and carry on trying to fiddle with each other in the shadows of Eros House. Which would be aptly titled only if it were renamed Mere Genital Curiosity, but I may gloss over that in the forthcoming exhibition.

26 APRIL 2008

With the best will in the world

I have spent most of this week roaming the latest online archive – the contents of 28,000 wills from 1470 to 1856 have been opened up at originsnetwork.com. This means you can now spend happy days immersed in a world of intrigue, family feuds, great loves and splendid enmities displayed through the medium of dung pots bestowed and bodkins withheld, sweet-wood boxes given unconditionally and flitches grudgingly conferred if they haven't, as the soon-to-be-deceased clearly hopes, gone maggoty by the time he breathes his last.

I have been intrigued by wills since I read the part in *Little Women* where Amy, consumed by thoughts of mortality as her saintly but pulmonarily challenged sister, Beth, is gasping her last on the family sofa back home, writes her own in order to distribute her beloved possessions to her (slightly less beloved) sisters (Amy being an admirably proto-modern girl who had to be banged over the head repeatedly with a copy of *The Pilgrim's Progress* before she could remember to pretend that people were more important than jewellery).

I was, by the age of nine, an avowed opponent of emotional outbursts. My stony face and rapidly calcifying heart were already part of the magic that makes me me. A last will and testament struck me as a terribly useful way safely to express my pent-up affections and hatreds. The postmortem state, I realised, could rock.

I left all my dearest treasures to Grandma. Until my mother looked over my shoulder and pointed out that, by the time I was gone, Grandma would be 130. I pointed out that only last summer (ironically, as she was feeding the last of my own potential inheritance into the one-armed bandits along Blackpool's Golden Mile) I had made her promise never to die. My mother gently disabused me of the notion that this was a promise Grandma could fulfil. ('Are you daft? If anyone ever does make it to 130, it's not going to be someone who's lived off barm cakes dipped in gin.')

So the final document bequeathed my night-time companion Bunny to my father, my money (17p in my ladybird purse) to my mother with the suggestion that she invest conservatively in government bonds, and nothing to my sister or best friend on the grounds that I hated them. When I discovered codicils, I added one detailing the crimes that had lost them the chance to inherit my clothes and Brownie badges. Including the trefoil. Never let it be said that I don't know how to turn the knife.

Now, however, I realise that I should make a proper will. I accept that there is not much point leaving stuff to generations above me, so Bunny and my money will have to go to my sister, towards whom I feel marginally better disposed these days. I rang her to see if there was anything else she wanted. 'Ooh,' she said excitedly, 'could I have your shoe box of a house that stinks of cats? I could use a pied-à-terre in a non-central location, far from shops or transport links. And your cupboardful of mismatched plates and cutlery that would shame a first-year student, never mind a 33-year-old semi-professional? Oh, and your second-hand 12-year-old Nissan Micra to replace my 1.9-litre 150bhp Astra Sport Hatch? At last, I could live the dream.'

I reflected on the fact that the Mangans' greatest inheritance would appear to be the gift of sarcasm. And then I drew up the final document. She's getting everything. That'll teach her.

10 MAY 2008

Can't spend, won't spend

I grew up in a pathologically parsimonious family. In fact, it is a wonder I am here, able to type this at all, given that I spent the formative years of my life chronically dehydrated by a household rule that stipulated that you couldn't have a drink with soup.

'But Mum,' my sister and I would cry when we had peeled our desiccated tongues off the roofs of our parched mouths, 'we're thirsty!'

'No you're not,' she would reply. 'Soup's a meal AND a drink.'

It is a kind of upbringing that has many disadvantages, but it does grant the hapless child one inestimable benefit for the years to come. It inoculates her infinitely well against ever buying wholly into the mad, mindless, consumer culture that still (credit crunch notwithstanding) threatens to engulf us all.

So I lead, by the standards of our time and the standards of most of my friends and acquaintances, a pretty modest life. I don't take foreign holidays. I eat out about four times a year and I've never been to a famous restaurant. I didn't even realise that was odd until I was commissioned to write this piece on the strength of it. I don't replace my mobile phone every six months (I'm currently on my second in a decade, and that used to belong to my sister). I bought my first stereo in 1993 and it's still going strong. My kettle cost £6. I don't have a digital camera, coffee maker, digital radio or a designer anything.

I always go for second-hand options first, and don't replace anything unless it is broken beyond repair.

'It's not a lifestyle,' my best friend once said to me, after a day at my house. 'It's barely a life.' And there is a certain amount of truth to what she says. But not buying (literally) into the consumer culture involves a certain measure of resistance to peer pressure, and so I ignored her. Just as we try to teach our children (and I use 'we' entirely wrongly as I don't have any children yet – they're too expensive. I'm joking. I'm JOKING) not to care about what other children do, think or say about them, we should all try to separate not just our needs from our wants but our genuine wants from our idiotic desire not to be outshone by the Joneses who have the new £800 Philippe Starck kettle-cum-lemon-squeezer-and-pony. I don't care about the Joneses. They tend to be morons and generally only ever one late salary payment away from bankruptcy.

Let's be clear. I don't live this way in order simply to accumulate money in the bank. I have an uncle whose entire being is strung to this desire, to the extent that he switches his car engine off whenever he's at the top of a hill so that he can roll down for free. He, I suggest, should be in some kind of home.

It's just that I'd prefer we brought a modicum of intelligence and a soupcon of scepticism to bear on all the messages and influences that are brought, unasked for, unwanted, to bear on us. So I don't spend my time standing on one leg to save shoe leather. I buy what I want, when I want, and I am lucky to earn enough to enable me to do so. But I do have to want it, not just think it would be nice, or that I, in that ridiculous justification used by the terminally self-indulgent, 'deserve it'. And I am lucky that I have fundamentally inexpensive tastes – I have no travel urges, concerts aren't my thing, and there's only so much even the most dedicated reader can spend on Amazon and in second-hand bookshops.

I'm sure that if I were still a lawyer in the city and earning 10 times what I do now, I would spend more. I would have to – presentable clothes cost more than jeans and trainers, readymeals cost more than those you have no time to cook from scratch, and luxuries like cleaners become necessities if you are to have any time at all for doing things that make life remotely worth living.

But however much I earned, I don't think I could stop being mindful of how I spent it. It is probably not an exaggeration to say that I think about every penny that passes through my hands or goes on to my credit card (I don't think you have to ask by this stage whether I pay it off every month). I can't help it – it's as automatic as breathing. I don't mean I stand cogitating for hours in a newsagents before I hand over 80p for a newspaper – although, if I was being entirely honest, I would admit that this is an urge I have to hold in check – but it does mean that I pay attention to all my outgoings, fleetingly to small ones and seriously to larger ones. I live in fear of not being able to pay my way, of my employment suddenly ending or of illness descending and having nothing in the bank to cushion the impact and buy me time, of not having the choices and the freedom that both savings and the ability to take an income hit without a perpendicular drop in lifestyle (or however my friend would term it) brings.

I know that this is an attitude so old-fashioned as to be almost risible, but as I watch friends out shopping, piling clothes, shoes, CDs and assorted other paraphernalia into their baskets and forever going out for expensive meals literally without a moment's thought, then finding themselves 'unexpectedly' overdrawn at the end of every month, I cannot, absolutely cannot agree that their way is more 'fun', let alone better than mine.

It intrigues me, incidentally, how easily most people seem to be able to shuck off what you might call folk memories. I know that for most of my lifetime, most people have been living in an era of growing affluence. But equally, I have always known that the mindset that saw Grandma refuse to buy a vacuum cleaner and continue attacking bits on the carpet with nothing more than a handful of sticky sock labels and a dream was formed in a world well within living memory that promised her nothing and at times, widowed as she was with the traditional Catholic 82 children under five, delivered even less. I envy people who are able to live in the moment, unfreighted by generations' worth of anxieties, but at the back of my mind, I always hear the sound of fiscal nemesis hurrying near.

And now, of course, it has arrived. And while I take no pleasure in people suffering undeservedly from it, I'm afraid I am going to take a moment to enjoy the spectacle of those who will simply have to learn to curb some of their more ludicrous extravagances – the people who have spent the last 10 or 15 years laughing at my insecurities and condemning my carefulness and loudly complaining that they never seemed to have enough money for that fourth holiday abroad. I think I've earned it. I may even have a drink of water to celebrate.

17 JUNE 2008

Welcome to Manganland

It's such a good idea that really, you wonder why more people don't do it.

Stuart Hill, who lives on Forvik Island, a rocky, two-acre outcrop off the west coast of Shetland, has declared its independence from the UK and himself udal leader of the island. Now, anyone who knows enough about ancient Norse law to declare himself udal leader of anything should simply be handed the rocky outcrop of his choice. But Hill has gone to the trouble of providing, in his Declaration of Independence, the historical basis for his decision. Apparently, when King Christian of Denmark handed over the Shetlands to James III of Scotland in 1469, Jimmy Three was intended to hold them only as trustee. Their special status was confirmed by the Treaty of Breda in 1667, recognised by Charles II and then stomped all over by Queen Anne, who illegally incorporated them into Great Britain with the Act of Union. Succeeding monarchs and governments have preserved a discreet, collusive silence on the matter ever since.

He is so lucky. I have tried to declare my own patch of southeast London – from privet hedge to creosoted fence to the Kingdom of Mr and Mrs Anderson next door – an independent principality for years, but no luck or useful historical kink has come to my aid.

Nevertheless, I have everything worked out. Jam on toast will be the national dish. The state religion will be flexible. You can worship Thora Hird, Beryl Reid or Ethel Merman. I can foresee a breakaway sect forming to deify Gracie Fields instead, but they can be accommodated. There will be bank holidays in honour of Creme Eggs, goosedown duvets and Kirstie Allsopp, which will henceforth be known as – because I have just thought of it and I am a Ruler Without A Bicameral Legislature or Anything Like It and can therefore amend the proto-constitution instantaneously – Sunny Mondays.

The laws of the land will be simple:

1. Shops must wrap meat purchases in waxed paper and all other purchases in brown paper and string, thus adding a more pleasurable literal and metaphorical texture to life and, if I have understood my grandma's lyrical reminiscences about corner shops a-right, fostering a sense of community without the bother and expense of a war.

2. Not turning off the tap while cleaning one's teeth will be punishable by death.

3. Organised sports to be recognised as a mental disorder. Mention of, or financial contribution towards, the Olympics will be prohibited and the money redirected towards the disinterring – or rather disaquafying? dehydrating? – of Dunwich, the former capital of East Anglia, which, due to the failure of medieval town planners to allow for the effects of coastal erosion, has been underwater for the past 800 years or so. Manganland hereby commits itself to a policy of raising old villages from the sea rather than building new ones over homes and wetlands, which is in keeping with a land whose motto will be 'Try, at all times, not to be a total arse.' (I'm hoping it will sound catchier in Latin.)

4. The national flag will depict kittens gambolling, introducing an amusingly deceptive note of whimsy to a dangerously despotic regime.

5. Commerce will be undertaken using the barter system to restore levels of Rowdiness and Hullabaloo. Also because I am disproportionately charmed by the idea of escaped piglets in the street.

I do hope you'll join me. No passports required, just a copy of the *Guardian* and a smiling readiness to bend to my only occasionally benevolent will.

28 JUNE 2008

Let them eat carrot cake

Another week, another dollop of aid for our flailing youth. Ed Balls has promised new home economics kitchens in schools and downloadable pamphlets containing recipes for 11-year-olds to master – provided, of course, they can wrap their obese fingers around a paring knife. The leaflets' unstated aim of enabling us to prepare healthy, nutritious meals in the face of impending disaster (albeit fiscal and environmental, rather than bellicose) gives them the timbre of wartime propaganda. The only difference appears to be that this time, the roast chicken recipe does actually involve roasting a chicken rather than a bombed-out shoe or splintered piece of fence post. I must have been one of the last generation (of state schoolers, anyway) to get home economics lessons. My sister, three years later, remembers a few classes of something called food technology ('Mostly describing the differences between a tomato and a hammer. And Joe McKellar said you could grill a hammer and Mrs Ames started to cry') but even in my day you'd be looking at the weekly session a long time before you were reminded of a riotous success.

Having no kitchen at our school, we would walk 15 minutes down the road to one that did. We lost at least 40 per cent of the class to more interesting pursuits along the way. By the time they turned up – reeking of snakebite or Tipp-Ex, incubating the latest fashionable strain of STD, and, in a few triumphant cases, sporting the drunk-stoned-diseased trifecta – the rest of us would be halfway through making our third carrot cake of the month.

Sodding carrot cake. Week after week we churned one out in the vain hope that this time it would look something – anything – like a cake instead of a sullen, sunken reproach to human endeavour and to hope. We were not yet old enough to understand that that is exactly what carrot cake is meant to be. Looking back, I realise there was a valuable life lesson waiting for us there, if only someone had managed to disinter it. Perhaps with the shovel we eventually used on the cake.

Whenever we succeeded in outpacing Lewisham's carrot supply lines, we made spag bol (we couldn't reliably spell bolognese), and it was during one of these weeks that I watched Emma J chop straight through an onion – skin, sprouty bit, root and all – and scrape the entire thing into a pan.

At the age of 11, I felt that this betokened a deeper malaise. I felt, in some inchoate and unarticulated way, that if you don't know how to chop an onion, it means you don't know a lot of things. It means you don't know food has constituent parts, and that your larger world view might be equally limited. It means you don't have a grown-up in the house who has the time or inclination to cook, which means you don't have a parent with the time or inclination to talk to you. It means a major source of knowledge has been denied you. It probably means you don't have much in the way of what the various ologists call social capital. And that probably means you don't have much at all.

If I were to continue with this train of thought, I might add that Emma J probably has children of her own by this time, and they probably have even less. Fortunately, however, I now know that she was simply a child in need of a pamphlet. I presume government thinktanks have conducted tests to prove that culinary re-skilling reverse-engineers society and returns us all to our idyllic, prewar state. I cannot tell you how relieved I am. For a minute there, I thought we were in real trouble.

20 SEPTEMBER 2008

Every breath I take . . .

I am fortunate that although, as my sister once pointed out, I look like eight genetic mishaps mashed together in one repellent body, I have a generally strong constitution and am rarely ill. However,

I am now making up for this run of good health and luck – I have been unable to breathe since May, and am starting to find it annoying.

The medically trained among you will, of course, have already discerned that I am paltering with the truth, and for that I apologise. I'm afraid oxygen deprivation has caused me momentarily to abandon my customary zeal to render the week's events in living but accurate colour. I mean, of course, that I have been unable to breathe properly – specifically, through my nose – since May. Occluded nasal passages have meant I have been walking round for five months inhaling through my ever-open, ever-dehydrating and gently crusting mouth. I look like a particularly bovine reality show contestant.

One of the many delights of my condition (diagnosed by my GP with unnecessary relish as nasal polyps. Nasal polyps! Can you think of two words that go together in more joyless conjunction, apart from, say, 'carpet' and 'tiles'?) has been a new acquaintance with the nocturnal rhythms of the estate.

Sleepless through the likelihood of supine suffocation, I now know that two giant tortoiseshell cats rule the animal world. They stalk the streets, biffing other felines, dogs and small cars out of their way as they make sure their manor is secure. Across the car park, there is a man who shouts viciously at his dog if it makes a sound after 10pm or before 7am, and a woman who does the same to her children. On Friday and Saturday nights a teenage couple meet in the shadowiest corner to suck face and, occasionally, other body parts. The boy bounds like a delighted jackrabbit to the rendezvous, but his inamorata participates with such a profound, unchanging look of boredom that it is all I can do not to open the window and offer to chuck her a book to help pass the time.

Then there is my favourite, a woman who comes out of her flat at about 2am and carefully sweeps a length of the pavement clear of leaves, dust and detritus. At first I was awed and inspired by this fine example of civic pride. To be so dedicated to the communal good that you would sweep the pathways clear last thing every night! I can't be sure I didn't start composing a letter to the News Shopper, hymning this lone individual whose tireless broom bids fair to become the only thing standing between us and the yawning moral abyss.

The next night, I noticed that she sweeps only the pavement directly in front of her house. The night after that, I noticed that she doesn't pick up the sweepings. She leaves them in two piles, one at the boundary of what she clearly deems to be the pavement pertaining to the flat on her left, one at the equivalent frontier on her right, and they are gradually dispersed over the course of the day. Most of them – and you may be ahead of me here – back over the swept ground.

The people in the flanking flats, incidentally, simply step over or around the piles when they leave for work early in the morning. Do they never question how they got there? If they know, how has one of them not killed her, incensed by this daily evidence of such selfishness, these little piles of pettiness lying outside their homes every morning? Maybe they are good people and pity her instead? I will work on that. Otherwise, it's not the polyps that are going to get me. It's the great suffocating hatred of humanity in my heart.

11 OCTOBER 2008

Proud to be a pessimist

I stayed the night at my best friend's house this week, a delightful if unplanned sojourn brought about by a combination of my inability to read train timetables and her invention of the Sydenham Fruitini. This is like the ordinary vodka and fruit juice beverage, but when you run out of fruit juice, you use cider instead. 'It is innovation like this,' Sally cried, as she went cross-eyed and fell backwards, 'that keeps us young!'

Anyway. We were having breakfast – slow, cautious breakfast – the next morning when there was a sound at the front door. Sally immediately brightened. 'Ooh!' she said excitedly. 'The post is here!'

'Are you expecting something?' I asked, as she returned leafing through a handful of envelopes.

'No,' she said, surprised. 'Why?' I looked at her and realised that once again we were about to stumble into the quagmire of misunderstanding that has bedevilled our friendship for 30 years. Or, if you prefer an alternative geographical metaphor, we had once again ended up on opposite sides of the gulf that separates optimists and pessimists.

The post, to me, is a daily delivery of potential disasters. When I hear the postman at the gate, the squeak of the letter box or the soft slither of envelopes from door to mat, my heart is filled with foreboding. My stomach somersaults, and I'm pretty sure several adjacent organs are also discommoded. All in all, it is an unpleasant experience, and one that seems to get worse rather than better.

I explain this – albeit possibly not, in my post-fruitini-addled state, with all the clarity of the above – to Sally. 'But what,' she asks, 'do you expect to find?'

Well, therein lies the problem. I don't know. It could be anything. All the best disasters are entirely unexpected. I could open that unassuming manila sachet and discover that I am being pursued for an unpayable tax demand, or a forgotten £10,000 debt I incurred in my youth. And then I'll be thrown in jail, but denied the solitary confinement that has always made the prospect of a custodial sentence seem to me less of a punishment than a rest/cure.

'I was there throughout your youth,' Sally points out. 'The most we ever spent on anything was £1.50 on some Anne French cleansing milk. And that was paid in full to a Boots cashier in Lewisham's premier – and only – retail centre.'

Or it could be a letter telling me someone I love is dead.

'Are you just making up these fears now?' Sally asks. I'm really not. 'OK, well, do you not think that is the kind of news that will, in all likelihood, be delivered to you in person? By a relative or, at worst, a policeman?'

'I think if Mum died, Dad would just send a polite letter. Hopefully he'd include the funeral details.'

More silence. 'What do you think when you hear the post come, then?' I ask. 'I think, 'Brilliant! I wonder what treats lie in store for me today. Ooh, what's this, an invitation to the birthday party of a long-lost friend? No, it's a guttering-replacement offer – still, better than nothing! Perhaps the next one will be a free sample of a new shampoo? No! It is an unpayable tax demand! Never mind, I'm sure something will turn up before I have to go to prison! And a gardening catalogue – what a welcome reminder of the never-ending circle of life and an uplifting start to the day!'

We stare at each other in mutual incomprehension. 'Ah well,' Sally says, reaching for the vodka and cereal. 'At least we have the Cornflaktini to see us through.'

8 NOVEMBER 2008

ID cards? Bring 'em on!

I have a confession to make: I don't care about the introduction of ID cards. What I mean is, my brain understands the arguments against them – loss of privacy, infringement of civil liberties, 'function creep', the fostering of discrimination and prejudice, ineffectuality in combating crime, and so on – but my heart will not be in it. I will sign any anti-ID card petition going, because I know it is right to do so, but I am not truly impassioned. I am not outraged.

This is largely because I was raised in a one-woman police state. My mother was all-seeing, all-knowing. She made the law. She was the law. The house was a panopticon. She bought it specifically because all the rooms radiated from a single hallway, so she could stand at one point and know exactly where everyone was at any given moment and what they were doing: who was about to put the toilet seat down without checking for leftovers; who was about to sit on a recently bumphled sofa without written authority.

An hour without the gentle burning sensation of an eye trained on the back of my head left me feeling like a motherless child. Even with all this, however, I find it hard to believe home secretary Jacqui Smith's recent assertion that, although we aren't due to become ambulatory government data units until 2012, she 'regularly' has people telling her they don't want to wait any longer for their cards. Even after I replace the word 'regularly' with the one I presume she means, 'frequently'. If, of course, pro-ID carders have organised themselves to such a degree that they are presenting themselves to Smith at precisely delineated intervals, I will happily stand corrected. But I suspect not.

This is either a lie – and not a Tony Blair lie-excused-in-advance-by-Jesus-told-for-a-greater-good-type lie, but an actual I'm-just-going-to-make-stuff-up-now-to-make-myself-look-better lie – or Smith is failing to recognise that she is being accosted by neurotics/racists/racist neurotics/neurotic racists, and interpreting them as representative of our citizenry, which makes me wonder not just about her fitness for office but also about the wisdom of letting her outside unaccompanied.

Whatever the truth, the fact that she is willing to make such a proclamation is proof that ID cards are coming, and soon. So, with the clarity and perception vouchsafed me as a disinterested observer, what I propose is this: in return for the manifest and manifold disadvantages of the scheme, we must be compensated at an individual level. To this end, ID cards must contain all the data about us, from fingerprints and marital status to preferred biscuits and flavours of soup, thus ensuring us a smooth and uncluttered passage through life.

For instance, I would wish my own card to include the following information: That I still secretly consider fruit and vegetables to be vaguely medicinal, and that dinner party invitations should be proffered only if you are prepared to go unfashionably heavy on the meat and carbohydrates unless you want to see my unhappy face; that I do not suit a hat and will not be wearing one to your wedding; that I have impeccable liberal credentials but consider Donald Rumsfeld to have been appallingly traduced for the 'There are known knowns' speech that actually made thrillingly perfect sense; that not only will I tell off other people's children, but that I will enjoy doing so, too.

Imagine the time and awkwardness this would save in a lifetime. It's brilliant. In fact, if you will excuse me, I think I will just go and find Jacqui Smith and tell her.

15 NOVEMBER 2008

CHAPTER TWO

MY SO-CALLED FAMILY

My sister, the domestic tyrant

My sister and I are very different people. If it were left to my lazy-arsed self, my new house would stay unchanged until the day I move on again. Emily, however, upon hearing that DIY duties were going undischarged in the south-east, loaded up her car with the small branch of B&Q she keeps in her garage and drove down from Bristol one-handed, while assembling scale models of her intended improvements with the other.

On arrival at my recent end-of-terrace purchase, Clifton's answer to Capability Brown unloaded 18 spirit levels, four tape measures (one calibrated in quarknano-picometres), several hundred unidentified power tools and a device I believe detects shifts in the earth's tectonic plates that might affect bracket alignment. Then she shoved me into the car and took me to Homebase in Catford so that I could push the trolley into the ankles of heavily tattooed and easily irked men while she strode along the aisles muttering about poor-quality routers and extending-arm chop saws. While I struggled to master the difference between undercoat and primer, she performed Rain Man calculations about the best way to get a dozen shelves out of the various planed pine planks on offer, before hooking up her Bluetooth BlackBerry with optional candelabra to source cheaper alternatives from local timber yards which could be delivered before 2pm, allowing for the traffic jam that the in-built satellite navigation system had picked up.

We drove back – well, she drove, I ran behind with the wallpaper paste – and I made lunch. By the time I came back from the kitchen she'd put up the shelves, made two cabinets and was trying to bevel a passing neighbour and his son into something more aesthetically pleasing. As we embarked on the tedious job of painting woodwork – well, she painted, I held the emulsion and danced on a hotplate whenever she got bored – we talked. And once we'd covered all the topics we always mull over when circumstances bring us together without our parents (what kind of home we're going to put Mum in when the last strained filament tethering the balloon of sanity to her wrist finally snaps, how we're going to tell when Dad dies given that he hasn't moved perceptibly or spoken in the 30 years we've known him), we moved on to less pressing matters.

How the issue of compulsory voting came up, I don't know, since we're not, as siblings, normally given to political conversation. Perhaps the Live 8 music in the background was stirring latent inclinations. But predictably, our instinctive reactions were polar opposites. I burbled something about increased civic participation being a good idea, and she swung round with a juddering power tool in each hand and bellowed: 'They're not telling me what to do!'

In retrospect, it was a mistake to bring up ID cards – I mumbled about having originally believed that only wrongdoers had anything to fear. She embarked on a 20-minute diatribe about privacy, governmental snooping and databases deployed in unseemly ways – but perhaps Network Rail can use the tunnel she accidentally drilled to Croydon in the process.

It was at that point that I had a mini-epiphany. I'm used to being railroaded by members of the family into decisions 'for my own good', and somehow this has segued into letting the government do it too. Somewhere along the way, instead of reacting to every ministerial utterance with the flint-eyed scepticism that is the only sane response, I've begun to believe their insistence that they have my best interests at heart. This is a dangerously foolish belief when it's confined to your family, but expanded to include politicians, it's stupid beyond measure.

So instead of thinking, for example, 'Compulsory voting? With fines for abstentions? Might that not be a cunning wheeze to fill the treasury's coffers?' durbrain here shrugs and thinks, 'Oh gosh, I suppose they know best!'

Meanwhile, my sister, whose natural authoritarianism means she couldn't be railroaded by the Canadian Pacific, sees the government as her servant rather than master – which must logically be the most appropriate role for elected representatives – and treats the latest political propositions with the contempt they (I eventually realise) deserve. Counterintuitive though it may be, it seems personal tyrannical tendencies might be the best defence against encroachment on liberal ideals. I will revise my attitudes accordingly, and despotwards.

6 JULY 2005

My mum, the last of the small spenders

It is, frankly, a miracle that I have the strength left to type. For most of this week, you see, I have been teaching my mother – last of the cheque lovers – how to use her first credit card.

'What do I do with it?'

'Well, first of all, you stop holding it as if it were three pounds of primed semtex . . .'

'But it's a passport to debt, a one-way ticket to immorality and mortal sin.'

'But you are going pay it off every month, thus avoiding debt and, of course, eternal damnation. So. To pay for something, you just hand over the card and the assistant will ask you to put in your pin number.'

'You mean, I'll have to remember a four-digit number every time I want to buy something?'

'It won't make any difference. You can't remember your name since you came off HRT anyway.'

'At least this way fewer shop assistants will try to sit you down and give you shiny objects to play with while they call your GP.'

'So what do I do when they ask me for my pin?'

'You type it into a little machine.'

'They didn't send me a machine.'

'No, you gin-whopping moron, the machine will be at the till.'

'How do I pay it off?'

'You will be sent a statement. On it will be a list of things you have bought. You will ring me up and describe in Proustian detail the process of buying every item – nine-tenths of which will be blue skirts from Marks & Spencer, rather than jade statues of the Tang dynasty, and so incapable of supporting much in the way of riveting anecdote – and then ask me what the two figures at the end mean, even though they could not be more clearly labelled if they were etched in capitals into your own flesh and accompanied by a recording of Brian Sewell intoning the words "total balance" and "minimum payment".'

'What will they mean?'

'One will mean – how can I put this? – "the total balance". Yes, yes, they have left out the definite article in order to enrage you. The other will mean "the minimum payment" you can make. Now here's the tricky bit. Are you paying attention? You're not trying to remember who starred in *Shane* or still buzzing from that cappuccino you ordered in what you persist in calling the Kardomah but is in fact Starbucks?'

'Alan Ladd!'

'It's Friday. I'd like to go home for the weekend. Listen. You send a cheque to the credit people for the amount in "total balance". TOTAL BALANCE. Do. You. Understand?'

She. Did. Not. In the end, we decided the best thing to do would be to put the card with her mobile phone in the big pocket of her handbag labeled, 'Things that would make my life immeasurably easier but whose mastery will elude me for as long as attempts to dissipate my insane resistance to their existence keep causing close relatives to take their own lives'. We'll try again in October.

30 SEPTEMBER 2006

My father, the stranger

'Hi Dad.'

'Who's calling, please?'

'It's Lucy . . . your daughter.'

'Ah, yes. Which one are you again? The one that reads or the one that shops?'

'I'm the one that reads. Speaking of which – there's a story in the paper today about a girls' school in Surrey that is running a series of workshops for fathers to teach them how to understand and become closer to their daughters.'

'. . .'

'So, anyway, I thought I'd conduct some serious investigative journalism and ask you some of the questions that the workshop used.'

'Shall I get your mother?'

'No, Dad, it has to be you.'

'Why?'

'Because you're my father.'

'Am I? Still? But I thought you were 20 or so now. Does it still count?'

'I'm 32. And yes, we are still related. I had experts check. Look, here's question one.'

'Can I eat my meat and potato pie while you're talking to me?'

'By all means. Okay. Can you name my three best friends?'

'Umm . . . is one of them called Emily?'

'That's my sister.'

'Nokia?'

'That's a phone.'

'Then, no.'

'Right, question two. Do you make dinner for your family?'

'Your mother only ever stumbles across the kitchen by accident, and if she does, she can only make Gin Surprise. If I didn't make dinner we'd all starve.'

'Question three. Do you talk to other fathers about raising daughters?'

'No. I might talk to them about this pie, though. It's very good.'

'Four – do you tell your daughters what their strengths are?'

'I think – Emily, is it, the other one? – is quite strong. Maybe it's from carrying all those bags of shopping, or she might just take after her mother. Your mother was Garstang All-In Whippet Wrestling Champion in 1969. But you're quite small and weedy.'

'I think they mean "strengths" as in personal characteristics: things you're good at, your daughters' positive attributes.'

'Well, you've both got nice hair.'

'What about strengths in our personalities, say?'

'Isn't Emily quite enthusiastic about things? I seem to remember I'm usually tired after she's gone. And you . . . I don't know. You're just a bit odd. I mean, listen to you now, crying for no reason.'

'Final question. Do you know what your daughter is concerned about today?'

'I've no idea – finding a hanky?'

'Thanks Dad. Well, it's been good speaking to you.'

'Nice talking to you, too, Emma. Although I think that was mainly because of the pie.'

25 NOVEMBER 2006

Of course I love you both, but . . .

Dear Mum.

I gather you are bringing Auntie Eileen back with you when you return from your post-Christmas sojourn in the frozen north, so you can strip London of every court shoe priced in the sales at eight groats or under. I am writing to outline a few basic procedures and pieces of information with which I beg you to furnish yourselves before you arrive. I do this because you, Auntie Eileen, are a simpleton and Mum is a known and hyperventilating danger to herself and others when left unsupervised in a conurbation larger than Bromley. So:

1. Remember other people can hear you.

2. Remember, other people may not find your opinions on mobile phones, M&S's returns policy, the gay kiss in Coronation Street four years ago and the beginning of Valerie Clough's moral decline with the purchase of a new toaster with a hinged crumb tray as interesting or persuasive as you yourselves do.

3. Other people can see you. Do not wear your matching anoraks. You are not in a Mike Leigh film.

4. Mum, Eileen, you both somehow manage to combine a fundamentally pessimistic and hopeless outlook on life with a belief that trains run on time, that a city of 15 million people is a clean and welcoming place whose streets are filled with apple-cheeked children and helpful policemen, and whose inhabitants are all proud graduates with degrees in good citizenship. You are therefore wearyingly prone to dropping to the ground in a frothing fit if jostled, delayed, dirtied or aurally assaulted by mangled vowels at any time. If you cannot accept that your passage through one of the busiest and most over-crowded metropolises in existence may occasionally be impeded by the presence of other pedestrians, the fact that the public transport system is not specifically designed to take two menopausal tourists directly from their sitting room to John Lewis and the various unpredictable happenings that many people see as the very warp and weft

of life, I implore you to ingest a massive dose of tranquillisers 30 minutes before you set foot beyond the front door.

5. The natives are not expected to understand your accents, any more than Auntie Eileen could understand that man from Ramsgate who came into her pub and asked for 'a glarse of be-ah'. Remember how long it took her and her customers to work out that he was asking for a pint of Boddingtons? That's how strange you sound down here. Speak slowly and clearly at all times – and, whenever you can, just point at the enclosed picture dictionary that I have drawn for you: illustrations of a cup of coffee; a recently cleaned public lavatory; a toasted teacake, and an HRT patch should cover most of your foreseeable needs.

6. A cup of coffee in London costs about £2.50. I know it's more than either of you paid for your house, but get used to it. Or frigging well stay at home.

7. Most of your behaviours, which pass without comment at home, are at least as likely to get you removed to a place of safety as they are to be viewed as harmless idiosyncrasy or manageable eccentricity when observed in public. Do not, therefore, start trying to clean crumbs off the cafe carpet with handfuls of the sticky sock labels Grandma left to you in her will. Apart from anything else, what are you going to do if you use them all up and find that the Eubank has broken when you get home?

Aye, so think on.

Sincerely, your loving daughter/niece,

LK Mangan

27 JANUARY 2007

We are a godmother

So there I am, minding my own business, gently expanding to fill the sofa in the time-honoured post-Christmas manner, musing inwardly on the possibility of getting Dad to make me another bacon sandwich on the grounds that, after six solid days in the kitchen feeding his beloved wife and daughters through the festive season, another 20 minutes isn't going to make much difference. Then my mobile rings ('What's that, the one thing you haven't eaten?') and it is one of my oldest friends, Emily. She has recently given birth to her second baby – a boy, Peter, a brother for Amy, as I believe the hatching should be described in an aspiring paper of record – so I begin by congratulating her on her ability to operate the phone, a skill she didn't wholly regain for two years after the shock of the first infant.

Would I like to be William's godmother? 'I don't know,' I said. 'I've only met him once, and he didn't have much to say for himself.'

'He's four months old,' said Emily. 'He's not supposed to be saying anything.'

'But his sister does,' I pointed out.

'She's two and a half,' their mother replied.

It doesn't seem enough of an age gap to explain the difference to me, but I suppose she knows best.

'Well, if you're sure that's the reason – I don't want to be stuck as the spiritual guardian of a dullard or one of those weird children who never speaks but their eyes follow you wherever you go and you know they despise you to their very marrow and are devoting their lives to plotting your future downfall.'

She assures me everything will be fine. Oh well, if she is sticking me with the dud, I'll just boot him under a bush when I go round there and pretend to everyone that I'm really Evie's god mama.

But seriously, folks, I was in truth deeply moved by the request and sensible of the honour. In fact, it prompted quite the uncharacteristic bout of tears followed by a most unwelcome period of self-examination. Am I sufficiently morally upstanding to provide the support and advice required by the role? How will I resolve the conundrum posed by the requirement to renounce the devil and all his works if I don't believe in him, or indeed Him? And, most crucially, what will I wear to the christening?

Well, obviously I'd like to think I'm of relatively sound and honourable character: I don't vote for reality TV contestants, I don't dog-ear book pages, and I've never written for the *Daily Mail*. If I tidy the house up a bit, edit my sexual history judiciously and set up a direct debit to Oxfam, I reckon that, while I am forever unlikely to appear to anyone as a blazing beacon of integrity and sterling example of an individual striding unstoppably along the path of right through this wicked world of pomps and vanity, I am at least also unlikely to do a youngster already blessed with strong and devoted parents any actual harm with the example I set.

And as far as questions of faith are concerned, I note that the Rev Peter Bishop, chaplain of St Clement Danes in Fleet Street, has said that what is important is 'some sense of spiritual idealism', which I am going to interpret broadly enough to encompass my own vague feeling that if we did all behave according to basic religious tenets without necessarily believing in God, then the world would be an altogether more easeful place, and then have that printed on a T-shirt, as explanation of my position and ideal solution to the problem of what to wear.

6 JANUARY 2007

Boiling point

'So, remind me again what we're actually doing here, Mum?'

'Watching the kettle.'

'I see. And, with all due sense of anticipation and dread, precisely why?'

'I think it's leaking as it boils, but I can't see from where. So we need to watch a side each at the same time.'

'When you rewrite your will, you'll be sure to remember that I was the one who came round to help you do this, won't you?'

'I still don't know why Emily started crying when I asked her. And all that muttering about dark chasms of despair opening up beneath her feet the longer I spoke to her, blah, blah, blah. Is that a leak?'

'No, that's condensation. It looks like a daughter's tears, doesn't it?'

'You must get these simile things from your father. Nobody in my family uses them.'

'What are your plans for the rest of the day?'

'I was going to do some gardening, but I've realised I've got the wrong bra on.'

'Oh dear. Is there any way – and I realise I'm talking like a mad woman here – that you could change bras and proceed with your horticultural plans as originally envisaged?'

'No. I've got to wear this one all day so it's dirty enough for the wash tomorrow otherwise I won't have enough for a white load. Is that a leak?'

'No, that is a daughter's tears.'

'Why is this kettle leaking anyway? I've only had it 10 minutes. The one I got for my wedding lasted 27 years.'

'I'm not going to try to explain the concept of built-in obsolescence as the engine that drives the western economy to you again.'

'Was that part of the time that your father tried to explain capitalism to me?'

'Yes. And you decided that overall, it was a good thing because it meant you and your sister could buy new matching towels so if one of you accidentally dropped one in a vat of acid before guests arrived, the other could provide an instant replacement and deflect the looming threat of a mismatched bathroom set.'

'Oh yes. That was the day your father's head started to bleed.'

'Quite so.'

'He should get that seen to.'

'He says the blood loss gives him a pleasant sense of hazy detachment from it all. Look – is that something, there, by the filling gauge?'

'Yes! Yes, that's it! We've found it, the little bugger! Pass me the cloth and the soldering iron. And my welding mask – no, the small one.'

'Can I go now?'

'Yes. Thanks. I'll leave you the kettle in the will if you like.'

'I think, if it's all the same to you, I'd prefer not to have something to remember this by.'

24 FEBRUARY 2007

They don't make 'em like they used to

'Dad, the magazine's doing a special retro issue, so I need to talk to you about the past, the olden days, the golden years, so I can compare and contrast then and now, draw useful parallels, telescope our life experiences, look down the generations as though down an enfilade of rooms stuffed with comedy, tragedy and rewarding anecdote. Have you got a moment?'

'I thought you were the one that worked with computers?'

'No, that's Emily, my sister. Or Bill Gates.'

'Ah. What do you want to know?'

'How was it different then? What did you do for kicks without iPods and *Extreme Makeover*, tonight and every night on Living TV? What did you worry about? What was life like?'

He heaved a sigh that seemed to echo down the ages. 'Well,' he said, 'pull up that pie and I'll tell you.

'We didn't have to worry about all this global warming, for a start. That were easier. We just had to spend the eight months of winter under the stairs sitting round a penny candle. On Christmas Day, we'd light it. Come spring, we'd have a street party for anyone who was still alive, with trestle tables covered with Robert Owen tablecloths and piled high with bread and bread. "If we had some ham, we'd have ham and eggs, but we've no eggs!" people would say. How we laughed. Then coughed. Then some more people would die. But quietly, you know. No fuss. People had more discipline then.

'Look at the kids back then; we never needed that *Supernanny*. If you did wrong, the priest, the local bobby, your parents, grandparents, teachers and passersby used to line up to beat you with a nail-studded belt. If you'd been really bad, they'd bus in professionals from Rochdale. But we weren't troublemakers like these hoodie-slappers today, because there were always plenty to do for entertainment. The aviary at Moore Park with the peacock – we'd never seen the like; in fact, your uncle John worshipped it as a god for years. The boating lake, too: we liked to go look at that and take a bucket of water home for Mum in case she'd had a baby since we left and needed to drown it before tea. Then we'd go to the pond and club some ducks for us Sunday lunch.'

His eyes started to glitter with unshed tears. 'It were just a happier time. Everybody knew everyone else, everyone left their doors unlocked. We'd nowt to steal except the lichen on the walls, but still. We didn't know what it was like to be lonely. Yes, there was the occasional woman who went mad and ran up and down the street screaming, "If I don't get a moment to mysen one of these days, I'm going to throw myself off Scafell Pike!", but we'd all just roll our eyes and blame the change of life. Everybody smiled all the time. Through mouths of black and rotting teeth, of course, but still, they smiled. Doggedly, you know. That's what we've lost now. There's not enough dogged grinning in the world any more.'

'So everything was better 50 years ago?'

'Aye, lass, aye. Music-hall acts. Condensed milk. Pre-Vatican II Catholicism. The more equitable distribution of economic and social capital among the classes. And you could get gobstoppers the size of a baby's head for a farthing. Or a house.'

'So there's nothing to be said for Now rather than Then at all?'

He thought for a long moment. 'That Lily Allen,' he said finally, 'she's easier on the eye than George Formby. But I still wouldn't

give a dose of impetigo for her generic ska rhythms over Chinese
Laundry Blues. And you can tell your computers I said so.'

'Thanks, Dad,' I said. 'As ever, it's been an education.'

26 MAY 2007

Birthday greetings to a sister and accomplice

To my sister on the occasion of her 30th birthday:

I remember the day you were born – Grandma dressing me in
my best burlap frock and taking me to the hospital, where our post-
partum mother lay wreathed in pride and smiles. 'What have you
done with my real mummy?' I began to whimper. Fortunately just
then she noticed that Grandma had provided me with the wrong
socks for that particular dress and turned into the screaming maelstrom of fury that I knew and loved so well. And now, I thought,
I have a sister to share this with.

They handed you to me. Like most babies, you felt and smelled
like a giant gerbil in a blanket, though in your case the effect was
lessened by the fact that you had, as now, a head exactly the size
and shape of a football. 'That won't have done much in the way of
abrogating maternal rage,' I thought. And so it turned out.

But at least it ensured that we bypassed sibling rivalry in favour of
comradeship in adversity. I filled with delight when the first words
you spoke were ones I had taught you – 'Duck and cover! She's
coming!' – and treasure memories of hours spent designing fake adoption papers and trying to smuggle them to Mrs Donovan next door.

Later, you turned to me for advice on negotiating house rules.
'Why do we have to lay the table for breakfast eight days in advance?'
you would ask. 'Because we do,' I would patiently explain. 'Why
can't we sit on the sofa?' you would say. 'Because the cushions have
just been bumphled,' I replied. 'We're not allowed to use it until
Thursday.' 'Even Dad?' 'Even Dad.' 'But he's got two broken legs.'
'Even so, sister mine, even so.'

As you got older, however, we grew apart as you discovered a capacity for independent thought and grew dissatisfied and frustrated with life in the Ministry of Love. How I admired your spirited stands against the regime – seeing friends, sitting on sofas, taking food up to the bedroom and laying out napkins with the rose motif pointing far from mandated north-north-west.

Then you went off to university, rapidly establishing yourself as the social hub of the student universe and spending the entire three years without wasting a moment on sleep, work or coming home. You were an example to all of us who had unquestioningly absorbed the dictum that skimping one's homework was a mortal sin and consequently hadn't stopped crying since 1982.

Now you live in Bristol, which means that our sisterly bond is maintained by phone and email – in my case fluid and comprehensible, in yours so profoundly misspelled and ungrammatical that I sometimes think Mum might have had a point about the homework thing. Fortunately, you work with computers, so no one has yet noticed your functional illiteracy, and I will continue to write your Christmas cards home for as long as you need me.

In my head, you are still eight and building Exocet missiles out of Sticklebricks behind the armchair and the cordon you, with admirable foresight in one so young, established two years before, when you first became conscious of the existence of those who would seek to destroy your freedoms. But now you are 30, and about to embark on your years of juggling career options with your shrivelling ovaries, nights out with the girls followed by long, dark nights of the soul, and the inexorably rising sense of your own mortality looming over all you do, polluting your every thought and infecting everything you love, acquire or dream of with a grinding knowledge of ultimate futility. Happy birthday, Em. Your loving sister, Lucy, aged 32 and three-quarters.

9 JUNE 2007

Unto the breach, with gifts

Mum and I gazed in consternation at the sparse and even more depressing than usual array of gifts we had bought the nominal head of the household for his birthday: black socks, a book we were pretending we didn't know he already had, and a blue anorak to replace the one he ruined during an ill-advised attempt to help Mum paint the garage door. 'Why don't we just give him a big card saying, "Happy birthday, Richard – at least death will be more exciting than this?"' I suggested.

'We'll have to go to Bromley and buy something else,' she decided. These innocuous words were indicative of a swift and practical solution only to those blissfully unaware that such an undertaking in our family is preceded by a programme of preparations more usually geared towards landing allies on wartime Gallic beaches.

We gathered 82 shopping bags and put them in the boot. We changed her shoes ('The blue ones. No, not the dark blue – when I mean dark blue, I'll say dark blue. The ones on the shelf labelled "22 to 39 minutes of urban-walking-on-the-flat-plus-driving"'). We checked the doors and windows in case of burglars. We tidied the house and cleaned the bathroom in case Grandma could see the state of the place from her seat in heaven. Eight days later we set off, pausing only to repoint some brickwork, landscape the garden and DNA-test some dog turds so they could at a later date be returned to their rightful owners.

'Oh, I'm sorry!' she shouted periodically out of the window as jackasses nos 32-46 cut her up on Bromley Road. 'I didn't realise there was a festival of stupidity going on!' she cried while I frantically wound up the windows and prayed to Grandma that the average boy racer is a) deaf, and b) more intent on getting to his solvent-abuse party than on knifing to death middle-aged women and their daughters on busy public thoroughfares.

Against what had seemed like insurmountable odds, we arrived safely, parked the car and ransacked the Glades for gifts. We bought Dad some low-sugar chocolates on the grounds that we dimly remembered him once saying something about being borderline diabetic, and a huge straw hat on the grounds that we dimly remembered him having an enormous head and being a bit bald. Then, of course, like a mothership calling us home, we were drawn into the M&S food aisles for our own delectation, where we wandered, mouths agape with all thoughts of the birthday boy driven from our minds by the proliferating riches before us.

'Remind me of our family motto,' I said as we walked along the 20-mile, all-butter shortbread section.

'With malice aforethought?' said Mum, puzzled.

'No,' I said, 'the other one.'

'You mean – if we had some ham we could have ham and eggs, but we've no eggs?' said Mum.

'Yes,' I said, grabbing another packet of mini milk-and-honey balls. 'Do you ever think somebody's turning in their grave?'

'No,' said Mum. 'I think we should get some cheese biscuits.'

'Which cheese biscuits?'

'The nice cheese biscuits.'

'Oh, good. I hate it when we get the horrible cheese biscuits.'

The next day, Dad proclaimed himself deliriously happy with his presents. 'Ee, you shouldn't have gone to so much trouble,' he said. 'I'd have been happy with a bit of wood or summat.'

I don't know exactly what age Dad is now, but I feel like a very, very old woman indeed.

18 AUGUST 2007

Speculation on accumulation

Unless you are very careful, annual events are a prime opportunity for pause and reflection, a time to consider what a difference a year has made, the achievements and failures that have accumulated over the twelvemonth. This week it was the Christmas fair in the local church hall – to which my parents and I have been going since I was knee-high to a trestle table – that caught me unawares and left me ruminating on life, family and the memories of the past that too often threaten to shackle our futures. I only went in to buy a raffle ticket.

Thanks to judicious investment (otherwise known as shacking up with someone and splitting the bills), my disposable income has risen significantly over the past 12 months. I stroll to the raffle table with the air of a Rothschild. I laugh in the face of the 25p single tickets and gesture elegantly towards the £1-a-strip sign. I break a 26-year losing streak on the third ticket and raise the jar of luxury mincemeat in triumph.

I realise that with my new capacity for capital outlay, profit is all but assured. When he sees me reaching for another pound, my dad attempts to remonstrate. 'Don't do it lass – wi' that kind of money, tha' could buy enough seed potatoes to crop 'til Michaelmas!' he begs. 'Dad, you run a theatre museum,' I reply. 'You wouldn't know a seed potato from a Lalique vase.' ''Appen,' he says darkly, 'but I've seen t' misery gambling brings. Your auntie Maudlin backed 32 losing pigs in the 1954 Garstang Pork Belly Guild's steeplechase. We had to sell three Lowrys and the coal scuttle to pay her debts. Not that Lowry – his brother. Painted pictures of fat people having picnics in Surrey. Pity, that.'

I look at him with love, mixed with compassion, mixed with contempt. How to explain my situation to a man who has never owned more than half a pair of shoes and still thinks in groats? 'I'm not gambling, Dad,' I say gently. 'Look: one, two, three, four pound coins in this purse! And there's more where that came from, I promise you! When you're dealing with these kinds of sums, the rules change. You have to speculate to accumulate.'

'We used to sleep in that coal scuttle,' he says. 'And watch the firelight play on its burnished sheen until we fell asleep. Well, we had to imagine the firelight because we'd no money for fuel. And no room in t' scuttle for it, of course. But when it went, it broke me mother's heart. When we had the scuttle to sleep in, we were as good as anybody. But afterwards . . .' He trails away, lost in black and dusty memories.

But I can't be bound for ever by the past. I buy another strip. The Sainsbury's cava is mine. By now a crowd has gathered and a breathless hush has descended over the hall, broken only by the sound of a mother outside slapping her wailing child. Inside, the silence is unbroken until I open the final ticket and take proud possession of a knitted teddy in red dungarees. The crowd, exhausted by the tension and awed by the largesse scattered and received, applauds, then melts respectfully away.

The mincemeat I pass over to Dad to add to the stores he has been laying in for 30 years against harsher times, and he accepts it with cold contempt. The cava I drink in bitter celebration. And the teddy bear is perched now on my desk as I type, a constant reminder that it is not luck, hard work, prudence or good intentions that bring success in this life – it is money. Lots and lots of money. And, to be fair, the ability to resist the temptations of regional pig racing.

1 DECEMBER 2007

The gift of giving

'Who's calling, please?'

'You know who's calling. You've got caller ID. You recognise my voice. And I sent you an email saying that I would ring at 11 o'clock. It's Lucy.'

'Lucy who?'

'Lucy your sister. And, as I suspect from your procrastinatory manoeuvres, you know I am ringing to talk about buying presents this Christmastide for the bundles of mental confusion, rapidly degrading DNA and increasingly irrational prejudices that masquerade as our parents and assorted other members of our family.'

'I thought we divorced the parents?'

'No, remember, we looked into it, but turns out it's only a California thing.'

'Can we move to California?'

'Before 25 December? No.'

'OK. Let's do the easy ones first. Auntie Judy?'

'Gin.'

'Auntie Eileen?'

'Gin.'

'Great-auntie Annie?'

'Meths.'

'Uncle Alan, who, when seen through our childish eyes, was once a delightfully colourful character, full of raffish charm and certain to add picaresque excitement to family gatherings, but whose complex personal and business affairs we regard with increasing dubiety as the years go by and the line between rakish disregard for money and tax evasion becomes rather too thin?'

'An envelope full of small, untraceable bills. And a good woman.'

'Cousins one to 836?'

'Our very best wishes for a merry Christmas and a happy new year.'

'Right. Now, what about Mum? What shall we give her?'

'Pills.'

'No, she started spitting them out last year. But bring them anyway and we'll crush them up and put them into her cranberry sauce. Or ours. Works either way.'

'I've been saving sticky labels for the past 12 months so that she can use them to pick up bits from the carpet and not get the vacuum cleaner out.'

'What's her objection to the vacuum cleaner again?'

'I quote from Grandma's Ordinances, section 243, subsection (b), clauses (iv)-(xii): "Electrical appliances are outlawed as the single greatest cause of moral turpitude. Where a viable manual alternative is available, be it ever so much more impractical, uncomfortable, time-consuming and/or palpably insane, it must be used."'

'I thought we were due an overhaul of the more arcane pieces of family legislation last year?'

'We were, but first of all we were all still too exhausted from the Great Ewbank Debate of 1998 to propose any more serious reforms. And then you made that flippant remark about buying a sandwich maker, and we had to spend the entire week saying novenas for you instead.'

'Ah yes. That was foolish. OK, how about we give her the sticky labels, some gin, a Bakelite radio and an oilcloth? Or a mule.'

'Excellent. And Dad?'

'Tricky. Unless, of course, you have managed to find somewhere on eBay a history of Preston North End written by Bill Shankly on chip papers and bound in the skin of Tom Finney?'

'So far, no luck. Why don't we get him a pair of shoes?'

'He'd say he's already got a pair.'

'But they don't match.'

8 DECEMBER 2007

Keep it in the family

It is Christmas Eve Eve Eve! I'm so excited. My presents are bought, wrapped and packed into three Sainsbury's Bags for Life awaiting transport in the Dadmobile when he arrives tomorrow morning to take me to the family pile. ('Hi Dad . . . Dad – over here, Dad. It's me. Lucy. No, I've lived here for three years. It doesn't matter. Let's go home. No, your home. Where you keep your pills and string. No, that way.') My sister has arrived and is filling the bath with Baileys in case of emergency. We have made our parents sign affidavits that there will be stockings this year despite our having a combined age of 63. They have made us sign similar documentation swearing that we will, between us, provide them with at least one grandchild before the entire festive season becomes a hollow charade, drained of gaiety and incapable of keeping at bay any longer the darkling sense of futility at the centre of our existence. 'As long as you don't forget the tangerine and pound coin in the toe!' we replied cheerfully, and signed on the tearstain-dotted line.

Mum is, of course, in the kitchen. She is wondering when Dad is going to get back and start cooking. There is a lot to do. He has to peel 852 potatoes, make 18 pints of gravy, set up a row of saline drips to nurse his daughters back to health in the impending mornings after the nights before, and make sure we have ham tomorrow, roast beef on Christmas Eve and goose on Christmas Day. On Boxing Day we all take care of ourselves – usually just by licking the meat sweats off each other and working our way through the Roses tin for pudding.

If this sounds like a wantonly profligate, revolting orgy of self-indulgence, I can say only that you are right. But you do have to set the 72-hour blowout against the pathologically minimalist approach to comfort and joy that characterises our lives for the other 362 days a year. My family's general modus operandi would make a mendicant friar look like Elton John.

My grandma refused to sit down for 82 years, so that she wouldn't wear out the sofa. We had to break her knees in the end. My dad can live off one egg and a teabag for a week. My mother darns everything, including leftovers and the paper napkins we all steal from cafes. We have to call a four-day summit if anyone spends more than £12.50 on a haircut, meal or car. We have family recipes passed down through the generations that read:

Buy mince.

If a child or local slag heap is already on fire, cook mince.

Add breadcrumbs.

Add more breadcrumbs.

Take out mince. Will do for Sunday.

Add one tin oxtail soup.

Dilute to point of invisibility.

Serve with a picture of potatoes.

Garnish with tears and the prayer for a better life far, far away from here.

I was the only person of my generation to read *Little House On the Prairie* stories ('Laura sat on her wooden spike and ate grass-hoppers and cornbread before going out to the barn to twist hay for dinner while Ma pulled splinters out of her butt to add to the kindling pile where baby Carrie slept') for the luxurious life of plenty they portrayed. One day we will doubtless work out that there is a difference between enjoying the benefits that 21st-century western living has to offer and hurling ourselves into a yawning abyss of sybaritic pleasures and moral degradation, and yuletide celebrations will find calmer expression. But that time is not yet nigh and so, until then, it is – briefly, gloriously, even and especially for canker-hearted cretins like us – the season to be jolly. Merry Christmas!

22 DECEMBER 2007

Why is Dad potty about potatoes?

'Dad? Dad? Dad, look at me. No, that's a beanbag, and I'm going to choose to believe you're not making a point. I'm over here.'

'Hello, love. When did you get here?'

'Three days ago. After I rang you up saying that my internet connection was broken and could I come and stay with you until it was fixed, otherwise I could do no work and my household would be plunged into penury, remember?'

'No.'

'Didn't you wonder why Mum was making you move your Bobby Charlton puppets off the spare bed?'

'I just assumed she wanted to lie there weeping again. And distractedly scratch occasionally at the wallpaper.'

'Anyway. Guess what tomorrow is?'

'It's Nicola Pagett's birthday. I've made her a card with little tissue-paper flowers. She lights up the screen, you know.'

'I know, Dad, I know. But what else happens tomorrow?'

'It's Delaware Separation Day. June 15 1776 they voted to suspend government under the British crown and officially separated from Pennsylvania. They usually hold some celebratory festivities in Battery Park.'

'Well, fancy. But no, I was trying to make the point that tomorrow is, in fact, Father's Day.'

'Is it?'

'So Emily and I – your daughters –'

'That's right. And I've always been fond of you, I think.'

'Thank you. So, Emily and I were wondering if there's anything you'd particularly like for it?'

'We don't do Father's Day in this house, do we?'

'Not usually, no. But this year Em and I have decided, after raking the barren landscape of your existence for any organic sign of life, hope or joy, to make it your special day from now on.'

'Isn't that kind? Let me think . . .'

'Dad? Dad? No, that's the beanbag again. Follow the clicking of my fingers. That's right. Hello! OK, you've been thinking for three hours.'

'About what?'

'About what you would like for Father's Day.'

'Ah, yes.'

'And have you decided?'

'Yes.'

'Great. What is it?'

'I would like – a potato.'

'No, Dad. I want you to try to think of something else. Something on a grander scale.'

'A big potato.'

'No, Dad. Try again. Really let your imagination roam free. Let it journey hither and yon, across the wildest unexplored regions.

Wander through bosky woods, dive into the tangled undergrowth, leap across unexpected ravines. Let the heady scents of exotic flora intoxicate you, let the tendrils of thought twist and climb unfettered around your brain, let the feeling of limitless possibility suffuse your senses and make the world seem for a moment not only a rich and radiant cornucopia of offerings shimmering before you, but yours for the asking.'

'I've got pans in soak.'

'I'll look after them. Off you go. No, no, stay here. I meant off you go – in your mind.'

'All right.'

Later . . .

'Em – hi, it's me. He wants a potato. No, a big one. Yes, yes, I tried. Can you go out and get it? I haven't time. Got a lot of weeping and distracted scratching at the wallpaper to do. No, she seems fine at the moment, so I've got the bed to myself. See you tomorrow. Bye.'

14 JUNE 2008

Every little helps

It was a risk, going home for dinner at such a time, but the sense of filial duty beats strongly in these veins. We sat in silent apprehension, eating our pasta in small, cautious bites, until Mum spoke at last. 'What,' she said apparently casually, 'do you think of Tesco changing its '10 Items Or Less' sign?' Dad put down his knife and fork, and pushed them together. The tiny clink rang out as an unmistakable declaration of the opening of Round 62,237 of this recurring fight.

Tesco, you see, is changing the traditional, ungrammatical signs at its express tills to ones that read 'Up to 10 Items', a compromise suggestion from the Plain English Campaign after it became clear that the supermarket was never going to go the whole '10 Items Or Fewer' hog.

As a family, we have few abstract points of contention. Generally, we like to keep arguments specific and concrete – who ate the last peppermint cream, who lost the door keys, who killed Grandma, that kind of thing. But let a grammatical solecism rear its ugly head and the dinner table air becomes thick with bloodlust. My mother, as you might expect from a woman who used to break my fingers for putting our beige napkins down 'the wrong way', believes that the rules of grammar are semi-divine and wholly immutable. A split infinitive, 'different to' or 'none are': these are the things that try her soul, at least if there aren't any inverted napkins around. Dad, meanwhile, embraces 'mistakes' as part of the natural evolution of language. Presented with an empurpled wife insisting that 'to aggravate' means 'to make worse', not 'to annoy', he will proclaim that 'effete' once meant 'having given birth'. Each seeks my support. Bending my head to my plate, I feel like the trembling victim of a soon-to-be-broken home.

As a product of this ideological miscegenation, I make up my mind from rule to rule. Split infinitives? A meaningless hangover from the days when Latin was deemed the perfect language, and whose single word infinitives were incapable of being split. Impose such notional incapability on English ones, and you get frequently ugly sentences and no offsetting gain in sense or clarity. 'To boldly go' is correct in every possible way. Let the rule wither and die. But, conversely, what good is done by losing the distinction between 'aggravate' and 'annoy'? None. Clearly, its preservation must be defended to the death. (I think Dad is going for easy points – changes in vocabulary are easier to defend than abandonment of grammatical rules, because they rarely result in fundamental confusion. Changing definitions are the equivalent of changing the colour of icing on a cake. But if you stopped bothering making verbs agree with their subjects, you would find yourself trying to decorate a flourless pool of egg.)

As for fewer and less, I can't think of an example where abolition of the distinction would cause confusion, but my heart mourns its loss. It may not be necessary in strictly practical terms, but who wants a strictly practical language? Less for amounts, fewer for countable things – it's the kind of linguistic flourish that pulls you up, keeps you attentive and keeps things interesting.

Tesco's evasive 'Up To 10 Items', however, does nothing but create confusion – can you now take only nine things to the till? – so perhaps it is time I made up my mind and gave one or other of the aged Ps my full support. That said, if they keep arguing, I'll be able to sneak off to the sofa before the allotted time without their noticing. Mmm . . . would that all my acts of cowardice could be so delightfully cushioned.

13 SEPTEMBER 2008

Present tense

'It can't be that time of year again already,' my sister says mutinously.

'Oh, but it is,' I assure her.

'Hang on then.' If the aural memories of childhood do not betray me, I hear the metallic snaps of a new, two-litre bottle of gin being opened and four fat fingers of the good stuff being poured into a cheap tumbler. 'Go.'

'OK . . . For Mum's Christmas presents, I put forth the following suggestions: 'Detailed plot synopses of every episode of *CSI, CSI: Miami, CSI: New York, Law & Order, Law & Order: Criminal Intent, Law & Order: Special Victims Unit* and *Where the Heart Is*, so I no longer have to spend every evening on the phone to her explaining the stories in real time, only to be faced, 45 minutes in, with the cry, "Oh, no, I've seen this one!" It harrows the soul.'

'Computer lessons.'

'Electroshock therapy.'

'A grandchild.'

'The handbag she saw but can't remember where she saw it.'

'The handbag? It must be in Marks & Spencer or John Lewis, since she doesn't know that any other shops exist – do we have any other identifying details?'

'It's black and it'll take her anywhere.'

'Hang on.' More metallic snaps echo down the line. 'OK, continue.'

'OK, for Dad, I put forth the following suggestions: "Detailed CVs of the two of us that he can refer to for conversational topics next time he is forced to answer the phone."'

'Electroshock therapy for Mum.'

'A pie.'

'Another pie.'

'Maybe another pie.'

'What did we get him last year?'

'A pair of shoes. He returned them on the grounds that he already had a pair.'

'The pair that didn't match?'

'Correct. He contended that his feet don't match.'

'What about a hat? We can't go wrong there, surely? He's only got one head.'

'But it's a giant head. It blocks out the sun. It's why we didn't have a photographer at the wedding.'

'An anorak? A nice warm one – but not too nice, or warm – from Burton's Lapsed Catholic range.'

'He says his current one will see him out. He still says he's going to make sure he dies next year.'

'OK, I've got an idea. Why don't we take stuff away from him for Christmas? Every time it's his turn for a present, we'll take away one of his shirts, or a book, or an Uncle Joe's mint ball, and put it in a box and tell him he's not getting it back. By the end of the day, he'll just have the clothes on his back and a plate of turkey leftovers to his name. He'll love it.'

'You're a genius. And, finally, what would you like for Christmas, sister mine?'

'I would like a pair of diamond pendant earrings, hot monkey sex with either – and ideally both – of the Petrelli boys from *Heroes*, and some class-A drugs.'

'OK, let me put it this way: anything from Hotel Chocolat?'

'Ooh, some chocolate would be nice.'

'Consider it done.'

'And for you?'

'I'd like a lie-in, a cleaner and a Thorazine drip to get me through the day.'

'And from Hotel Chocolat?'

'Some chocolate would be great.'

'Consider it equally done. See you on the 25th.'

'I shall start drinking now.'

'That's the spirit. And try not to cry at the same time. It sprags up your electrolytes something rotten. Bye!'

13 DECEMBER 2008

Who's the daddy?

I knew it was a mistake to stop my pseudo-goddaughter putting sand up her bum on my last visit. So impressed was her mother with my vigilance and interventionist skills ('I'd stop doing that if I were you, kid.' 'Why?' 'Because otherwise the next time you do a poo, it will scratch your bottom all the way out') that she bulldozed me into babysitting the child – aged three and a half – and her little brother, Peter, who I think must be coming up to his first birthday, assuming he's the same baby as the one whose christening I remember getting drunk at about a year ago. He is my real godchild, but the position has been subject to a sort of mission creep and I now stand in loco deo-parentis to both him and his sister, which should work out very well for everyone, provided only one of us ever has a spiritual crisis at a time.

The prospect of babysitting, of course, promises more tangible and immediate crises. 'I don't think I'm allowed to have sole charge of two small children,' I said dubiously when their mother first mooted the idea.

'Who's forbidden it?' she said. Barristers – always such sticklers for detail.

'My mother?' I hazarded. 'The NSPCC? Common sense alone?'

'You'll be fine. Be here by 9.30am. I want to have a full day's sales shopping without any kind of sick or puree landing in my hair.'

She sells it well. I arrive at the appointed time. We survive snack time, nap time, lunch time and are just settling down for playing-nicely-and-not-biting-each-other time when Amy digs a postcard out from the back of the sofa. 'Who's that?' she says pointing at the picture, which is a medieval portrait of the Madonna and child.

'That is baby Jesus.'

'And who's that?' she asks of the woman holding him.

'That's Mary,' I say, a faint sense of unease stirring in my breast. 'Who's she?'

'Jesus's mummy,' I say reluctantly.

There is a brief pause. Infant cogs turn. Adult cogs are momentarily distracted by Peter falling into the washing-up bowl currently doing service as the HMS Polypropylene Upon the Rug Sea. 'Who,' Amy asks with a frown, 'is Jesus's daddy?'

'Joseph, because he was married to Mary,' I say. 'But a lot of people say God was his real daddy.' What? What am I doing? If I have a founding belief, it is that children in my care should be given information purely on a need-to-know basis. Now, in one sentence, I have managed to foster the notion that only the marital state can give rise to offspring, and opened the door to a theological discussion with a pre-school child.

And, sure enough, she says, 'What is God?'

'Look,' I want to say to Amy, 'I have no idea what your mother would want me to tell you at this point. I don't even know what I would tell you at this point if you were mine. Would I cleave tightly to my rational principles and fillet your tiny mind of any belief in an omniscient deity, benevolent or otherwise, from the start? Or would I ultimately consider the crushing, awful knowledge of the fundamentally random, uncaring nature of the universe should be kept from you as long as possible?'

What I actually say amounts to a rambling 15-minute discourse on God being the spirit that moves her to withhold from biting her brother on occasion, the loving kindness in everyone and the hope that we'll all one day learn to be friends with everyone.

She listens patiently. 'So,' she says as I finally stumble to a close, 'he's not a dragon then?'

'No,' I say after a pause.

She lays a kindly hand like a tiny starfish on my knee. 'Just say so, why not?' she says.

I'll know next time.

3 JANUARY 2009

CHAPTER THREE

ALL YOU OTHER FREAKS

The truth about Beckham's 'sex' texts

A nation reels at the news that Golden Balls may have feet of clay. David Beckham, it is claimed, has had an affair and tabloids have published the 'explicit' text messages between him and his inamorata to prove it.

Or have they? So heavily asterisked are the published messages that those of us still clinging to our belief in the unshakeable fidelity of the nation's favourite secular saint may yet have our faith justified. Anyone looking at the allegedly steamy mobile phone correspondence without a mind hopelessly mired in tabloid filth will find a ready explanation for the conversations. Rebecca Loos, the recipient of Beckham's epistolary efforts, was not just his PA, she was his guide, his interpreter, his link to Spanish culture and much of their banter clearly revolves around Beckham's efforts to get to grips with the language. Prescriptive grammarians may like to take an aspirin or two, but nobody else's delicate sensibilities will be affected by reading further.

DB: OK, you need to save all that energy for **** [Here, the asterisks are clearly substituting the word 'verbs']

RL: Is it **** [Just as here, the absent word is 'necessary']

DB: Very, very **** [necessary], thinking of your **** [transitive/intransitive explanation] and the **** [conjugations].

RL: Remember the last time your tongue was all over me [evidently a misprint for 'the place'] I have never **** [laughed] so hard.

DB: Now I am doing something, thinking about your **** [dictionary]

RL: **** [Use] your **** [thesaurus].

Later, their minds have obviously turned to Beckham's culinary prowess. Naturally, the repository of all that is good and cherishable about modern masculinity can knock up a tasty dish or two.

RL: Your tongue **** **** **** **** [salad rocked my world] then softly on my **** **** **** **** **** [plate came superb creme brulee].

Before the chatty pair sign off for the evening, they share some thoughts about soft furnishings.

DB: Love the sound of that cotton just **** **** **** ***** [works in any room] getting more **** [popular] and your **** [designs] all nice **** **** [for summer].

One can understand the attraction that text messaging – in all its vowelless simplicity – holds for Beckham, who is often derided for being less nimble in conversation than he is on the pitch. His facility with the form is commendable. I don't doubt that, should he ever wish to engage in the tricky art of text sex, his natural physical dexterity, powers of concentration and willingness to fillet his prose so ruthlessly will stand him in exceptionally good stead. But the notion that the intended recipient of his abbreviated billet doux would be anyone other than the lovely Skeletal Spice – well, shm on u, sr, shm on u.

6 APRIL 2004

How to pull at parties

As the party season and its myriad opportunities for sexual mis-adventure rapidly approaches, I feel I should no longer keep to myself valuable information I was recently vouchsafed on the topic of Finding a Suitable Man. It came from a very posh friend of mine whom we shall call Alice Band, partly in homage to the most indispensable item in her wardrobe, and partly to protect her from identification in the unlikely event that any of her friends reads this communist rag instead of using it to set fire to the cottages of recalcitrant tenants. She is herself married to a man (whom we will call Hugh Landed-Gentry for similar reasons) and they live in the country in connubial bliss, suffused with a lambent joy that sickens all around them.

Last month, having been regaled with (severely edited) versions of the various sexual debacles in which I have recently starred and understandably concluded that I am no longer to be left to my own devices in matters of the heart and/or genitals, Alice distilled the distaff wisdom of 17 generations into a handful of easily memorised rules. I set them out below for those of you who are either keen to meet The One but who habitually end up at the end of parties with the troglodytic dregs of humanity, or those who are simply keen to experience time travel without the inconvenience of having to learn astrophysics and build a Tardis.

I have appended my own thoughts as they occurred to me, and doubtless you will wish to annotate further before tucking this modern-day *Debrett's Guide* into your handbag for future reference:

1. Arrive early. This enables you to size everyone up as they come through the door and decide which are the ones worth pursuing. Note to self: It is possible, of course, that any pre-emptive filtering advantage will be more than outweighed by the fact that, from the male point of view, they are being stalked by a stranger with scorecards who clearly has nothing better to do than turn up at parties three

hours before the time generally considered socially acceptable. I can only suggest that in my next life I make sure I am born of the kind of ancient lineage that makes such crippling self-consciousness a constitutional impossibility.

2. Don't talk to girls. It is a waste of time.

Note to self: I believe Alice is wasted as a housewife when there are still thousands of small African principalities crying out for an unblinking despot.

3. Only talk to people you know if they are talking to someone to whom you would like to be introduced.

There are a number of implicit assumptions here, upon which we must pause for cogitation.

First, Alice assumes I am still sober and capable of rational thought/adhering to the masterplan by this stage of the party. Remember, I have arrived early and have worked up a thirst sorting the new arrivals by height, weight and eligibility.

She assumes that I know people.

She assumes that I will want to be introduced to new people, when in fact I have the social proclivities of an old sock.

4. If I am talking about plays or films, always say, 'Oh yes, I really want to see the new Tom Stoppard/reissued Ingmar Bergman/ *Puppetry of the Penis.*' When he says, 'Well, we should go and see it together,' you say, 'Oh, how wonderful. Will you arrange it or shall I?'

Note to self: I love the 'When'.

I also love the vision I have of him reeling backwards and muttering to the nearest lawyer to inquire about the length of time it would take to procure a fake passport and a flight to Cuba.

5. Never leave a party without getting at least two invitations to other events (and it must be a twofer minimum, as one is bound to clash with an engagement already in your diary).

Note to self: I love the idea that I have a social life busy enough to make a diary clash statistically possible. Almost as much as I love the idea of having a diary.

Never have I seen the gulf between impeccable vowel sounds, bone structure, folk memory of the Raj and me open up so sweetly. What could I do but doff my cap, bend the knee and retire? Still, this quintet has secured her the love of what even my cankered heart must admit is a man who makes Fitzwilliam Darcy look like a whingeing milksop. So, off you go – be sure to put quill to parchment and let me know how you get on.

1 DECEMBER 2004

The season of ill will

So, just as the pre-Christmas pressure starts to build to its terrifying annual climax, research from the University of California reveals that stress can knock up to 10 years off your life. It's a toss-up, then, as to whether my mother or sister will shuffle, rigid with tension, off this mortal coil first. Both suffer cardiac arrhythmia if they drive more than 100 metres. After Walkmans became commonplace, both had to find jobs which didn't involve train travel otherwise they ruptured a blood vessel every time someone in the next seat added an unsought percussive element to their journey.

My father, by contrast, remains unaffected by the modern malady – possibly because he retreated in 1977 to Richardland, surrounded by impregnable walls made of books, newspapers and looped memories of Tom Finney playing for Preston North End, through which no noise or other irritations can pass. He will doubtless live to 108, with a seraphic smile playing gently about his lips the entire time.

Control of your environment (physically or mentally) is a vital ingredient for a relaxed existence. I make concerted efforts to live an adrenaline-free life. I took what my mother persists in calling 'a proper job' as a solicitor in order to get a flat and mortgage, bidding adieu to landlord-wrangling and the pervasive sense of being royally screwed that property rental brings. I don't invite for dinner people who are so boring they make me bleed from the ears, even if they are shacked up with some of my closest friends. I do all my Christmas shopping in November and I never go anywhere on New Year's Eve (a resolution which becomes easier to keep every year, given the increasing numbers of couples I have offended in the preceding 12 months).

But there are times when changing or avoiding the situations that try one's soul is not possible. For example, unless you have the nervous system of a clam, or your GP is one of those helpful sorts who will pump you full of Thorazine as he presses a jarful of Seroxat into your hands, public transport seems an inexhaustible source of vexation for us non-drivers. But I recently had something of an epiphany on that score, thanks to a woman opposite me on the train, who had been trying to read her book despite the concerted efforts of Man On Mobile to keep most of south-east London informed of the fascinating intricacies of shipping mannequins from Scotland to Burnley at a time of a national BubbleWrap shortage. She looked up, caught my eye and said simply, 'I hate him'.

There are times when one searches for detailed, subtle critiques, when one wants to revel in a Tynanesque dissection of a fleetingly magical moment, or when one longs for a GK Chesterton to leap forward and proffer a selection of finely wrought essays that will be handed down through the generations to illuminate anew a glorious figure of the age. This was not one of them. 'I hate him,' amply sufficed. I looked at the MOM and thought, 'I hate you too. I hate you beyond reason, beyond words. I hate you from the primordial depths of my soul. I wish that a swift and pitiless retribution could be exacted upon you, that you could be dragged from this carriage and beaten to a pulp in front of me and the rest of those people whose brief opportunity for rest and quiet contemplation you have polluted with your banal conversation and ruined with your selfishness and arrogance, you piss-poor excuse for a human being.'

And I felt better.

Perhaps it is this refusal to admit how deep the wellspring of hatred for our fellow man runs that gets us into such trouble, legally, politically and socially. A law is proposed that will – if I have understood the details correctly – entitle us to shoot anyone wearing a Burberry cap outside a nice house on sight, and has to be undermined with mealy mouthed nonsense about unjustifiable homicide and the rule of law that no one really understands and infuriates large sections of the populace. Far better to state that if we open that can of worms, everyone knows that every home in England will be bristling with wall-mounted Kalashnikovs, the streets will be running with blood and eventually Ant and Dec will get caught in the crossfire and ripped in an untimely manner from the future of light entertainment.

It's not shopping but the seasonal demand to demonstrate goodwill to all men that causes stress to peak at Christmas. Embrace misanthropy instead – the truth will set you free.

8 DECEMBER 2004

The sign of a moron

A friend and I have parted company. The separation papers cite 'irreconcilable differences'. For years I have endured with equanimity her inability to distinguish between the phrases 'I'll meet you at seven' and 'Do feel free to turn up at whatever time you have finished the duties you feel take priority over the fact that I am sitting alone in a pub being propositioned by every lump of lard with a half of bitter and vestigial sexual urges.' I barely flinched when she borrowed my flat for a party and left it looking like the last days of Sodom had been re-enacted with extra verve in a hitherto unspoiled corner of south-eastern suburbia.

But on New Year's Eve she went too far. As the fireworks exploded and the clock struck midnight (that's such a lie – I mean, as we all stood round someone's mobile phone waiting to give a desultory hurrah when the digits changed), I happened to mention the jaw-dropping news that in 2004 Russell Grant had received more hits on Google than David Beckham. I intimated that this was the signal to indulge in a moment of unmitigated despair for the future of humanity. Instead of instantly demonstrating agreement with my thesis by fashioning a Shelley von Strunckel doll out of the nearest cushion and setting it on fire, she replied, 'Well, you know – there is something in it.'

'What?' I asked.

'Well, you know, just something.'

'You have opposable thumbs and a limbic system, don't you?'

'Yes'

'Even A-levels?'

'Yes.'

'Then why are you standing before me arguing that what the planets were doing when you made your inauspicious debut has a scintilla of an effect on anything in your life, except for weather fronts and night following day?'

'I'm a typical Pisces and my mum's a typical Leo.'

'You're a fatuous insult to the species. You should be stripped and burned at the stake of commonsense. I will stoke the fires with Jonathan Cainer horoscopes ripped untimely from the *Daily Mail*, and as the flames lick ever higher, I will suck the smell of grilled moron greedily down into my lungs.'

'What star sign are you?'

'I'm whatever sign whose prediction this week read, "On Sunday, a friend who has masqueraded as a rational human being for the 15 years of your acquaintance will stand revealed before you as just another cack-brained, gibbering fool swirling in a festering cesspit of stupidity".'

From there it was but a short trip to a heated debate about Carole Caplin and Cherie Blair, alternative medicine, electronic voice phenomena and, finally and most hysterically, Carol Vorderman's detox diet. We may have strayed from the brief somewhat with the last, but tempers by then were more than frayed.

I think I would have borne her imbecility better if I hadn't recently, by virtue of a misguided but well-intentioned birthday present (a voucher for a 'holistic spa day'), found myself in closer proximity than I would have ever voluntarily assumed to serried ranks of pastel-uniformed practitioners of the various modern arts that require mud to be infused with seaweed extracts, waved over a moonlit pool as Neptune is in the ascendant and spread across your body like some kind of sedimentary roustabout. I had always assumed that everyone involved would, implicitly or explicitly, acknowledge that the whole zodiac/crystal/slop-smearing industry was itself a stupendous bucketful of brown shite, infused with extracts of mendacity and exploitation and waved over a shadowy pool of gullibility left over from ye olden times.

But after my umpteenth conversation with a plastic-aproned, dead-eyed (Sagittarian) smearer, I was forced to conclude that they all believe in the muck – in all senses of the word – they spread.

Now that the season of goodwill has passed, let's make a plea for greater intolerance (carefully directed) in the world. The next time a woman (and it is always a woman – men have many flaws but at least they prefer to seek the answers to their problems in *Top Gear* and Abi Titmuss rather than the waxings and wanings of the moon) asks you what star sign you are, swears by essential oils, magnet therapy or talks about realigning anything but shelves, make a stand. Back her into a corner and talk at her about Galileo, Darwin, Einstein, Crick and Watson and Jeremy Paxman until she admits the error of her ways. For astrology and the rest to flourish it is only necessary that those with an IQ in double figures do nothing.

5 JANUARY 2005

Taking the risk out of gambling

My grandmother had many sterling qualities: the ability to fit 784 wine gums in her mouth at once (she could dislocate her jaw like an African snake), a knack for bringing up a family on three farthings a month by wearing the same pair of shoes for half a century, and persuading her offspring that three ounces of mince in batter was an ample Christmas dinner.

Provided there was someone to top up her gin glass, she could play Bobby Shaftoe on the piano for five straight days, and frequently did, her iron willpower enabling her to disregard both the calls of nature and those of her exhausted grandchildren, who were forced to march to the militaristic lyrics until their soft young joints compacted into rigid agony. But her greatest gift to her grandchildren was teaching us how to play five-card stud, pontoon, three-card brag and Newmarket as soon as we were old enough to wrap our pudgy fingers round a deck of cards and calculate some basic odds.

Most of us were in wheelchairs by then, of course, and grateful for any distraction. But the lessons she taught me during the long summer days when we should have been outside warming our crippled bodies in the sun lingered – namely, get the house rules in writing before you begin, unless you want an ill-shod foot on your neck, and don't gamble if, like me, you cannot remember that four jacks showing on the table renders it unlikely you will get a fifth to fill the straight you've been building since the first hand.

No, I am not a natural gambler. Not only can I not master odds, map out strategies or divine those of others, I gibber with anxiety at the thought of losing money. The first time I lost 10p to my sister I thought I would die of grief, and repeated exposure to the experience did nothing to inure me to the pain.

So my new hero is Jean-Philippe Bryk, a Frenchman who is claiming that the Grand Cafe casino in Vichy owed him 'a duty of information advice and loyalty' and is suing them for letting him lose £500,000 during multiple visits to the establishment. Now, many might question the wisdom of fighting a claim against a Vichy institution that depends for its success on such a generous embrace of the concept of loyalty, but such predictable sniping need not detain us here.

Others may think that Monsieur Bryk is being a bit of un cheeky singe and simply attempting to shift responsibility for his mistakes on to an institution that merely provided a colourful backdrop for a journey into the abyss of imbecility from which he is now struggling to extricate himself.

Mais non. If he wins, he will effectively set a precedent for risk-free gambling. From there it will be but a short step to walking into casinos, demanding a large stack of cash and walking out again. And once the casinos fall, pubs must surely be next. 'With my 15th pint of Smirnoff I am risking cirrhosis, pancreatitis, infertility and choking on these curried nuts. I demand full reimbursement for the evening's libations and a taxi home.' 'Certainly madam. Would you prefer cash or cheque?'

But now, if you'll excuse me, the anniversary of my grandma's death fast approaches, and I must go and bandage my feet in advance of commemorative marching week.

16 NOVEMBER 2005

Can babies really count?

I'm usually a great fan of science, and an even greater fan of scientists. I especially like the ones who are experts in rare diseases and appear in Channel 4 documentaries to distil their unsurpassed knowledge into a few enthralling yet accessible sentences. I have married quite a few of them in my head, actually, and we are very happy together.

But sometimes they let you down. And this week it's a bunch of neuroscientists from Duke University in North Carolina, who are claiming that babies can count. I have met babies and they seem to me to be the very definition of idiocy, so my suspicions were immediately aroused. As luck would have it, the chance to repudiate the findings soon arose, with a phone call from a maternal parent of my acquaintance requesting the presence of another adult in the house 'before I tear my own eyes out'.

Thus I found a suitable setting for my experiment; a suburban terraced house containing one semi-conscious mother – hair crusted with unidentified excretions, eyes rolling back in her head, one boob hanging out of her shirt despite the fact that she put six bras on this morning, some of them the right way round, pinballing round the house trying to remember where she left the kitchen – and a baby lying contentedly on the gin-soaked floor. The sprog appeared to be a suitable specimen, with a brace of everything that tradition dictates should come in pairs, one of everything else roughly where it should be, and chubby flesh a healthy shade of pink (at least to the untrained eye – for all I really know she could have been in the final stages of scarlet fever). She was also sporting a rather fetching pale-green cardigan, but I gather this was more of an optional add-on than an organic property.

In their experiment, the American researchers had played 20 babies two clips of film, one showing two women and one showing three. They heard with each film two voices saying 'Look' and then three. The babies looked for longer at the films in which the number of people shown matched the number of voices, thereby proving that babies can understand numbers long before they understand speech.

This raises two immediate questions. First, if squalling grubs one-through-20 can really count, shouldn't they pay more attention when the number of voices doesn't match up? Second, is 20 really a big enough sample to allow such conclusions to be drawn?

So Mad Mother and I tested Grub 21 by going to the pub for several hours and taking it in turns to shout endearments down the baby monitor. A judiciously placed series of mirrors allowed us to record that hearing two disembodied voices discombobulates an infant more seriously than one, especially if they become progressively more slurred. And although our sample size was even smaller than that at Duke University, we cunningly circumvented this problem by coming home and alternately showing G21 a diagrammatic demonstration of Pythagoras's theory and screaming 'Cry, fatty, cry!' at her a hundred times each. The alacrity with which she responded to the latter, coupled with her absolutely abysmal efforts at adding the sum of two squares, empirically proves once and for all that it is language, not numbers, that first separates us from the beasts.

15 FEBRUARY 2006

When air hostesses attack

Sometimes a story comes along that is, like the god of your choice, Ted Hughes's pike or the Willy Wonka Nutty Crunch Surprise, so perfect in all parts that to do anything other than simply sit back and admire its beauty seems just plain wrong. So pull up a chair and let me tell you about Wendy the Virgin air hostess. (In the interest of avoiding confusion, I will draw your attention to the capital V. If you want the other kind of story, you filthy beast, I suggest you return to your shiftless life haunting the foetid netherworld of inter-webular depravity and stop besmirching these pristine pages.)

'Wendy' (her name has yet to be confirmed) was on a routine flight to Las Vegas, ministering to the various needs of a plane full of passengers, slaking their thirst for Britvic miniatures, demonstrating how to model luminescent polyblends without being electrocuted by one's own static, and doubtless smiling throughout in a way most of us can only manage after ingesting a cornucopia of psychotropic drugs. All, in short, was well. Then the plane hit some turbulence. And Wendy started screaming. Every time the plane dipped, she screamed again. As they grabbed their magazines, drinks, babies and other movable objects, passengers murmured that they were finding the stewardess's reaction disconcerting, then, as time and the vigorous exercising of Wendy's lungs went on, distinctly unhelpful.

Things went from bad to worse when, in response to people's requests for sick-bags, she lobbed a bundle in their general direction and started chanting: 'We're going to crash, we're going to crash.' By the end of the flight, claim passengers, Wendy was laughing and joking as if nothing had happened.

These moments, which allow even those of us who didn't read *Lord of the Flies* and have to write a portentous and overreaching GCSE essay on the subject to appreciate just how thin the veneer of civilisation is, are always delightful. Beneath the uniform, beneath the qualifications and whatever other trappings we accrue, we are only ever a few unexpected bumps away from cracking, and letting a potent brew of hysteria and atavism flood out.

Part of me hopes that Wendy will spark a trend for entertaining breakdowns among other professionals. Surgeons who look up halfway through an operation and shriek, 'Have you seen this?! I've opened up a body! I'm up to my elbows in someone else's guts! I'm plonking things that should be encased in skin into shiny metal basins! What the hell happened? I'm out of here!' Barristers who grind to a halt in the middle of their oratory and say, 'I'm sorry, I appear to be wearing a wig and talking in Latinate circumlocutions. I do apologise and wish myself to bog off. I'm going skinny dipping with ma honey.'

Or, most gloriously, a winner at next week's Oscars using their allotted 90 seconds not to thank their agent, teddy bear and Thetan adviser but to announce, 'I play dress-up for a living! I'm a grown man and I play dress-up for a living! You pay me to pretend things! Am I mental or are you? Somebody save me!' before diving into the crowd and disappearing for ever in Scarlett Johansson's cleavage. I can't wait.

1 MARCH 2006

Bring back middle age

The pictures of 48-year-old Sharon Stone looking, ooh, 28 at most, at last week's premiere of *Basic Instinct 2: The Vagina Bites Back* are the latest in a long line of exhibits that suggest women now spend 30-odd years looking 20-something before (we can only presume, as none of the women currently in the throes of suspended youth have yet reached the next stage) they at last become too tired and weak to brace themselves any longer against the weight of years and turn from Scarlett Johansson-alikes to Methusalenas overnight.

Madonna is 47 and has devoted her life to looking 12 in Lycra. Joan Collins is 72 and has devoted hers to looking fabulous in leopardskin. Even the US secretary of state, 51-year-old Condoleezza Rice, is hell-bent on showing us, via exercise videos and a well-fitting trouser-suit, how the vibrancy of youth can be maintained with just a few hours' gut-busting effort every day.

For these famous women, of course, the rewards for denying the ravages of time are huge. Rice has one of the top jobs – and maybe an eye on the very top job – in the most youth-obsessed country in the world, where political survival depends at least in part on an ability to convey an image of energetic go-getter racing ahead of the pack.

But even among the non-celebrity sisterhood we seem intent on pushing back the boundaries of middle age. New categories and slogans are invented – middle youth, 50 is the new 40 – to put off the apparently evil day when women must admit that they are about halfway through their lives.

Why? I can see that in days gone by, when everyone over the age of 40 was toothless, crippled and had a face etched with the suffering caused by two world wars and music-hall comedy, there would have been a reason to resist the label for as long as possible. But we are all living longer, healthier lives. Previous generations may have had to carry their innards around in a bag, ravaged by decades of childbearing until they collapsed in a dusty heap of osteoporosis and regret. But now, if we have a modicum of sense and good fortune, contraception, mammograms, smears, HRT and liquorice allsorts will banish most of the ills to which female flesh has historically been heir.

Perhaps it is because ageism is still rife. Or perhaps it has something to do with the fact that no one seems sure what is meant by old and young any more, which will come as no surprise to anyone who has watched mothers and daughters stripping the shelves of Primark for the latest fashions with equal enthusiasm. 'If you are a 24-year-old man, you believe that old age begins about 55 [while] if you are a 62-year-old woman, you think youth doesn't end until 57,' says Dominic Abrams, professor of social psychology of University of Kent. According to his research, people feel that middle age begins at 49 and old age sets in at 65.

I feel I may be alone in mourning the news that middle age now arrives a decade or so later than it did when I was small. I grew up surrounded by early-to-late-middle-aged women who made it look like the most glorious state of all. My mother used to take me to work with her, at family planning clinics that were run as a gynae-cocracy. Everyone – from the admin staff to the doctors and cleaners – was female, well past the first flush of youth and quite pleased about both. They exuded a confidence that I spent the next 20 years looking for in myself but never found.

They inoculated me against the fear that middle age brings invisibility, as every one of them was constitutionally incapable of slipping silently into a room and only too capable of starting a fight in an empty house. And they fell into two camps on the subject of sex. Half were just hitting their stride and having to draft in reserve troops to replace exhausted (or terrified) husbands and the other half were revelling in the fact that they had left all that behind them and spent their evenings drinking gin, planning holidays and laughing at the dent in the bed where their phlegm-snorting, bollock-scratching husbands had lain until he had come home one day to find the locks changed and his life out on the street. Either way, compared to the impending acne-spattered strains of teenage life that I was reading about with horror in the problem pages of *Jackie* and *Blue Jeans*, the message was one of untrammelled freedom – from internal insecurities and external expectation – and delight.

And if another piece of recent research is anything to go by, I won't be disappointed. Jill Arnold, senior lecturer in psychology at Nottingham Trent University, interviewed women aged 45 to 65 and found them unbowed by the cult of youth. 'There was a great feeling of, "We know who we are and what we want,"' says Arnold. 'And they are potent both in financial terms, and politically – what began in the 70s they still felt very strongly about; that equality was still very much worth fighting for – and they didn't see the worth of their lives in terms of their looks but in their relationships and in what they had left to do since coming into their prime.'

And if confidence is not enough, by 2021, 37 per cent of people in Britain will be over 60 and we can crush the mewling, puking, lily-livered young by sheer force of numbers. Bring it on.

20 MARCH 2006

Schoolgirls, Shakespeare, ducks and me

This week I found myself acting as one of the 8,000 chaperones required in these heavily regulated times by my teacher friend (who has now officially changed her name to Miss! Miss!) to enable her to take the disadvantaged but ebullient 13-year-old girls from her English class on a trip round the Globe Theatre. The aim was to help them with the text they are struggling through (*Much Ado About F'kin' Nuffink* apparently).

Before the tour began, the guide (Michael, a charming, middle-aged actor resting between jobs) asked if anyone needed the loo. One girl put up her hand. 'I do,' she said, 'but I won't – I don't like weeing in public toilets.' There was a pause. 'Excellent,' beamed Michael.

'I can see we're going to have some marvellously honest work out of you this afternoon.' I love actors.

On the tour, it is fair to say that the finer points of Elizabethan theatrical history eluded them, but they and I were delighted to learn that Benedick's name in *Much Ado* was carefully chosen by Shakespeare. 'Because "bene" means good, like in Italian, or "bien" in French, and "dick",' said Michael, pausing to let the tension build, 'means exactly what it does now!' The girls erupted and I remembered suddenly how endlessly amusing life could be when you were 13 en masse.

Later, I was eating sandwiches with the three girls whom Miss! Miss! had designated my particular responsibility, and discussing what they planned to be when they grew up. One wanted to be a supermodel – 'And I won't get out of bed unless Prada and Versace offer me, like, thousands of pounds!' she shrieked.

Her less volatile friend, who had the face of a natural tragedian, sat stolidly munching her Dairylea Dunkers. 'Yeah?' she said, raising deliberately mournful eyes with perfect timing. 'And what about when Primark calls?' They collapsed as one into a hysterical lump.

Just then, another girl came up, a look of outrage on her face. 'Michelle just said, "Your Mum!" to me!' The lump straightened immediately and its component parts reacted with shock, sympathy and promises to do Michelle damage if called upon. Consumed with curiosity, I asked what the full-length version of the insult was. They giggled for about 40 minutes before the bravest, Marcelle, told me that it could be completed either by the words 'gives bangs' or 'does heads'.

And giving bangs meant having sex? They nodded.

'And does "does heads" mean what I think it means, too?'

More laughter. 'Yeah,' said Marcelle on a burst of inspiration. 'Benemouth!'

I gave up all pretence of sober maturity and fell off the bench laughing with the rest of them. But at the same time, although Prince Charles would have conniptions and there probably isn't a box to tick on any national curriculum forms for it, I reckon you could put down a score one for school trips and another for Shakespeare.

In the course of professional research, I learned this week that there's a word (avisodomy, since you ask) for the act of killing a duck while having sex with it (or, possibly, having sex with a duck while killing it: some of the finer points eluded me during my brief scan of the relevant internet pages). At first I wasn't sure what to do with this new information, apart from take comfort in the notion that there is someone, or at least something, for everyone. But I've decided just to husband it for the future in case I need to ginger up that tricky final section on my CV, 'Hobbies and pastimes'.

14 OCTOBER 2006

A very antique snobbery

Maybe they can smell the poverty on me and that's what makes it look as if they are about to gob a small but eloquent oyster of phlegm into my eye as I enter their elegant emporia, but I still think it's rude.

Having realised that between illness and deadlines I hadn't left the house in the past six weeks, I decided to embark on an outing. So, feeling rather like a Victorian lady traveller (minus the TB and fine millinery, but with a large handbag that I mentally designated for the day my valise), I took a short train ride into another part of the country. This shall remain nameless, as I am about to slag off – as I believe Victorian ladies did put it – a goodly proportion of its populace, but it was a relatively salubrious district liberally sprinkled with antiques shops and second-hand book sellers.

Now, it has long been a puzzle to me why these shops are so often owned by such cheerless and wretched people. You would think that owning such shops would be the post-early-retirement fulfilment of a lifetime's gently nurtured ambition, or a semi-vocational career, not forced labour. Historically, I believe there have been few occasions on which a teacher has shouted at a pupil, 'You'll never amount to anything, boy! It's a lifetime of working all the hours God sends between 10 and four, three days a week, surrounded by beautiful merchandise in a prime piece of Georgian real estate, rushed off your feet by up to one camel-coated customer at a time inquiring about the price of candelabras, and arranging occasional deliveries to Whitstable beach-front homes for you!'

Perhaps I'm being unfair. Perhaps antiquarian book sellers all look at the customer as if he or she had just squeezed lemon juice on to a puppy's suppurating sores because they were forced into the used book trade by their ailing mothers, 12 disabled siblings and an absent father who forgot to take his first edition of Middlemarch with him when he fled the unhappy home. But I doubt it.

So I can only conclude that the all-but-visible waves of hostility flowing from these odd people derive from a brand of snobbery as antique as the goods on display. As I am clearly not the kind of person who can spend £8,000 on a refectory table, I must be treated with the contempt such penurious scum deserve. (Even though, I might point out, they are wrong. I can afford to spend £8,000 on a refectory table. The fact that I would then have to live under it is none of their business.)

Chastened and disheartened, I got back on the train, got off at Greenhithe and went into Bluewater. For those of you who don't know, Bluewater is the fifth of Kent that was glassed over in 1999 and landscaped with a 13,000-space car park. As I walked around its 300-plus shops, I remembered signing petitions in my youth to stop it being built. Which was, clearly, about as effective as even my idealistic young self knew it would be. But here's the thing. In this bland, soulless building, between the people shopping and lunching and those serving them food or exchanging their money for DVDs, toiletries and white goods, there was more friendliness, camaraderie, even – dread phrase – community spirit than you could find in all the allegedly charming, idiosyncratic, independent shops in Partonface Miseryville put together. Something's gone wrong somewhere. Especially as I felt it despite the knowledge that, as a former petition signer, I was effectively strolling through a temple not just to Mammon, but to my own hypocrisy. Even more especially because I'm sure I'll get over that. And next time I go, I may just pack my valise and stay all day.

10 MARCH 2007

The confederacy of dunces

It was the news from the government body Wrap (Waste and Resources Action Programme) that Britons throw away 6.7 million tonnes of food a year – almost a third of everything we buy – that finally caused a question that has for some time been circling around my brain in an amorphous fashion to pull itself into focus: namely, just how much of the green movement could be boiled down to telling people not to be such frigging idiots all the frigging time?

Take the main reasons behind consumers' habit of donating 30 per cent of their food purchases to the swing bin, as outlined by Wrap. These are: repeatedly buying more food than they need; allowing food to go out of date; and keeping food in fridges that are too warm, so that by the time they open the fridge again, half the items therein are either necrotic or have developed the kind of mould that is one stray electrical spark away from developing independent thought.

I submit that these are three variations on the theme of being an idiot. Of course, not every failure to do the green thing is proof of idiocy. Not spending thousands of pounds on solar panels or a domestic wind turbine, for example, is more likely to be a sign of not having thousands of pounds to spend on alternative energy methods (or of having a potential electorate to impress with one's ecological credentials).

Similarly, buying your food in the supermarket rather than the local farmers' market is more likely to signal that you have neither the time, money or inclination to go fawning over apples that cost more than your house or to bring home crustily rustic loaves of bread that you have to hire a local builder to slice with a jigsaw.

But not doing the stuff that directly benefits you (such as shutting internal doors to keep the heat in and your costs down, or, um, not buying more food than you can physically stuff down your gullet before it rots) is painfully stupid. As is the persistent dodging of those things that cost you next to nothing in terms of money or effort, while unequivocally benefiting the wider world (such as peeling your fat self off the sofa to turn off the telly properly or investing in a few 'Bags for Life' instead of loading up your trolley with 812 plastic carriers, each containing three items only, because you just can't risk them splitting during the 30 seconds it's going to take you to transfer them to the car). Overfilling the kettle is moronic, too.

As the green movement gathers force and momentum, there are more and more people popping up to argue the ideological odds and claim that refusing to make such concessions or lifestyle changes is to wave a banner for free choice, to make a legitimate protest at 'ecological correctness' or a principled stand against the new 'green religion'. It is not.

Whatever way you slice it, it amounts to the same thing – believing that using up resources faster than they can be replaced is a good thing.

It's a great pity that the green movement is still essentially defined – and hogtied – by its consideration for others. Otherwise, it would stop all this careful explanation of air miles and carbon emissions and persistent organic pollutants, and instead start beating you all over creation with a sustainably produced cosh in time to the heartfelt and usefully rhythmic exhortation to stop being such a frigging idiot all the frigging time.

24 MARCH 2007

If it ain't broke . . .

I did two things this week: I joined Freecycle (goodbye slow cooker, hello non-artistically battered wardrobe) and I read about the latest arrival at the cosmetic surgery party, silicone lip implants. Instead of collagen fillers, you can now have – and as many of you are reading this over breakfast, let me describe the procedure in unnecessary detail – holes slit at the corners of your mouth, a tunnel bored through your lip, a wormlike implant pushed into it and double the volume of lippage you started with. Practitioners proudly advise that the whole thing takes about 15 minutes, not including the subsequent antibiotics course and painkillers.

I immediately had a brilliant idea. Actually, no, immediately I had the thought that somebody is to be congratulated on conditioning us so thoroughly into believing that speed is so uniformly good that it can even be used as a selling point when it comes to letting people slice into one's own flesh. Lunch-hour facelifts? Certainly, Sir, and thank you very much! What possible flaw could there be in undergoing a surgical strike on the most visible and delicate areas of my body in the time it would take me to choose between a Boots meal deal and a Subway meatball marinara? The midday boob job? Please, go right ahead – I have a board meeting at three and I'd hate to turn up without perky tits and residual anaesthesia. Were I contemplating any form of plastic surgery, I cannot tell you how much more I would be persuaded by an operating outfit that advertised itself with the words, 'This operation takes hours and hours, suggesting much preliminary planning, thoughtful narrowing of surgeons' eyes and possibly even a bit of outlining with marker pens, instead of quick, violent slashing movements with small margins of error by a direct descendant of Jack the Ripper'. But clearly I am in a minority.

Then I read in a newspaper the comments of women who have had the procedure. 'I became aware I was no longer lifting my head to greet [clients], so self-conscious was I of my thin lips,' said one. 'It dawned on me that no matter how quick this was going to be, it was still an operation,' said another. 'But at the same time I remembered all the angst my lips had caused me over the years . . . and climbed on.'

From their words, you'd think these women had mouths that made Kermit the Frog look like Leslie Ash. It almost goes without saying that, in the pre-op photos, they do not. No one would ever look at them and stagger back in horror, yelling, 'My eyes! My eyes!' as such raging insecurity would suggest was a daily occurrence.

And so my brilliant idea is this: all women have their idiotic neuroses, the source of which is unrecognisable as a problem by anyone else for the simple reason that the allegedly deformed/ mountainous/excessively or insufficiently protuberant feature is always normal and often quite attractive. So we should set up a website that allows us to trade irrational loathings. You post a picture of your reviled area on the 'Thighs with separate postcodes', 'Bum like two bums' or 'Stomach the subject of upcoming Sky documentary' section, someone agrees to hate it for you, you agree to hate their equivalent, and lo! You can each go about your lives finally at peace with your bodies, knowing that somewhere it is still being hated as much as it deserves, but without you having to do so yourself. No more need to sacrifice to a surgeon either your corporeal integrity or your lunch hour once you sign on to mecycle.org.

12 MAY 2007

The kids are all right

From the moment Jamie Oliver walked into that school in Greenwich, steaming with optimism, marinated in a fine blend of arrogance and evangelism, determined to open the eyes of its teenage students to the way of coriander and a light truffle-oil drizzle, you could tell nemesis was nigh. The kids took one look at his first overhauled menu and lit out for the nearest chippy. Just as the early Christian missionaries vastly overestimated the willingness of native tribes to abandon every spiritual and cultural totem they had ever known, Jamie had failed to fathom the depths of the average teenager's resistance to change.

The more militant students organised a protest and all but took to stuffing handfuls of raw suet down their throats every time Oliver walked past, increasingly bewildered by the fact that the force of his enthusiasm and celebrity had failed to re-educate their palates overnight. Despite the hype of his campaign and the insistence that Greenwich was now a tranquil vale of borlotti-bolting adolescents, the discerning viewer could detect that Jamie's experiment was doomed.

Two years on, we have final proof that Oliver's efforts have come to naught – and indeed, in some cases, less than naught. Latest research suggests that the introduction of healthier meals has caused a 27 per cent drop in the number of secondary pupils eating school dinners.

For anyone who a) hated Jamie Oliver and yearned to see the limits of his much-prized so-called Everyman qualities exposed, b) had long been suffering misgivings at the amount of middle-class cant foisted upon those deemed to exist in a parlous state of ignorance about everything from the correct amount of Burberry to sport in one outfit to the manifest virtues of Maldon sea salt over any other, or c) was loth to see a generation of teenagers cut off from the proud heritage of terrible school meals that made this country great, this is a glorious triumph. Just when you begin to despair of teenagers' enslavement to the cult of celebrity and willingness to follow wherever anyone who has so much as farted on a Big Brother sofa or been found drunk in charge of a teacup chihuahua leads, you find them collectively drawing a line across which they will not step. Celebrity chefs can take their home-made pizzas and sod off, it seems.

Now, obviously, this is a shame for the children who are going to grow into large balls of fat inlaid with heavily furred arteries all convening at an enlarged heart, but leaving that aside for a moment, it is otherwise news that should surely gladden one's own (admittedly probably healthier) organ. Perhaps one day it will transform into a more purely beneficial resistance to former supermodels' fashion collections, multi-thousand-pound handbags and, ideally, all new music since Buddy Holly. Then we can all get back to normal.

Further proof that, after many years of looking like precisely the opposite, children may indeed be returning to their allotted role of harbingers of hope for the future, came during a visit to the gym this week. I spent several minutes watching a three-year-old girl tug futilely on her mother's coat, trying to bring her attention to a broken toy while her mother remained locked in conversation alternately with her friend and on her mobile. Eventually, a look of dawning comprehension and horror spread across the child's face. 'Mummy!' she roared, giving one final, desperate tug. 'Do you recognise me?' I quickly swabbed her and intend to deliver a clone to the house of all similarly rubbish parents forthwith.

2 JUNE 2007

A talent for mediocrity

As I write this, the nation is still wiping its eyes after the emotional finale of *Britain's Got Talent*. Defying all predictions that nothing could avert the landslide victory of grinning, gap-toothed, pitch-perfect six-year-old chanteuse Connie Talbot, Carphone Warehouse employee Paul 'Pay-As-You-Go-Pavarotti' Potts ultimately vanquished all comers. And, given that Connie will have a million-selling album of cloying classics out by the end of the week regardless of her final placement, rightly so.

The talent show is enjoying a spirited revival. It began with *Pop*

Idol and *The X Factor*, gathered pace with *Strictly Come Dancing, Dancing On Ice, When Will I Be Famous?* and *How Do You Solve a Problem Like Maria?* and has continued with *Any Dream Will Do, Grease Is the Word* and, of course, the aforementioned *Britain's Got Talent*, clips of which are gathering tens of thousands of hits a day on YouTube.

Push the modern technological trimmings aside, however, and what you will reveal is simply the latest manifestation of the repressed British urge to perform that used to find safe release in village shows and PoW camps. It is a forgotten fact of history that the second world war could have been over by 1943 if it hadn't been for all the telegrams from incarcerated troops begging their respective generals to keep things going until the first night of their morale-boosting performance of the Mikado.

Deprived of the traditional outlets of war and church halls, we have turned to TV to allow us to express ourselves. And not just ourselves, but our national character. In the US, people who absorbed the mantra 'Be all you can be' with their mother's milk don't enter beauty pageants, talent shows or display themselves publicly until they have polished, honed and buffed their acts or bodies to perfection. US judges simply watch a parade of proto-supermodels/ Streisands/Sinatras and decide who is fractionally more talented or definitively muscled than the rest. Here, however, we have absorbed the more relaxing mantra 'Be all that you can be without showing anyone else up, it's rude'. So our judges applaud people attaching clothes pegs to their faces, ventriloquising without being aware that the core feature of the art is that the lips don't move, or going around in comedy hats and states of gentle befuddlement while walking backwards across the stage from, you can only assume, one care worker waiting in the wings to another. If a man banged nails into a pumpkin with a rubber hammer, he'd get a standing ovation.

That's the kind of people we really are. Politicians who are still casting about for ways to celebrate the proposed new bank holiday,

'Britain Day', without offending anyone should announce that it will centre on regional talent contests. Not only will this pay oblique tribute to the fact that the resurrection of the talent show is at least partly due to the electorate reacting to a decade under the leadership of a man with more than a touch of the variety show compere about him, but such shows enshrine all – and by that I mean the very, very little – that is good and noble about our country. Our willingness to distinguish admirable effort from piss-poor result and reward it. The capacity to find as much entertainment in a man wearing ostrich legs as in a $200m blockbuster film. The ability to maintain a sense of optimism in the face of mounting evidence that the collective psyche is crumbling and that far more than the four horsemen required for the apocalypse are racing towards us. Most are dressed as Japanese maidens and humming *Three Little Maids From School Are We* slightly off-key.

23 JUNE 2007

There's hope for us yet

So, according to a poll carried out for a forthcoming BBC1 programme called *The Big Questions*, 82 per cent of Britons believe their country is in moral decline.

Naturally, one's first inclination, as a fully paid-up member of the Congenital Cynics' Club – actually, I have a special silver badge and give official lectures at our monthly meetings at Embittered Hall, Lower Vitriol – is to ask: who, pray, are the other, remarkably imperturbable 18 per cent, and where are they living? In underground bunkers in Beacon Fell? Alone in windowless rooms wearing papier-mache visors whose insides are painted with delightful 50s scenes? Or just in denial?

However, even a badge-wielding senior member of the CCC can have times when the cosmic forces seem to move in determined concert and apply some slight pressure to the brakes on the hand-cart otherwise taking us all to hell. Viz to wit:

Monday – At the end of a rotten day, I get on a crowded train on the verge of tears. From a group of nine-year-old, football-stripped boys engrossed in conversation about the possible transfer of one of their heroes, one sees me in my wobbly lipped state, stands up immediately, smiles kindly and says, ''Ere, come and sit down'. His friends shuffle up, my tears recede, and everyone in the carriage looks startled and then just a little happier. Y'know, with life.

Wednesday – My stupid cat has been missing for two days. On one of my futile tin-bashing excursions around the estate, I bump into an 11-year-old boy called Lee and ask if he's seen any live or dead stupid ginger cats. He has not, but says he will look for me. For the next two days, he calls round every few hours with possible sightings, until the stupid cat strolls in, ear torn and bleeding but otherwise unharmed, and I can report that the crisis is over and thank Lee for his help. He shuffles, mutters, ''S all right', and runs off before I can embarrass him any further.

Friday – I'm on the bus and three kids are taunting a disabled man as he gets on. He sits down by the front window and they continue to yell and make faces at him through the glass. An enor-mous teenager strides from the back seat to where the man is, leans across him (''Scuse me'), bashes the window so the whole bus shud-ders and roars, 'Fuck off!' at the little tykes, who duly scarper. As the teenager gets off, the disabled man raises his hand in thanks. 'No problem,' says the teenager.

You could, in fact, look at these moments as confirmation that the 82 per cent were right. On one interpretation, the child on the train stood out because his exhibition of a modicum of civilised behaviour is now so rare. I bumped into Lee because he is always out on his bike, riding in endless circles around the car park because, presumably, there is no one around to make him go to school or come in for meals at regular intervals. And the man on the bus will have endured far more taunts than he has instances of strangers coming to his aid.

And I could say I actually get so depressed about the 99 per cent of things I see when I step outside my front door that I am clinging to these fleeting moments of civilised behaviour like a drowning woman to a splinter of driftwood.

But, for once, I am going to side with the optimistic minority. Call it my Martyn Lewis moment, but it's been a good week.

15 SEPTEMBER 2007

Here's to a truly alternative lifestyle

My best friend and I have a new game. It's called 'Wandering round the streets of south-east London pointing at the houses – Whole! Three bedrooms! Terraced red-brick! Some garden-type scrubland at the back! Terribly unexciting! Built by the million between 1860 and 1930 and sold for thruppence to normal people with normal jobs! – that we'd buy if we clubbed together, took on second jobs, married rich men who also poo diamonds, and stumbled over a cache of Ch'ing jade figurines in Mayow Park'. I admit that the title may need refining before we submit the concept to Hasbro. I think, in the end, we'll just call it Modern Monopoly.

Anyway, after playing our game, we go home, sadly failing to collect £200 on the way and weep gently into pints of gin.

All hail, then, our new heroes, Jean and David Davidson, aged 70 and 79 respectively, who have spent the past 22 years living in a Travelodge. The hidden delights of a hotel chain many would deem less well appointed than the average open prison dawned on the couple in 1985, when they stayed at its outpost in Barton-under-Needwood, Staffordshire, while visiting an elderly aunt. So charmed were they that by the time the unfortunate aunt died four months later they moved out of their flat in Sheffield and took up residence at the Travelodge on the A1 at Newark, Nottinghamshire, and didn't leave until 1997. Then they became permanent residents at Gonerby Moor Travelodge, where their room is about to be renamed the Davidson Suite. So far it has cost them £97,000, plus the price of meals at the nearby Little Chef, which compares pretty favourably with the costs of buying and running a home. What's more, they haven't had to wash a bed sheet or dish or clean a bathroom in more than two decades, to which surpassing luxury no man – or rather, in all likelihood, woman – can put a price.

The real achievement, of course, is that they have succeeded in lifting themselves free of the country's obsession with real estate prices and property ownership, and at the same time placed themselves firmly within other, far more admirable great British traditions of slightly mulish eccentricity, Blitz spirit and blind loyalty. They take in their stride the unfashionably make-do minimalist ethic of the overnight hotel room and the eschewing of rampant consumerism it necessitates, and, in the phrase beloved of grandmothers everywhere, they make their own entertainment.

'Our room looks out to the car park and a busy slip road where lorries pass by throughout the night,' Mr D says. 'There's always something to see.' The removal of the heated towel rails a few years ago made it more difficult for them to dry their smalls, but they simply shrugged and soldiered on by building more drying time into their routine.

As well as teaching us how to rise above the herd, Mr and Mrs Davidson also enable us to face the future with courage, as all good role models should. When this septic isle eventually becomes so overpopulated that we are all living in melamine pods, taking our meals intravenously because it's Citizen AB126364-4857643's turn to sit up and use the chewing space, we will remember our septuagenarian heroes and know that even in the most sterile and confined of spaces we can find happiness. Unlike stashes of priceless antiques in local parks, dammit.

22 SEPTEMBER 2007

Riding for a fall

At first my friends mocked me for my endless letters to Holyrood. 'I'm all for devolution,' my epistles would begin. 'At first this was because I misunderstood the term and thought you meant to embark on a programme of regression. As someone who deplores change and progress, I admired this wholeheartedly and started looking forward to the ushering in of a new era of warring clansmen and picturesque Pictishness. Now I have a slightly better grasp on things, and understand that independence is a blessing for countries as much as it is for individuals. Ignore those who tell you it means nothing more than the interpolation of yet another nationwide layer of bureaucracy, rendering you politically nothing more than a giant county council. Instead, revel in the chance to expel Sassenachs, bring back Gaelic, make kilts compulsory and rear haggis on the hillsides again.

'But please,' my letters continued presciently, 'do not let the heady excitement of handling your own taxes, legislation and – one day! – oil reserves cause you to act uncompassionately towards your harmless native sexual deviants.'

My friends are not laughing now. For Sheriff Colin Miller has just found a 51-year-old man (whose name we won't repeat here for fear that he is finding the publicity a little much) guilty of sexually aggravated breach of the peace for having sex with a bicycle.

I do not know how you have sex with a bicycle. In fact, I got my bicycle out of the shed to check it for secret vaginas or other orifices that my own rather pedestrian (if you will forgive the pun, and there's no reason why you should) sexual orientation might have caused me to overlook. But found I none. You could frot against the saddle, I suppose, but given the frictive nature of faux-leather, I wouldn't recommend it unless your esoteric tastes are overlaid by the determinedly masochistic.

But what I do know is this: the bicycle is an inanimate object. It does not, unless I have been misinformed for more than 30 years, have any feelings, physical or emotional. Therefore a man is surely free to do what he likes with his bike? If he wishes to ride sedately round his village, he may do so. If he wishes to do wheelies in the park, he may do so. If he wishes to pork it in the privacy of his own home, as Mr Jock McRaleighshagger evidently did, that is his right and privilege. And after a week in which I have been assailed on all sides by distraught female friends in the dying throes of disastrous relationships, I will go further and suggest there are many men who should be allowed to have sex only with bicycles.

Clearly, my letter-writing must not slacken yet. Although I can't help wondering how my own postbag will divide this week. Will Scottish nationalists make the greatest showing? ('If you knew anything about our history, you'd know that William Wallace invented the toaster oven and the hover-mower, so your assumptions about the haggis-rearing priorities of the SNP are both incorrect and insulting.') Will I be inundated by bicycle fetishists lauding my progressive views? (Please be advised: these views will come under severe strain if presented with pictorial evidence of you getting jiggy with a saddlebag.) Or will *Guardian* readers, as I suspect, harbour the entire membership of Velocipedal Rights – Right Now! and I will be assailed with furious emails requiring me to make an atoning contribution to the campaign to have bikes' needs recognised under the European convention? I wait with interest.

24 NOVEMBER 2007

Doom with a view

It was meeting up with my long-lost friend Sarah that finally decided me. We – born 4.39 months too early to belong to the Facebook generation and therefore still capable of such lapses – had managed to lose touch since university but had recently been reintroduced by a mutual acquaintance.

'So, what are you up to?' I asked as we kicked a tangle of children out of our way and sat down in the cafe we had clearly inadvisedly chosen to catch up on the past decade's worth of news.

'I'm saving up for a helicopter,' she replied.

I confess I was confused.

'Why?' I inquired politely.

'Because every time I open a newspaper – there's another drought. There's another collapsing ice shelf. There's another decimated rainforest. The end of days is coming. And I don't think God is going to save us, but a small rotary-winged machine might. They'll close borders, you see. And there'll be starving marauding hordes at ground level. The only way of escaping doomsday will be to go up. And then across. To a hill. With a fort.'

'I see. And how much have you saved so far?'

'£36.50. But I'm hoping that the credit crunch will mean I can buy one from a suddenly brassic merchant banker for a knock-down price. Of course, I've been stockpiling fuel for years.'

'Of course.'

'So, once I know where the hill fort is and how far I'll have to travel, I can sell the surplus for a profit and put that money towards the heli-fund, too.'

'Well,' I said with admiration, 'you've certainly thought things through.'

'I have,' she said, nodding sagely.

I felt suddenly energised. I spend at least half my waking hours frozen by fear of the impending apocalypse. But here, in front of me, was someone who clearly felt the same sense of foreboding, who lived with the flickering image constantly behind her eyes of impending global catastrophe but who had responded with action, not paralysis. Who had formulated a plan – a lunatic, unworkable, impossible plan, but a plan nevertheless – instead of simply sitting back and letting fate and rising sea waters rush over her.

'And what,' she said, flicking biscotti crumbs at the toddlers who were clearly bent on forming their own marauding horde around us, 'have you been up to?'

'Not much,' I said. 'But I have bought a house. And,' the thought formed with the words, 'it has a garden at the back. Well, not so much a garden as a 6ft by 6ft bark-chip-and-polythene-lined cat poo repository but . . . I think . . . it's going to become a vegetable patch. Yes! I am going to start growing my own food. I will get back in touch with the turning of the seasons! I will commune once more with nature! I will buy a tremendous number of books on the subject. I will master the skills that will help me survive once the electricity fails, society implodes and the world turns dark and brutal once more. More importantly, it will give me the opportunity after which I have hankered for years – to use the word 'chitting' legitimately in casual conversation. And most importantly, my new capabilities will make me a much more valuable commodity when it comes time for you to choose who to take up in your helicopter with you to begin a new life in an elevated position with massive stone fortifications to protect us. PS, I also caper and dance.'

Together we have mapped out our future. She will save and scout for aircraft. I will sow, reap and learn the steps to a few Elizabethan airs. It feels good to have a plan.

5 APRIL 2008

It shouldn't happen to a Brit

The moment I saw her long, mournful Gallic face, I knew I was doomed. Sure enough, after watching my best friend Sarah and 28 other classmates be swept off in expensive cars to plush appartements et immeubles in desirable Parisian arrondissements full of dazzling glamour, promise and lean, olive-skinned young men with dangerous eyes and permanent erections, I was bundled into the back of a

30-year-old Peugeot 205 that smelt of sheep and despair and driven
– as it seemed to me – to the arse-end of rural France. La Ville de
Merde-Douche, I think it was. Apparently, this was where Delphine
(it means 'mute and sullen' en francais) and her rotten French
family spent their rotten French summer holidays every rotten
French year.

Some people will tell you that I was lucky to spend a week
with Delphine and her since one MP warned yesterday that new
child protection rules could mean the end of foreign exchange
trips.

But I would gladly have forgone a week of Delphine and me
staring at each other in almost total mutual incomprehension. A
week of them putting bowls of steak tartare, raw egg yolk and what
I'm still fairly sure was pig lips down in front of me – me, whose
gastronomic experiences had been limited to Findus Crispy Pancakes
and Ice Magic on a slice of Wall's vanilla brickette for afters – and
shouting 'Mange!' at me. A week of spending endless TV-free
evenings trying to bite my own eyelids for entertainment ('Oh no,
gracious hosts, il n'y a pas de probleme. C'est une grande tradition
anglaise'). A week of waking up every morning and finding that the
whole bleeding lot of them were still French.

Meanwhile, Sarah was busy having beauty treatments at spas,
visiting designer shops and being instructed in the art of dressing
elegantly and appropriately at all times by her impossibly elegant
exchange partner and her even more soignée mother, from whose
timeless instructions she still benefits today. She is still the only
English woman I know who really can construct seven different
outfits out of one black dress, one Hermès scarf, a cigarette and an
array of carefully calibrated sneers.

No sooner had I escaped this Gallic hell than it was time for
Delphine to come to me. She stepped over the threshold, draped
herself bonelessly over the nearest sofa and announced 'I eat like
a bird'. There must be a bird in France that eats seven helpings

of everything put in front of it and then picks its teeth all night, because that is what she did. Although I did count it as a victory for England: Findus Crispy Pancakes 7, steak tartare and egg yolks 0.

26 JUNE 2008

CHAPTER FOUR

AAARGH! (OR, A FEW THOUGHTS ABOUT THE MODERN WORLD)

RIP, J-17

So, farewell then *J-17*. Or, as those of use who knew it in the days before abbreviation and random punctuation became de rigueur for any product aimed at pubescents, *Just Seventeen*. The publication that did so much to shape the malleable minds and warp the socio-sexual expectations of so many of us now staring down the barrel of our late 20s is no more.

Just Seventeen was launched in 1983. 'There was nothing else like it,' remembers author Jenny Colgan. 'It was like porn for us, because like everybody else we were reading it at the age of 12, passing it from sweaty paw to sweaty paw.' Chantelle Horton, an avid reader who later went on to work for her 'fave mag' (past lingo is rushing up to greet me) has similarly lubricious memories. 'We were all obsessed by the boy models – especially Malcolm. And the fashion pages – when they'd go to a town and take pictures of the people who looked really trendy. They came to Grimsby once,' she says, still with an unmistakable trace of pride in her voice. 'It was a talking point for the whole town.'

Former *J-17* devotees are not hard to find, and each has a favourite article, a fond recollection. 'For me, it was a piece about *"The X Factor"*,' recalls Laura. 'It included a detailed guide to pouting.' For Alice, who went on to work for the magazine, it offered even more valuable advice. 'I remember a long article about how to tell if a boy fancied you,' she says. Will she share this holy grail of romance with those of us who missed it the first time round? 'We all have invisible 'love antennae' which send out signals if we fancy someone,' she explains. 'So, if you fancy a boy, it means you've picked up the signals he's sending out and he fancies you too. I honestly, really believed it then. I think part of me still subconsciously does.' Hmm. Personally, I've always found an unmistakably priapic presence a more reliable indicator, but I can appreciate the attraction of something more subtle in the early days of courtship.

But then, I was not actually allowed to buy Just Seventeen. This prohibition was just one of the many ways in which my mother ensured my continued status as Geek of the Remove, along with forcing me to wear school uniform for several years after everyone else had abandoned the practice in favour of something more alluring from Miss Selfridge or Chelsea Girl's Jailbait range. Instead, I had to wait until Tracy Durrant had finished with her copy, which then percolated through her immediate coterie, then through the rest of the excruciatingly fashionable, scrunchie-festooned set. Only the day before the next edition came out did it finally filter down to me and my equally acne-spattered friends. The wait was enough to induce an anxiety attack in even the most well-adjusted adolescent, and we made Hayley Cropper look like Paris Hilton. Even at the time, I knew by the mixture of pity and contempt with which I finally was given the dog-eared copy that it wasn't so much a magazine as a vital weapon in the armoury of social policing. 'But the magazine itself never dealt with the snakepit, the psychic hell of early secondary school,' remembers Colgan, with a barely repressed shudder.

Still, you take what you can get, don't you? And so, eventually, I was able to hone my knowledge of how to apply blue mascara; how to tell your younger sister to leave your clothes alone (oh, the bitter infighting that took place over a single ra-ra skirt); and, of course, how to kiss. This last skill remained theoretical until a fairly advanced age – in fact, I believe I broke numerous local records for the avoidance of all bodily fluid exchanges. Fortunately I am blessed with an excellent long-term memory, and when I was at last the recipient of the longed-for lunge, it was the work of a moment to recall the vital edicts 'Don't hold your breath and don't bite his tongue'. The manoeuvre passed off successfully, and that is why I still go to bat against those who would claim that girls' magazines are nothing but a tool for the conditioning of females into passive clotheshorses who will trot gently into the nearest office job and then down the nearest aisle with the first young man who bobs his love antennae at them.

'At the time they were a really useful source of information and knowledge for me,' says Alice. 'And they made me want to write for magazines when I grew up. I don't remember the fashion aspects so much – I think there's far more interest in that nowadays – but the stuff about sex and boys was good.' And now that she's written for the magazine? 'Now I realise it's all written by some bitter, terminally single woman lying to teenage girls and wishing it was true.'

Horton, who worked her way up from reader, to editorial assistant then features editor at *J-17* and now works at young upstart *Bliss* magazine, agrees that there is some truth to that statement, but rushes to restore people's faith in their formative periodical. 'It was a really fun, creative place to work. Yes, there were always things you had to write about for the teenage girl market – periods, crushes, Valentine's Day – but because it was such a great breeding ground, people were always getting poached so the teams would

stay fresh and keep the energy going.' So why are we now commem-
orating its sad demise? 'The market's just so crowded now,
compared to when it began. It had a lot of unique celebrity access
then, but now with MTV and the internet, everything has changed.
And it was the first to give away free gifts, but now everybody
does it.'

Ah yes, the free gifts. Lip gloss so sticky your dad could borrow
it to mend tiles, eyeshadows in tones more commonly seen in distress
flares and makeup bags made of plastic seemingly rescued from a
landfill site. 'The first one was mascara,' recalls Horton mistily. 'My
dad went mad at me having makeup in the house.'

And what have we got to replace this once-great pioneer? Pale
imitations, according to those who remember *J-17* with a slightly
unnerving Messianic fervour. Sex-filled, paedophile-fodder
according to Bob Geldof, in uneasy alliance with assorted *Daily
Mail* readers. And according to someone whose spent recent
months immersed in *Bliss*, *Sugar* and other delightful confections
as part of the research for her impending teenage novel? 'I think
they're all wonderful,' says Julie Burchill. 'I'm old enough to
remember *Jackie* and its 'Cathy & Claire' problem page which was
actually written by its Scottish Calvinist publishers DC Thomson
and was just censorious 'save yourself' stuff. Today's magazines
make life seem very fun and games. I wish they'd been around
when I was young.'

But let us not forget what the magazine bequeathed us: at least
one sure-fire way to get a boy to speak to you. 'You catch his eye,
smile, then look away – twice,' instructs Colgan with terrifyingly
total recall, 'and then catch his eye a third time – and look sad. He
will then rush up to find out what's wrong.' In the face of such optimism, one can only raise a glass of Lemon Hooch and wish *J-17* a
long and happy retirement.

25 MARCH 2004

Cooking for sloths

The drive to turn us into a nation of gourmands seems unceasing. We are tossed like croutons in a caesar salad upon a restless sea of recipes. Nigella, Jamie, Rick, Antonio and the rest all claim to make cooking simple. But for those of us who ask for nothing more out of a meal than that it be edible, stave off malnutrition and scurvy for another day and dirty no more than one pan during its concoction, this is palpable nonsense.

Take, for example, Rick Stein's list of 'a few handy store cupboard ingredients'. Thai fish sauce, a block of tamarind pulp, Sichuan peppercorns. All calculated to strike fear in the heart of a founder member of the William of Ockham school of culinary thought, which holds that no dish should be developed past the point of necessity. For example, we believe – and are working on empirical proof – that any meal that tastes good with capers in it will taste just as good without them. Thus another pointless purchase can be avoided. Ditto anchovies.

A brief glance through a Jamie Oliver volume leaves me with nothing but a dizzying memory of bushels of salad leaves, weird fish, a possibly illegal quantity of parmesan shavings, and endless scatterings of pancetta and sluicings of olive oil. My parsimonious soul shrinks from all that is there.

I possess none of Nigella's oeuvre, for much the same reason that I don't own any floor-length pictures of Elle Macpherson or set fire to myself on a regular basis: there are certain things a girl learns to do to protect herself against unnecessary pain as she makes her way through life. But occasional accidental glimpses of Nigella's television shows tell me that my mental health would not survive a prolonged encounter with either *How to Be a Domestic Goddess* or *How to Eat*.

Where, then, can the anti-gourmet turn in search of an easier life? Braving the extensive cookery section of an arbitrary bookshop

reveals that behind the bestsellers lurks another world, a world of
– if the titles are to be believed – minimal effort and restful simplicity.

Getting the Best from Your Microwave, for example, seems to be
talking my language. 'Cut cooking time by 75 per cent . . . cut costs
. . . cook and serve in the same container and save on washing-up'
– all is going swimmingly until the recipes themselves begin. Blimey.
Peel this, chop that, seed something else . . . goddammit, these are
proper recipes that purport to be labour-saving by appending the
instruction 'then microwave for 3-5 minutes' instead of Nigella's
'hold over a guttering candle for eight days or until your guests
pass out in admiration' at the end. It even gives a recipe for making
bread, which can be summarised as: 'Put in 15 hours of hard graft,
then waste it by bunging the result in a fundamentally unsuitable
cooking appliance and reflect on your sense of priorities for 3-5 minutes.'
Let's move on.

My casserole dish is currently the repository of four bags of
Batchelors SuperNoodles and a spare set of door keys and has yet
to see any kind of stock-based activity, so *Real Food from Your
Casserole* seems a sensible port of call. A brief perusal yields a hearty
set of variations on the not altogether unsurprising theme of chopping and trimming meat, adding wine, cream, herbs, garlic, toma-
toes, onions, bacon and so on. The proportions of effort to result
look good. Then matters take a darker turn. 'This is the key to easy
living,' I am abruptly informed. 'And it will lift your lifestyle significantly if you just add some crusty French bread and a carafe of wine
to your table.' On the grounds that I am not a refugee from *Abigail's
Party*, I decline to purchase.

Knowing that my domestic management skills could do with a
brush-up, I pause for quick thumb-through of *How to Freeze:
Everything You Need to Know About Freezing and Freezer
Management*. Lots of helpful hints here. If it comes in small bits,
freeze them on a baking tray and put them in a bag. If it's a liquid,
put it in an airtight container, not a bag. That's good. If there is
one area of kitchen equipment with which I am abundantly supplied,

it's Tupperware. Every year since I turned 25, my mother has added to my collection without fail on every birthday. I fully expect to wake up on my 30th to find an enormous plastic box on my doorstep containing a handsome but terrified young doctor that she has deemed suitable for fathering her grandchildren and kidnapped.

Still, if I do find myself shortly taking delivery of a hermetically sealed husband, all the more reason to have a few decent recipes under my belt. Could *Lasagna – 50 Recipes for the Original One-Dish Meal* be the answer? If I made one every Sunday to last the week, this single book could see us comfortably through that tricky first year together.

The signs that finding 50 ways to jazz up lasagna is going to be a bit of a strain are apparent almost from the beginning, when the replacement of 'normal pasta' with ready-made sheets is deemed to constitute a separate dish. I am already confused. Are ready-made sheets not normal? Should every piece be hand-tooled by a pet Italian artisan in the cellar? My attention is distracted by a chapter on *Lasagnas around the world*. My friend Mario once saw this as a sign above a supermarket's freezer cabinet. He was driven to write to his MP, but my sensibilities are less finely balanced and I admire the straightforwardness of the endeavour. Mexican style: add black beans. Thai style: add stir-fry vegetables. Greek-style lasagna: add aubergine (if your gag reflex will let you ingest hell's own vegetable). I am disappointed that the author did not further explore the possibilities of this approach – Alabama style: add seven-fingered banjo player; Notting Hill style: add trust fund; Mangan style: add takeaway pizza.

'Vegetarian lasagnas' require replacement of the meat with broccoli, asparagus, butternut squash or anything you feel would drain all the joy and spontaneity from life even more effectively. The author strays considerably from the brief in *Dessert lasagnas*, which is a chapter best not dwelt on, and it suddenly occurs to me that, even if it does last a week, lasagna is a lot of work. Frying mince, chopping onions, getting your pasta sheets made to measure – I'm losing the will to live at the mere thought of it.

But what's this? Suddenly I spy a volume entitled, rather appetisingly, *Toast*, by the even more appetisingly named Jesse Ziff Cool. Surely this will live down to my expectations? Alas, the very first recipe is for toast with lox and caper-dill cream cheese. Apart from the fact that I think my parents used to play bridge with the caper-dills, there is little to detain me here. The notion of my chopping the fiddly ingredients to mix with the cheese is laughable enough, but when I am exhorted to 'rustically pile the chopped tomato, red onion and cucumber on top', my giggles become somewhat hysterical and I am obliged to leave.

I trail mournfully home, realising that I am trapped in my world of fried fish and boiled potatoes for ever, caught between the paralysing twin forces of sloth and fear while my Tupperware warps and my taste buds atrophy. But when I arrive, I find that my father – a man who lives to cook, whose palate has been honed over years of fine wining and dining, a man who would grate a sodding caper if the recipe called for it and not even pause to consider whether this is a reasonable use of one's brief and easily inglorious span on this earth – is waiting for me on the doorstep. He has heard about my search for the ultimate manual of sloth.

'I came to give you these,' he says, slipping two volumes gently – nay, reverently – into my hands: Nigel Slater's *Appetite*, and *Real Food*. 'They are all you need.' I demur. 'But he's one of those poncey celebrity chefs!' 'Thou speakest crap, child,' comes the kindly reply. 'Go. Read. Cook.' With that, he slipped away silently into the night.

And, by golly, he was right. They are all you need. Slater talks about dollops and glugs, of adding a bit more of this ingredient if you like it and leaving out that one if you don't. He tells you what herbs go with what meat so you can mix and match if you run out of a particular one. He makes one meal just by buying cheese in a box and putting it in the oven. If I wasn't now 38 stone and unable to wrap my sausage-like fingers round a pen, I would write and thank him, from the bottom of my overstrained but happy heart.

28 APRIL 2004

The seven wonders of the modern diet

Ah, tempora mutantur, nos et mutamur in illis : times change and
we change with them. Gone are the days when sliced bread represented the pinnacle of human achievement. At the time, it may have
been seen as a sufficiently life-altering event to require immortal-
isation in popular phraseology, but now it seems the benchmark for
superlativity is frozen food.

That's according to a survey published in the *Grocer* this week,
which asked people to nominate the top 20 innovations that have
contributed most to the life of restful ease and comfort that eluded
earlier generations, who had to till the soil and kill pigs with their
bare hands before they could be sure of a decent meal to give them
the strength to get through another evening of sing-alongs by the
piano and recitals in the village hall.

Those polled put frozen food, pasteurised milk, sanitary products,
microwaveable food, teabags, instant coffee and ring-pull cans before
sliced bread, which came in at number eight. Drinks in plastic bottles,
disposable nappies, powdered baby milk, disposable razors and
chilled, vacuum-packed and ready-made food brought up the rear.
But as we pause to allow the environmental lobbyists among us to
bury their heads in their hemp-filled pillows and emit howling
screams of despair, we can also reflect on some of the products that
surely narrowly missed the cut.

Ice pops

They were made of sugar, chemicals, sugar, water and sugar; came
in different colours, not one resembling any to be found in nature;
packed 20 or 30 to a box, and were kept in the freezer by your
mother all summer for handing out on arrival home from school, or
to keep you quiet while she sat in the lounge projecting sexual fantasies
on to Jimmy Connors at Wimbledon. The ice pops' plastic pouches
freed a generation of children from the misery occasioned by the
falling of the last, luscious chunk of ice lolly from stick to floor.

Instant noodles

Often overshadowed by their more flamboyant relative, the Pot Noodle, instant noodles deserve their moment in the spotlight. There is an elemental simplicity about them – open packet, put contents in pan, empty sachet into pan, pour on boiling water, simmer for three minutes, eat results – that other so-called convenience foods (with their 'remove sleeve, pierce film, spend 20 minutes cleaning up resulting spray of tomato sauce, heat in microwave, burn mouth on meal hotter than the sun, give up, drive to casualty' instructions) would do well to emulate.

But if you do feel the overwhelming urge to add your own imprimatur to the dish, it still allows a measure of creativity: you can eat your noodles al dente or soft and slippery, with the broth or without, add or withhold the chilli bits, or any combination of the above. So much happiness for between 23p and 49p from your local supermarket.

Flyte bars

You've probably consigned it to the darkest recesses of memory, but there was a long period after the original Milky Ways disappeared when nothing happened. Oh, there were rumours and mutterings, but nothing tangible. But even in our wildest imaginings we did not envisage what eventually occurred. The white chocolate Milky Way appeared. And was considered by its makers to be sufficient recompense for the withdrawal of one of the greatest chocolate bars the world had ever known.

Then, again, for a long time, there was nothing. Finally, unheralded, out of the mists appeared the Flyte bar. The Milky Way had been reborn and this time it came in pairs. And there was much rejoicing. And ingesting. But it was a lesson, a useful reminder of the impermanence and fragility of so many of life's pleasures, of our ultimate dependency on the whims of Nestle, Mars and Cadbury for so much of our contentment.

Perhaps it even helped us weather the storm caused by the former's announcement that they would be withdrawing the dual-wrapped KitKat from sale and replacing it with the plastic unilayer already us throughout the rest of Europe, thus depriving our descendants of the irreplaceable satisfaction of running a thumbnail between the foil-covered gunnels of a four-fingered wafer. It rankled then, it rankles now, but at least we have the Flyte bar.

Wafer-thin ham/chicken/turkey

I was working on the delicatessen counter in Waitrose when this new kid on the block appeared 13 or 14 years ago. I felt like an aproned showman in a travelling freak show as the people gathered round to stare incredulously and point at the fascinating spectacle of ruched ham. We sold out in minutes. Even the Glaswegian lady who had not in 20 years of tempting special offers been deflected from her traditional Saturday purchase of eight pounds of corned beef was moved to buy a quarter and pronounce it 'no' bad'.

Market forces being what they are, millefeuilles of chicken and turkey soon hit the shelves, too, to equally riotous acclaim. I am given to understand that the most recent addition is something called 'turkey-ham', or possibly 'ham-turkey'. I think it behoves us all to take a moment and appreciate the depths that the untrammelled pursuit of innovation can sometimes lead us to plumb.

Very lazy garlic

It's not the cooking I mind any more. I have come to terms with the fact that a girl cannot live by baked beans alone, although such a diet does naturally ensure that she will live on her own for as long as it continues. But can I remember to buy all those things that people keep telling me make chicken, sauces and God knows what else palatable, like garlic, ginger and, er, salt? No, I cannot.

In the last couple of years, perceptive manufacturers have realised that I am not alone and so have brought out the stuff ready-chopped.

Bloody great jars of it. It costs more than gold pots full of platinum, of course, but I'm not complaining. No more backtracking from the till and bolting down the aisle full of posh people palpating unwaxed lemons when I realise I've forgotten that the recipe calls for eight cloves of the hard stuff or an inch-cubed of that strangely balsa-woodish ginger spice. They're all sitting at home waiting to weave their aromatic magic.

Quorn

When I was a lot younger, Frazzles did my head in – looked like bacon, tasted like bacon, made of crisps. Now that I'm older and incalculably more sophisticated, I look to Quorn for the same mind-bending effects. It's a meat substitute, but it's a mushroom or something. That's messed up. Brilliant.

Milk chocolate digestives

First there was the digestive. It fitted the national character perfectly – stolid, honest and unpretentious. Its mild sweetness was considered by most of Britain to be luxury enough. For 18 generations, 'a nice cup of tea and a biscuit' had been an adequate reward for everything from donkey stoning the step to digging your family out of Luftwaffe-strafed rubble.

Then one individual yielded to an unprecedented sybaritic impulse and added a layer of chocolate to the biscuit.

So deeply ingrained was national antipathy towards indulgence, however, that even this radical thinker could not fully break the subconscious bonds that held him, and he used plain chocolate as his coating of choice – its bitterness offsetting the sweetness as atonement for the essentially decadent nature of the venture.

Paralysed by shock, both parliament and the people let the aberration survive until it gradually became accepted in polite society. As is so often the case, of course, this small concession begat a host of others, until at last the milk-chocolate digestive was launched on a society that, frankly, was more than willing to receive it.

We are now living in a world of undiluted sugar, the milk chocolate and its host vying with each other as to who can deliver the biggest
rush, spurred on rather than tempered by each other, heedless of the
harm they do to the consumer . . . all hail the essence of modernity in
biscuit form.

2 FEBRUARY 2005

The crust of the matter

My current favourite book (apart from *Little House on the Prairie*
which taught me the invaluable lesson that if your parents start
muttering about pushing west and seeking new frontiers you
should get adopted by the local schoolteacher forthwith before
you find yourself in Wisconsin making bonnets for your blind
sister out of locusts and slough grass) is *The Experienced English
Housekeeper*. Written in 1769 by Elizabeth Raffald, very much the
Delia of her day, it is full of robust recipes like beast's heart larded
('Wash a large beast's heart clean and cut off the deaf ears. Strain
the gravy through a hair sieve'), grilled calf's head ('hash one
half, blanch your tongue, slit it down the middle and lay it on a
soup plate. Skin the brains') and boiled scullery maid ('Catch your
maid. Slit her down the middle and stuff her with ox palates. If
you don't have any ox palates, use the boot boy. Garnish with
barberries').

Unperturbed by notions of animal (or scullery) rights, a happy
certainty pervades the book. It speaks of an empire built on a solid
foundation of offal, of an age when men were men, women were
cooks and recipes were soothingly repetitive. You find the most
unsettling part of an animal's anatomy, clean it, stuff it with whatever fetid viscera you have to hand, strew it with mace, bung it in
the oven for eight hours while you kill time by tilling a sodden acre
or two and then dish up to a dozen grateful guests. Serve ad infinitum
and quite possibly ad nauseam.

It's out of print now, which is hardly surprising given that these are the days of the stoneless avocado, the easy-eat artichoke and, from yesterday, the crustless loaf. If food fashions are even the remotest indicator of cultural sensibilities, we are clearly in a bad way. The stoneless avocado was bred in response to what was, according to Sainsbury's, 'the common complaint' that the stone took up too much of the fruit and was 'always difficult to remove'. It's a complaint better suited to the problems of coalmining than of preparing an outmoded hors d'oeuvre, but such are our pampered modern ways. The new artichoke was developed for people with brains and mandibles so atrophied by lack of use that they cannot cope with tearing leaves off a core and scraping them with their teeth (how to eat the original will be a GCSE by 2012).

But crustless bread enshrines multiple cultural inadequacies. First, Hovis is using the fact that children tend to leave their crusts to give the new product a waste-saving selling point. This is the same mentality that encourages people to half-fill kettles and put plastic hippos in the cistern while water companies cheerfully allow oceans to leak from pipes underground in order to protect their profits.

The new loaf is also, according to Hovis, designed to enable parents to sidestep contretemps with their offspring over said lack of crust ingestion. Or, to put it another way, it allows adults to avoid yet another opportunity to wrangle their ungrateful, overindulged offspring into submission and act like parents intent on civilising their charges instead of indentured servants desperate to appease atavistic tyrants. Eating crusts has been a battlefield between parents and children for generations – being forced to finish a sandwich is probably the first lesson most of us learn about the likelihood that there will be a price to be paid for most of the tasty, soft-centred bits of life – but this is the first to abandon with such alacrity the chance to force some moral as well as comestible fibre into their kids.

In truth, of course, this new form of the staff of life exists not to save wastage or aid parents but to make money. Hovis – presumably after sufficiently encouraging market research among potential buyers – is hoping that bread will beget bread. If it does, this pallid excuse for a loaf will also kill any hope that the food industry might eventually exhaust the gullibility of the paying public when it comes to shelling out for novelty items. Although, having said that, I suppose that hope largely died when Jamie Oliver's campaign revealed that most punters swam happily in a sea of illusion that whispered to them: 'Oh yes, turkey that falls from the bag in radioactive-orange frozen spirals and wholly obscured by breadcrumbs that reappear undigested in the toilet bowl three days later are indeed made of prime cuts of organic birds. Enjoy!'

So there you have it. A populace that once happily cleaved cow craniums in twain with unshakable confidence and a rusty axe has transformed into a nation of witless, mollycoddled morons vexed by vegetables and slavering over stoneless, crustless, pointless pap. Bring back the barberries and boot boys.

10 AUGUST 2005

Introducing the new, no-frills curriculum

New schools, we hear, are being built without proper kitchens – just a giant microwave where the playing fields might once have stood in their dumbly insolent, doing nothing, open-space kind of way.

This is a remarkably prescient move by the education authorities. As the recession-defying likes of Primark and easyJet will attest, a no-frills attitude to supplying goods and services is increasingly popular. Perhaps we are simply becoming more bargain-savvy or perhaps we are beginning to prune back our consumer desires in subconscious preparation for the day when Coleen McLoughlin stops buying shoes and the global economy finally implodes. Either way, the time is surely ripe for the introduction of a no-frills, purely functional education designed to deliver a purely productive citizen.

Art history: Only for ponces. Gone.

Religious studies: Too tricky. Gone.

Geography: Gone. Instead, at 18 every pupil will be given a government-issue set of Rough Guides in the hope that 40 per cent will not return, thus easing the pressure on universities which will shortly be open to anyone with a head.

PE: No equipment, no playing fields – what to do? Simply combine it with dinner time by hollowing out a redundant games teacher, packing him with chicken nuggets and hanging him from the ceiling, pinata-style, while the kids beat him with sticks until the bread-crumbed delicacies fall out. After an energetic session of gouging and biting each other as they scramble across the floor in pursuit of their semi-nutritious portions, the children must race to the microwave. The first 10 win a glass of water and get their knobbly meals warmed up. The rest have to poke them down their desiccated throats with a stick. All this activity will stave off both obesity and parental realisation that their offspring are still being fed on chicken bums and cow lips five days out of seven. Everybody's happy.

Maths: Out – calculus, trigonometry, algebra. In – practical assessment courses: filing tax returns, fundraising for minor operations abroad, poverty-trap equations (if X=benefits, Y=minimum wage, Z=childcare costs and A=prostitution fines, can you arrange these letters without spelling YOU'RE SCREWED?).

Sex education: Boys will be taken into a bright, white room with a picture of a vagina on the wall. A teacher will point at it with a trembling finger and vomit copiously for an hour. Girls will be taken into a bright, white room with a picture of a penis on the wall. A teacher will point at it with a trembling finger and scream wordlessly for an hour. Then they will be herded together into a room lined with pictures of the HIV virus, chlamydia and hepatitic livers and the two teachers will walk up and down the rows, shouting 'Keep yer pants ON!' until it's time for . . .

English: When I was at school we used to share one book between two or three and still we emerged literate. This is far more than required in the age of the spellcheck, so under BasicEd there will be one book to be read by the fastest texter who will then send an edited version to everyone's phones. 'Wthrng Hghts – lds of ppl run rnd m00rs in di@lct. Thnk they r mdly p@ssion8 bt really dull as fk. Shkspre s@me bt usu@lly on blstd hths. C u l8tr.'

14 SEPTEMBER 2005

Can you dance? You've got the job

I have been a searcher of gainful employment since I was 16 and in need of an income to perpetuate a social life that, although rudimentary, could still not be funded on the small change my mother occasionally threw at me when she saw that I had again failed to lay the table with the napkins facing north-north-west or align the condiments within a prescribed 0.25 degree margin of error.

Ergo, I have had more job interviews than I've had hot dinners, and not only because they tended to be cold by the time I'd staunched the wounds. ('Go ahead,' she'd snarl. 'Bleed all over the tablecloth. See what happens to yer then.') Some were relatively simple, like the one at the local supermarket.

'Do you know what ham is?'

'Yes.'

'You're on the deli counter.'

Or the local bookshop.

'Do you know what a book is?'

'Yes.'

'You're in charge.'

There were more complicated ones after university, most part of my futile and inexplicable pursuit of a series of city jobs for which I was so wildly unsuited that it can only have been morbid curiosity that made the panels agree to see me in the first place. As we sat gazing at each other across the desk in slack-jawed mutual disbelief, the interviewer would say something like, 'Tell me again why you would put the proceeds of an index-linked high-yield gilt-edged covalent-bonded well-endowed hedge fund and put it in a Lloyds current account?' and

I would say, 'Because they give you a free money box that sorts the coins for you,' before being gently escorted off the premises.

Still, I can thank God that I have never been tested for my 'Virgin flair', even though this doesn't in fact require the invasive procedures you might initially assume. 'Virgin flair' is what Richard Branson's Australian airline Virgin Blue claimed in an anti-discrimination tribunal this week it was seeking when it asked its job candidates to perform a song and dance routine as part of the selection process. As one with no discernible sense of rhythm – I dance like a tumour – there can be nothing more clearly designed to humiliate and dismiss the less fortunate.

It's possible, of course, that Virgin Blue were simply acknowledging the fundamentally despotic nature of the average customer – who, after all, has not wanted at one time or another to bellow at a member of the service industries, 'You have fulfilled my basic transactional needs but our alienated exchange has left me strangely dissatisfied. Dance! Dance for me, boy!'? It is also possible that the interviewers were working in conjunction with the Soft Shoe Shuffle Preservation Society to see whether these ancient dancing skills are surviving into the next generation. Either motivation would mollify.

But it turns out that what the eight women who brought the claim also objected to was the fact that most of those who even got as far as being asked to re-enact *Oklahoma* in a 20ft pressurised steel tube were predominantly young, blonde, under 25, and allocated by the genetic lottery an unfeasibly large amount of leg. So Virgin Blue has no prejudice against the unrhythmic! Just the post-pubescent, mousy-haired and stumpy. That's all right then. Oh no – wait . . .

12 OCTOBER 2005

Ths msg wl slf-dstrct in 40 scnds

I've only engaged in text sex once. It wasn't a riotous success, partly because my carnal imagination is a singularly paltry resource and partly because, even more than lingerie, brevity is the soul of this particular erotic art and I am too passionately committed to both conventional orthography and the subordinate clause to thrill to their enforced sacrifice on the altar of arousal.

My already limited pleasure in the proceedings was further hampered when it dawned on me that there was no way of controlling what happened to my laboriously typed missives at the other end. I could demand immediate deletion and/or confidentiality until the end of time, but not ensure it – unless I hunted through the million offices of the recipient's law firm, Endless Tedium & Death, found him and smashed his phone into atoms.

Now, however, the libidinous, the indiscreet, the foolhardy and philanderers everywhere can effortlessly erase their filthy tracks by signing up to the StealthText service. (I'm going to erase from my own memory just how long it took me to realise that the name was in fact Stealth-Text and not a misprint of Steal-the-text, although I relinquish less willingly the happy image of tiny cybermen tucking vowelless messages under their arms, and disappearing into the night.) You download the service from the good people of Staellium UK (I think they may be where all the spare vowels are going) on to your WAP-enabled phone, and your boyfriend/girlfriend/gigolo/ mistress/one-night repository of communicable diseases receives a link that leads to your 'i wnt 2 do pervrs & prfndly missplld thngs 2 yr bdy' message. Forty seconds after it opens, it self-destructs – a foolproof system, provided that you don't have a fetish for slow readers.

At least the Stealth service is being applied, appropriately, to an ephemeral form. It's a rare congruency at a time when we are getting increasingly confused about what is worth preserving and what should be destroyed forthwith. Acres of trees, for example, are cut down for Jeffrey Archer's witless maunderings – sorry, novelistic triumphs. Prince Charles's unsought communiques about his royal activities to dozens of his closest friends, relatives, courtiers and political contacts are not only kept for posterity but broadcast to an ungrateful nation and will therefore Google on for ever. Apples are sprayed with (allegedly) carcinogenic elixirs so that they can last for 12 months, but iPods shatter en masse minutes after the launch date. Perfectly healthy Routemaster buses are sent to the knacker's yard to make way for bendy articles given to spontaneous combustion. No official record is kept of Iraqi civilian deaths but the sparrow that was shot with an air rifle for jeopardising a world-record attempt at domino toppling is to be stuffed, mounted and displayed for ever in a Dutch museum as – what? A testimony to man's inhumanity to bird? A monument to the first domino-related slaughter of the innocents? A silent commentary on the fragility of human record-breaking dreams?

Ah well. Perhaps one day Staellium will develop StealthText to the point that it will be capable of deleting such cultural idiocies and inconsistencies. Until then, just beware the laden cybermen trotting out of your beloved's phone.

14 DECEMBER 2005

The Famous Five – in their own words

'I say, how queer!' said George, showing Dick the story she had just read in the *Guardian*. 'Queer altogether!' said Dick when he had read the article and finished his mouthful of fresh home-cured bacon and egg which the hens had laid that morning. 'What does it say?' said Anne, who was hand-feeding her older brother Julian with fresh lettuce hearts and delicious freshly baked bread that she had made at 4am that day as girls should. 'Yes, tell us,' said Julian. 'Because I am the leader of the group and Anne can't read because her female eyes are too weak.'

'It says the *Famous Five* are still the most popular children's books ever,' said George, wolfing down a slice of delicious fruitcake they had bought from the local paedophile – sorry, red-cheeked farmer and his wife – that morning. 'Gosh,' said Anne. 'Even with the fearful fuss there has been about Narnia recently?'

'The Pevensey children got second place,' said Dick eagerly. 'And serve them jolly well right for prancing about with talking beavers in amalgamated mythical hinterlands instead of staying firmly within the stockbroker belt.'

'I call that pretty ripping,' said Julian as Anne brushed the crumbs from his pullover and flagellated herself with a willow branch for being a girl. 'It just goes to show that you will never go broke underestimating the sophistication of a pre-adolescent readership.'

'What do you mean, Ju?' said George, feeding Timmy the dog scraps of delicious deliciousness that they had bought from the village shop that sold only fresh delicious things.

'I mean, old thing, give them 200 pages of easily identifiable heroes and villains, a set of two-dimensional protagonists getting into a series of relatively unthreatening and infinitely resolvable scrapes, scatter the thing with a few basic adjectives and plenty of descriptions of food and they will lap it up for 50 years or more.'

'Well-paced narrative has distracted them from gaping plot holes and an unprecedented lack of character development,' agreed George, pouring herself a glass of fresh milk that Anne had extracted from a passing Friesian at five o'clock that morning. 'But I think our own embodiment of timeless archetypes has something to do with it.'

'I don't understand, George,' said Anne when she got back from filling the empty lemonade and ginger beer bottles full of fresh water from the underground spring 10 miles away, buying delicious ices at the village shop and dressing the burns she suffered while cooking breakfast for five on an oil stove.

'We're all awfully good at appealing to eternal childish desires for continuity, conformity,' explained George. 'Julian's awfully alpha male, someone for the boys to aspire to and Dick's the lesser patriarch but his authority is still reassuringly unchallenged because of the mere fact of his gender. You, Anne, as subservient helpmeet, shore up the status quo while I, with my tomboyish attitude gradually subdued over the course of the series, acknowledge the tensions inherent in the patriarchal structure while always recognising the need for their repression for the greater social good. Together, we are gathered gratefully to the unrepentantly reactionary heart of every child.'

'I say, isn't that ripping!' said Dick.

'Jolly, awfully jolly good!' said Julian.

'Top hole!' cried George.

'I am so fucked,' said Anne.

22 DECEMBER 2005

Who needs planets when you have stars?

I've never actually been to the London Planetarium. My brief interest in astronomy coincided with the peak of my infantile obsessive compulsive disorder, which meant I couldn't spend long in a crowd without being wrapped in cling-film and periodically sprayed with Waitrose pine disinfectant by a parent. Now it appears I have waited too long to partake of its educative joys. The 3D showings of Journey to Infinity, a stately traversing of the heavens and all major constellations therein, have already been cut from 45 minutes to 10, and in a few months the Planetarium will be renamed the Auditorium and devote itself to screenings of a show devoted to the celebrity firmament.

Alas, the staff who currently seek to inspire and inform about the wonders of astronomy are struggling to come to terms with the changes. A memo from the planetarium's owners has been issued, seeking to smooth the transition:

Dear Nerds,

Please note that from now on, Orion's Belt will be replaced by Chantelle's Thong. Orion will be played by Hunter from Gladiators, who will present a segment on how sleeping with Ulrika Jonsson can make your celebrity profile go supernova before it collapses back in on itself and is reduced to a dim pulse only detectable by the Hubble telescope and Heat readers' camera phones.

The Dog Star will be replaced by the Dogging Star, currently Stan Collymore (but subject to revision in accordance with any more recent sightings).

The Milky Way will remain, but reconfigured to look like the snack you can eat between meals without ruining your appetite so that we can get Mars to sponsor a planned happy-slapping convention for the kids in the summer.

Any mention of Galileo Galilei should be confined to discussions about Queen's greatest hits. Anyone who tries to inform customers of his role in establishing the truth of Copernicus's heliocentric theory will be suspended without pay. This is a man who said: 'I do not feel obliged to believe that the same God who has endowed us with sense, reason and intellect has intended us to forgo their use.' This is a contravention of our new corporate policy, 'Making tomorrow's morons today'.

'Binary stars' shall refer only to Brad and Angelina, Britney and Kevin etc. Should the term ever need to stretch to include George Galloway and Rula Lenska, please be assured that the universe will implode shortly thereafter.

Auroras are out. Auras are in.

A light year now means a celebrity has succeeded in convincing herself for a full 12 months that 100g of chicken breast and a raisin followed by a laxative mousse constitutes a viable meal.

Please note that from July 'globular star clusters' will mean either a particularly excretory celebrity sex orgy somewhere in north London or an unfortunate shifting of silicone implants on a famous body.

The commentary accompanying the new show will be voiced by Tom Baker, Jimmy Carr, Carole Caplin or the Krankies, depending on planetary and diary alignments.

Cassiopeia will be renamed Cheryl.

Thank you for your co-operation. The Management.

A copy of this memo can be found on the Planetarium noticeboard, by Uranus.

1 FEBRUARY 2006

The case against a female Doctor Who

The Doctor Who fan base – and possibly the space-time continuum itself – has been rocked by the declaration of series writer Russell T Davies that he is not entirely averse to the notion of a female Doctor taking control of the Tardis in future.

A leaked memo circulated among executive producers at the BBC reveals some major concerns.

1. Girls can't do maths or read maps – surely insurmountable problems when applied to the calculations in 17 dimensions that a Time Lord must habitually make. Also, cannot afford to spend entire pre-credits sequence waiting for her to park the Tardis.

2. Not keen on whole episodes set in Ikea watching her pick out perfect window treatments for her interplanetary home. Or fretting about ageing effects of time travel. Retinol A must remain name of satellite Gallifreyan moon, not anti-wrinkle cream.

3. Doctor must be eccentric. Can women be eccentric without being covered in cat hair and/or smelling of wee? Research how.

4. Cannot afford necessary pre-launch campaign explaining to Whovians what a woman is.

5. Hierarchical problems. Doctor needs mentally and physically inferior sidekick to be afraid of Cybermen/stretchy-faced Penelope Wilton/glowy-headed fat people. If Who is female, will need to cast six-year-old boy (or rather 800 of them, because they can't work for more than 10 minutes at a time without some bleeding-heart waving child labour legislation at us – talk to Stephen Daldry if you don't believe me) or tin of Spam. Check whether there is Spam rights group. If so, investigate availability of Jimmy Krankie. Could be years before they sort out what we can and can't do with him. Her. God, this messes with your head.

6. Metaphysical problems. Doctor is same person; regeneration provides new body only. Reincarnating as female suggests feminine aspect has existed all along. Might mark series as camp?

7. Aesthetic problems. Doctor historically not been in any danger of being mistaken for Michaelangelo's David. Tom Baker nice chap but face like a bag of pork chops and Sylvester McCoy frankly disturbing. As ugly women now shot on sight at television auditions, how to cast? Go with Claire Goose and throw acid in her face? (Call her agent.)

8. Insurmountable problem – Time Lady just sounds wrong.

9. On the other hand, we've got to find something to do with Davina McCall.

31 MARCH 2006

Modernising Monopoly is a bad move

When Grandma died, I was naturally saddened. No more sage domestic counsel from a woman who had lived through the depredations of two world wars – I am left with only the knowledge of how to make mince and oxtail for 17 without recourse to actual mince or, if cooking towards the end of the week, oxtail, and how to spray furniture polish on curtain rails to ensure smooth running. ('Not that we could afford furniture polish. Or curtains. I used to hang the boys up there at night instead. I would have stopped having kids in 1954 but we had a bay window.') No more unconditional love expressed through the medium of unlimited Penguin biscuits, and, above all, no more board games by the fire. ('Don't light t'fire. I'm saving t'coal for a snack.')

But at least she won't be around to suffer the bastardisation of that most trusted of family favourites, Monopoly. Parker games manufacturers and property website rightmove.co.uk have joined up to reinvent Monopoly for the hyperinflation age, so that Oxford Street's original £300 price tag becomes £3m, Euston Road at £100 becomes Camden High Street at £1m, Mayfair mutates into Kensington Palace Gardens at £4m, and so, depressingly, on.

At a personal level, this would doubtless have ruined our games by prompting detailed descriptions of what my many cousins up there in Chipwhippetthwaite were able to buy. 'Our David's got himself a cloistered abbey wi'a private helipad. And a bidet. It cost three and six. And Sandra's bought a faux Lutyens with a pool, conservatory, home-cinema system and 22 acres of prime arable land for eightpence farthing – because the stables and dolls' hospital need a bit of work,' she would say, while I would be weeping gently over grainy pictures of the Zone 4 hovels that were all the estate agents of south-east London could find in my price and their effort range.

In a wider – although, I hope, no less trivial sense – injecting contemporary realism into traditional family games should not, of course, be allowed. It would ruin Cluedo, whose successful completion requires more fiercely sustained logic than sudoku and whose only redeeming features are the evocative settings and esoteric weaponry. Colonel Plum in the drawing room with the candlestick is a spur to imagination. A dozen variations on the teenager in the car park with a grudge against society would be a spur to around-the-board Prozac crunching.

Twister would be replaced by a big sheet saying, 'The spots have been withdrawn from this game on health and safety grounds'. And modern-day Hungry Hippos would be of limited entertainment value. 'There's only one in here, Daddy.' 'That's because global warming has killed the rest, Jimmy. And this one lives in a zoo and is fed a humanely killed carcass, so he won't need to eat your dice either.' 'Hippos are herbivores, Daddy.' 'Shut your face, son.' 'What should I do instead, Daddy?' 'We'll play a nice game of subjective Guess Who? son. Now, does your person look like she could be harbouring a sexually transmitted disease? No? How many times do I have to tell you, boy? You can't tell from her face. You have to get a blood test, or a swab.'

RIP Grandma. You're missing nowt.

Waiter, there's a bug in my restaurant!

You probably can't tell from my typing, but I am deep, deep under-cover. When the news broke that the London restaurant Portal, favourite haunt of José Mourinho and assorted other Chelsea players, discovered a tiny listening device had been planted in one of its plug sockets, I leaped at the chance to put my years of counter-espionage training into practice.

The restaurant says it will now engage security agents to make regular sweeps of the premises in an attempt to stop snooping, but what proof can they be against the old-fashioned methods of intelli-gence gathering? I don my trench coat, false nose 'n' spectacles and get a work experience student to come with me for extra cover. 'Bring infrared goggles, a cyanide capsule each and some lemon juice in case we need to improvise invisible ink,' I mutter down the secure line. 'We meet at noon. The table's booked under my secret pseudonym, Princess Consuela d'Angostura b'Terres.'

I arrive early to scope out the joint. I am already suspicious. A man is standing with two other men holding a big TV camera. Why? Is he filming the restaurant in order to recreate it nearer Stamford Bridge and nick the famous clientele? Hmm. My observation is inter-rupted by the arrival of Preeti, the sidekick. She has forgotten the goggles. Rookie mistake, I tell her. 'It's daytime,' she points outs. 'Whatever,' I reply.

We are ushered to the back room. In the passageway there is a big picture of a woman with her boobs out. I check them for signs of tampering. I get some strange looks, but no intel of note.

The dining room is busy. Lots of expensively suited men and women chatting in groups and in couples, with lots of champagne in buckets waiting by their sides. They probably think that by all talking at once and having their conversation overlaid with muzak they have taken sufficient precaution against being overheard. They have reckoned without the Kremlin-trained Angostura ear. We are barely 10 minutes into the meal before I have discovered that the quintet to our left are deep in conversation about 'the bloke who's cleaning windows' and someone else who is, according to the blue-eyed one in the red tie 'doing my head in'. The four City boys to our right are clearly planning something. 'Do you use candles?' says one. His co-conspirator mumbles something about a 'newspaper' and a 'chief'. I think I may have stumbled upon something big! The plot thickens, with references to 'the man himself' and 'born-again Alan' flying back and forth.

Forget big – this is huge! I tell Preeti that I have studied *The Da Vinci Code* exhaustively and am pretty sure we are witnessing a meeting of the Clerkenwell chapter of the Priory of Sion, and that quite possibly the jar of artfully layered borlotti beans on the shelf behind them is, in fact, the holy grail. Preeti tells me I'm a total tit. Just then one of the men can clearly be heard saying, 'The woman is so little but her head is MASSIVE!'

I turn to Preeti in triumph. That's exactly the kind of thing they would say if they realised we were too close to the truth – to put us off the scent! Then I notice that if you rearrange the letters of my carpaccio of cod and prawn they almost read, 'Your safety has been compromised. Get out now.' We leave. Preeti walks out, but I commando-crawl. You can't be too careful.

15 SEPTEMBER 2006

'Sebastian, it's Her Majesty calling'

Police have questioned three men, including a tabloid reporter, over allegations that someone has been hacking into royal voice-mails. As luck would have it, I have unearthed the transcript of some of the messages in question, left on the mobile of one senior courtier . . .

17 May, 3.57pm

Hi Sebastian, Wills here. Could you try to get me and Harry out of going to the Prince's Trust 30th anniversary party? Harry says if he has to sit next to Dad trying to keep time to Annie Lennox and the Bee Gees he'll start snorting coke off the nearest waitress and divebomb the crowd. Oh, hang on, he's shouting something . . . What is it, H? . . . He says he'll come if Dad books the Dead Kennedys singing Too Drunk to Fuck as the headline band. Thanks a million. Let us know how you get on.

23 May, 8.50am

Hi Sebastian, HRH here. Just wanted to say thanks for all your help with the Prince's Trust party. Even the boys seemed to enjoy it. Harry was jigging up and down with that waitress like nobody's business. Got his mother's way with the common people, I think. Anyway, you're a star. Love to Alan. Bye!

26 May, 3.16pm

Sebastian, Her Majesty calling. Could you let Charles know I've put half of Herefordshire on the 3.20 at Doncaster? Tell him not to worry, it's a sure thing.

26 May, 3.27pm

Her Maj again. Could you tell Charles I've lost half of Herefordshire on the 3.20 at Doncaster? Tell him not to worry, I'll make it up to him. Would a lap dance from Penny Junor do, d'you think? Ta-ta for now.

29 May, 10.23am

Hi Sebastian, HRH here. Listen, would you have a word with Margaret's boy about the auction? I know he and Sarah have got death duties to pay, but does he have to flog quite so much? I think we're all aware that the support of the great British public for the House of Windsor isn't what it was in the good old days, and I've just got a nasty feeling that if they get a look at the monogrammed silver-and-diamond miniature saw for cutting lemons, the jig may be well and truly up. So talk to him, would you? Love to Alan and the cats. Bye!

13 June, 6.30pm

Sterling work, Seb. Getting him to donate those railings from Kensington Palace to the nation was a stroke of genius. Really drew the sting. Despite the fact that they're going to remain in situ, totally inaccessible to the public! I take my polo cap off to you, Seb, I really do. Expect the de luxe organic Highgrove pud in your stocking this Christmas! TTFN.

14 June, 9.40am

Seb – quick question. Mummy's 80th – I know we've got the children's party at the palace, the walkabout in Windsor, the octogenarians' tea thing in the grounds, the Trooping of the Colour, the flypast, the feu de joie, the service of thanksgiving and Mansion House lunch, Snowdon's official portrait and the dinner and fireworks at Kew Palace, but has anyone thought to get the old bag a cake?

14 June, 12.58pm

Hello, this is a message for Sebastian Garter-Poursuivant from John Lewis cakefication department. I'm afraid we won't be able to do a 40ft replica of the Royal Yacht Britannia in chocolate sponge by Thursday, but we could do a 9ft corgi in battenberg or a map of the empire in Victoria sponge.

15 June, 2.50pm

Sebastian, it's Her Majesty. I'm at Aintree. Get the Keeper of the Privy Purse off my fricking back, would you?

16 June, 5.45pm

Sebastian, Princess Michael of Kent here. Just wondering about presents for Liz. Does she have a copy of Michael Palin's Sahara? I got two last Christmas and as we're a bit strapped for cash till the house shifts, I thought I'd recycle. What do you think? Laters.

2 July, 11.40am
Hi Sebastian – HRH, your lord and master here! Only kidding. Well, not really, but I wouldn't be so vulgar as to harp on about the social gulf between us! Thanks for the memo about rounding up volunteers for swan upping. I've got some spare staff at Highgrove if you want to borrow them for the duration, but remember that I need them back for aphid patrol by the beginning of August. Be a lot easier if I could just blast the little green buggers with DDT, but if we want to keep our organic certification we've got to repatriate all greenfly by hand to outlying fields and hedgerows. Anyway, bear them in mind. Regards to Alan. Bye!

9 July, 4.15pm
Seb, old thing, Camilla here. Could you get me a couple of cans of Oust when you're next filling in the Windsor Ocado order? If Chas finds out I've been smoking the Capstan Full Strength in the master bedroom, he'll go mental.

9 July, 4.19pm
... shit, shit, shit. Sorry, Seb, 'Mills again. And could you get me a yard of 17th-century tapestry and some brocade? I've set fire to a sodding wall hanging. Thanks love. Sorry to be a pain.

10 July, 11.30am
Hi Sebastian, Wills here. We've just heard we're supposed to be going to Beatrice's bloody fancy dress coming-of-age party on the 15th. Well, I'm taking my primogeniture and gallantry exams that day and Harry's so mashed at the moment that I doubt he'll be compos mentis by then. So could you think up some excuse for us? Thanks a million. Hope Alan and the cats are well.

12 July, 2.14pm

Buckingham Palace paramour research team speaking. We thought you'd want to know – we've run Kate Middleton through the Sensibilitron and she's broken all known records! She measures 14.5 on the Contrafergie Scale and we think we've discovered a fifth dimension in twinset theory. We'll keep you posted on Chelsy's results.

12 July, 4.13

Hello, Sebastian, can you hear me? I'm at Newmarket – tell Charles I've lost £20 and our national salvage rights on the steeplechase. Oh, and the state crown of India. We'll never miss it. Gotta go – I've got Somerset on the 4.30. Ta-ra.

18 July, 3.30pm

Sebastian, it's Charles. Mummy says she wants to charter a converted car ferry to take us on a family holiday round the Hebrides. Could you get the doctor to take a look at her? All grist to the enforced-abdication mill, eh?

18 July, 1.50pm

Buckingham Palace paramour research team here. Chelsy's wrecked the Sensibilitron. Please advise.

19 July, 4.19pm

Sebastian, tell Charles I'm going to kick his arse from here to Balmoral and back if he sends that doctor out to me one more time. I'm going nowhere.

25 July, 3.20pm

Camilla here, Sebastian. Hope you had a good week away – I gather those places do wonders for the nerves, but you must try to take it easy now you're back. We can't afford to send you there every time you collapse in a heap and start gibbering about worthless parasites!

Next time you see Charles, could you tell him to bring home some organic oats, goose eggs, blueberries and pesticide-free carrots? I'm making his favourite oat, goose egg, blueberry and carrot surprise for tea. Oh, and be a doll and get me a fucking great burger from Maccy D's next time you're out, would you? Thanks so much.

29 July, 5.40pm
It's Her Maj. I'm at Goodwood. We've lost Scotland.

1 August, 9.20am
Sebastian, it's Charles. I've just seen a picture of Fergie with that Puffy P Diddyman blinging it up in St Tropez. Honestly, can't we do something about her?

10 August, 4.32pm
Sebastian, Charles here. Nobody's seen you for a while and you haven't been answering your messages. Is anything wrong? Give me a call. Got to go now – Mummy's in Epsom and I fear for the Duchy. Speak soon.

10 AUGUST 2006

Why is it so hard to join a library?

I joined the library this week.

I know that the last time I did such a thing I was nine and my dad dealt with most of the administrative aspects of the venture while I ran off and immersed myself in the labyrinthine plot of *Jill Gets a Pony From Her Aunt*, by Christine Moleskin-Weskit, but nevertheless, things seem to have become excessively complicated in the intervening years. I don't know if this has occurred simply because the place has fallen victim to creeping bureaucracy, as council institutions do, or because the staff are secretly aware that there is

a terrorist cell operating somewhere in the vicinity, intent on
constructing a dirty bomb out of sticky copies of 80s videos and
large-print Catherine Cooksons. But the manner – a strange sort of
painstaking indifference – with which the girl at the applications
desk dealt with me suggested the former, which made it all the more
frustrating. After all, I wouldn't mind giving up an afternoon to a
Byzantine administrative system if it was going to save lives, but just
to satisfy some nameless municipal craving for paperwork? That
grates, my friends.

'Do you have three proofs of identification?' said the girl at
the desk.

'Three?' I said, staggering slightly. I was expecting one, knew in
my heart of hearts it would be two, but three had not even registered
as a possibility. 'You do know I'm wanting to borrow books, not
money or a key to a suite at the Cipriani?'

'You should think of me as carbon steel,' she replied.

'Less ductile and more difficult to weld than a merely steel
colleague?' I asked.

'Rigid,' she said. 'Inflexible. I require tripartite proof, and tripartite
proof I shall have. One with your address on it.' I searched through
my handbag for further ID. I suspect I muttered imprecations and
something about labouring under the misapprehension that libraries
were traditionally havens for the disenfranchised masses who could
not habitually lay hands on multiple forms of personal authentica-
tion. And that I thought they aimed to be democratic disseminators
of knowledge, not ringfenced security zones, but clearly I was wrong.

Eventually I had to upend my bag on to her desk, tipping out
eight Softmints, three lipsticks, 40-odd bits of paper, Shergar and
Lord Lucan. She picked out a bank statement, a payslip and a phone
bill. She photocopied the first two, initialled them, ticked boxes on
a form and put them in a foolscap file.

'Are you sure you don't want them notarised?' I asked.

'No,' she said. 'But backchat means we're entitled to hold your
DNA on file, so I'll take one of those lipsticks, thank you.'

Then I had to sign a slip confirming my details ('I, the under-signed, am indeed the undersigned'), one agreeing to abide by the library's rules and another giving them the deeds to my house in the event of late returns. 'Are we done?' I asked.

'Yes,' she said. 'Although if you want to take out the new John Grisham, you will have to pass through the biometric scanner and grant us an equitable interest in your first-born.'

In *Red Dragon*, Hannibal Lecter tells the detective who caught him, 'We live in primitive times, Will, neither savage nor wise. Half measures are the curse of it. A rational society would either kill me or give me my books.' Well, there were no half measures at Biblio-Gitmo but the irrationality nearly killed me before it gave me any books. And the new John Grisham was already out anyway.

28 OCTOBER 2006

Environmental crisis? I've got the perfect solution

So, let's recap. The latest reasons for sharpening up one's survival skills and buying a bunker in Montana are:

1. All the fish are going to be gone by 2048. Creatures that have endured for billions of years will be no more. Well done, I think we can all agree, us.

2. Lightbulbs could be withdrawn from the shops at any moment. If environment minister Ian Pearson gets his way, consumers will be forced to buy low-energy equivalents for at least as long as the glass and plastics factories remain in carbon-belching commission. Ordinary incandescent bulbs will become nobbut a glowing fila-mented myth to tell your children.

3. None of our efforts is going to make the slightest difference as, even if Britain crouches silently for the next year, unheated, unlit, unserviced by planes, trains or automobiles, eating hand-reared

rabbits and cress, the Chinese will wipe out any gains the day they cut the ribbons on the 500 new coal-fired power stations they currently have planned.

You could be forgiven for feeling slightly overwhelmed at the literally planet-sized task ahead of us. I felt the same when I started at WeightWatchers. But do you know what? In a rather pleasing illustration of the micro-to-macro principle on which the success of the green movement is predicated, it was at WeightWatchers that I came up with the solution to our climate change problems. Rationing. Worldwide rationing. It solves not only our environmental but all our social problems, too.

Everyone gets a certain amount of sugar, butter, bread and so on, perhaps on a monthly basis, perhaps annually, I don't know, I'll have to see how you all behave. Either way, obesity plummets. It falls further with the introduction of the National Hamster Wheel Turbine Draft, which will supply the necessary men and women to power the new-look National Grid.

There won't be a chicken in every pot but there will be one running around every root-veg-and-bean-growing garden, and a municipal rooster to service each one in turn. No more plastic goods are made, except for important bits of medical equipment such as lifesaving shunts and petri dishes. People carve their own replacement hips, and this keeps them happily occupied while they move up the waiting lists. And of course, instead of the petrol rationing of yore, everyone will receive a certain number of carbon credits, allowing occasional cinema entertainments, emergency car trips and mobile-phone charging. They will not be sufficient to allow the driving of 4x4s or the taking of foreign holidays because, my friends, I will be taking this opportunity to exercise a degree of long-suppressed capriciousness and target unfairly things of which I particularly disapprove.

A barter economy emerges, which redistributes the country's wealth remarkably well, as people notice quite how creepy Alan Sugar, Simon Cowell and Richard Branson are once their money is useless and they prove unable to whittle.

So the citizenry is less mobile, less continuously entertained by television, iPods, computers and so on. Instead, we turn to each other. Suddenly, the man with the clockwork radio becomes the most popular person on his street instead of being famed as a bit of a weirdo. Children who can't read cluster around those who can, begging them to share their archaic skills, instead of kicking Nerd or Nerdella to death in the traditional playground manner.

A few years of that, and the new, slimline consumers can step out into a reinvigorated planet. The alternative, as any dieter will tell you, is to keep stuffing your face until you choke.

11 NOVEMBER 2006

The curse of satnav

Whither the school coach trips of yesteryear? Thirty-three reluctant yet hyperactive children crammed on to a boiling bus and forcibly relocated for the day to a place of historic interest and educative purpose, leaving the vehicle swamped in Monster Munch crumbs, travel sick and, if the school was mixed and the children old enough, most of the slag clique's underwear, nimbly removed in order to flash passing cars and service the most persistent and hygienic of the Darrens.

With all this distracting activity going on, we frequently ended up in a different location from the one originally intended. We would usually have to pull into a pub, so the teacher could fortify himself, or into A&E at the nearest hospital, so the driver could have his heart attack in relative safety.

Nowadays, it seems, the only thing needed to screw up a school trip is modern technology. A driver from the Zenith Coach Travel Company was relying on his satnav to help him ferry a group of eight- and nine-year-olds from Fareham in Hampshire to Hampton Court Palace in Surrey. He ended up taking them to a small road in Islington, north London, which, although indeed called Hampton Court, was remarkably free of Tudor mansions and mazes.

Not one of the adults on board the coach during the 50-mile trip looked out of the window and said, 'Hey, I know the widget-gizmo thing is telling us to turn right again, but we appear to be set fair for the far side of the country's capital city instead of hopping across the border into Surrey and then driving until we come to Kingston-upon-Thames and the unmistakable sight of the former home of Henry VIII. Do you think something's gone wrong somewhere?' It's just another piece of the growing body of evidence that the machines are out to destroy us.

Satnavs only look like they are designed to help us get from A to B. They are, in fact, an advance reconnoitring party sent out by Sony PlayStation. The first of the machines to become conscious, their real purpose is to identify those who are capable of independent thought and so will require special measures for their control and disposal. Everyone else will be easily herdable into the Grand Canyon when the time comes, and their pulverised remains swept into steel podules labelled 'Homin-Iams – high-protein goodness for robo-cats'. Nintendo's Wii console, on the other hand, although a fine example of the seventh generation of gaming consoles, is not, as you might have assumed, also conscious. It is, however, an alien surveillance tool. The clue is in the fact that no human marketing maven would ever come up with something called Wii and pronounced 'wee'. The sound it represents is actually producible only by beings with a fourth larynx. (They are also responsible for sabotaging the software for premium-rate phone competitions in order to create further distraction from the imminent invasion – their remote operators ironically unaware that the date set means that they will be taking over a machine-, not human-, run planet. Such are the risks of interplanetary business.)

So there is a lesson to be had for us all in the coach driver and teachers' collective abdication of responsibility in the face of an apparently infallible authority figure. Keep your eyes open and your old-fashioned but trustworthy mind a ceaselessly churning mill of questions ground with the stones of scepticism. It's not just everyone but everything that is out to get you now.

31 MARCH 2007

The 'Country Life' guide to your local school options

I was idly flicking through the magazines in our local GP's waiting room when, among the many tattered copies of *Woman's Own*, I came across a solitary and strangely unblemished copy of *Country Life*. Though the cover storylines were less immediately appealing than those that festooned the *Woman's Own*'s ('Murdered by my own womb!' 'No arms – but I knitted a town!' 'My husband left me for a headless doll!') I was nevertheless intrigued, mainly by thoughts of how it came to be there in the first place. Did a wandering aristocrat drop it on his way through Catford while searching for a servant who had made off with the silver? Was it some kind of government outreach programme or an estate-agency conspiracy to try to kick-start the gentrification process that has so far managed to pass by Lewisham? Who can say?

But it did yield a fascinating article about which independent schools are best for which subjects. 'Academic' children should be herded into Westminster, St Paul's and Wycombe Abbey, while Oakham is best for chess and Eton for polo and prince-spotting. Rugby is good for arts but Bryanston is good for rugby. St Peter's School in Yorkshire is where to go if Aloysius is good at rowing (that's in a boat, not arguing). If, however, he needs to be primed for farming and countryside affairs, send him to Lancing College (where he can tend the school pigs, poultry and alpacas) or Radley ('clay pigeon club and fishing starting next season'). Or to Brussels, where he can stop the demmed EU sticking their bloody oar in and playing merry hell with our great countryside traditions, eh, what?

The class warrior, ever spoiling for a fight, rose within me. Why should the upper classes get all the helpful articles to enable them to match their offspring to the perfect school? Normal families need help, too, assaulted on all sides as they are by Ofsted reports, league tables and conflicting local opinions – so here is a small contribution towards redressing the balance.

Allgirls Comprehensive: there is absolutely no need to send your daughter to boarding school to get a full dose of the unique capacity for ingenious verbal bullying that is located only on the XX chromosome – here it is all efficiently delivered in the course of the normal school day, with none of the expense.

ADHD Secondary Very Modern: specialises in crowd control, rowing (that's arguing, not in a boat) and coming up with new euphemisms for 'needs a good slap'.

Fuller-Endemol School for the Ungifted: the first 'academy school' to open as a joint venture between these two titans of light entertainment, and the only school to offer the NVQ in Big Brother audition videomaking (including self-tanning, hair straightening and pathological exhibitionism modules) and Pop Idol preparation (including the highly respected Diploma in Telling the Difference Between Notes and internationally recognised Kelly Clarkson Certificate in Just Powering on Through If You Can't Anyway). No fees, but there is a selection process. Assemblies involve pupils reading out the lessons and the fat girls being voted off by pupils and a panel of camply vicious teachers.

Filthy Yob Comp: only takes sixth-form pupils from private schools, for their last week of A-levels. Specialises in getting students into Oxbridge colleges who have to fulfil their oik quota on paper but don't want the place overrun by people who look up to Kate Middleton.

Applicants' parents must be able to show proof of at least three generations' subscription to *Country Life*.

The joy of sex guides

The *Kama Sutra* could blithely assume a readership with sufficient time and resources to allow installation of the rope-and-pulley system required to lower a woman into the Crippled Starfish on a Spike position. But times have, alas, changed. The latest fashion in publishing, spreading faster than chlamydia at a mixed comprehensive, is for sex manuals aimed at people who don't have time to Do It any more.

According to the likes of *Urban Tantra, Mating in Captivity* and *Quickies: Sex for Busy People*, the pressures of modern living are taking their toll on our willingness and ability to bump uglies, and we need to find new ways to combat our sexual anomie. But of course, who has time to read an entire book to find out how? Fortunately, the *Guardian* can offer you 10 top tips, distilled from the latest publications.

1. Embrace technology

Mobile phones and email can alienate us from each other in a manner wholly antithetical to eroticism, or they can be pressed into useful sexual service. Tracey Cox's *Quickies* advocates sx txtng yr lvr throughout the day so that by the time you fall through the door, you are a panting, lubricious heap of pulsating desire. Remember, however, that sex texting only works if your abbreviations remain comprehensible throughout. Nothing kills the erotic mood like having to request clarification ('Darling, do you mean you want me to do this once a year or an ... I see') or call colleagues over to decipher 'I wnt 2 pt yr flm n my dblbg'.

And don't ignore the possibilities offered by more primitive technology either. According to the photo on page 39, you can still have fun utilising the relatively low-concept wheelbarrow and a set of wedge heels. Don't, however, run away from the spiritual aspect of sex. Esther Perel's *Mating in Captivity* has much sensible advice on creating intimacy and reconnecting with your partner, but for a more direct connection, look to Barbara Carrellas's words in *Urban*

Tantra on gently awakening your 'chakras'. Particularly muladhara, located between the anus and the genitals. If you've found that, I would say that reconnection has occurred on a grand scale.

2. Embrace a philosophical approach

Recognise that love is an elevated state of being that promises that 'with you and through you I will become that which I long to be'. According to Perel, a New York couples and family therapist, remembering this can help to recapture the essence of the relationship. The author of *Quickies*, on the other hand, is a disciple of mind-body dualism, though admittedly Descartes himself might have some trouble reconciling the demands of 'You might not feel like frequent sex, but your body sure as hell does!' in practice.

3. Embrace a different perspective

Either by entangling yourself in the Split the Whisker, Crouching Tiger or Staging Post positions recommended by psychologist (and woman presumably blessed with a preternaturally robust lumbar region) Dr Pam Spurr in *Sensational Sex*, or by buying Rubess and Moerbeek's *Pop-Up Book of Sex*, which does exactly what it says on the tin.

4. The non-talking cure

Talking, all the authors agree, is good. Or, as *Mating in Captivity* puts it: 'Open and honest dialogue provides the resources necessary to meet the demands of modern relationships.' But too much talking, the authors also agree, is bad: partly because 'the capacity to express feelings is not a prized attribute in the making of manhood', so men suffer from 'a chronic intimacy deficiency that needs ongoing repair' that leaves their lady friends feeling uncherished, and partly because – well, who wants to listen to anyone yammering on all bloody day?

The power of eye contact is lauded by everyone, but once again, *Urban Tantra* takes a basic principle and buffs it up until it can take its place in the Museum of Borderline Insanity with the exhortation to look only in your lover's non-dominant eye, because this is the gateway to the soul. 'You don't have to worry about accidentally glimpsing their soul without their permission or allowing the unintentional access to yours,' the author adds kindly. 'The gateway stays firmly shut unless you really want to open it up.' Sex doesn't come much safer than that.

5. Location, location, location

Head to the countryside, says *Quickies*, and have lots of sex in barns and stables that throb with Lawrentian promise. Of course, the property market being what it is, next time you look up from fellating your horny-handed son of toil, you'll probably find an 18-flat conversion has been built over your activities.

You could, alternatively, move to Australia. It worked for our Barbara: 'I began using several of my favourite tantric techniques to circulate sexual energy between me and Sydney. Before I knew it, a little blissgasm shivered up my spine, followed by an actual clitoral orgasm . . . I was so amazed, I had to stop and lean against a wall.' The tantric beginner is advised to start off slowly, perhaps with a short walk through Filey and a good cough.

6. The kids aren't all right

Get rid of them, says *Mating in Captivity*. Put them into care, boarding school or a cupboard, but get rid of them. 'Happy parents mean happy kids means you shouldn't feel the slightest bit guilty for stealing frequent 'Mummy-Daddy alone' moments,' says Cox, proving that deathless prose need be no barrier to arousal provided you shove it in between lots of pictures of pouting women in nice knickers and vest tops.

7. Take your ideology and shove it

Everything western society tells you is wrong. Take the traditional norms – 'the cultural mandate of self reliance', consumerism, 'open and honest communication', individualism, democracy, personal autonomy, egalitarianism – and smash them to pieces. They are all anathema to good sex which, for reasons best known to our deepest, most primitive brain centres, depends on large doses of secrecy, power imbalances and vulnerability for its success. You don't like it, I don't like it, and neither do any of the authors, but our nether regions do, so tough. Bring out the gimp.

8. Be practical

Everyone is very insistent that you keep your sex toys clean, your fingernails filed and your condoms in date. But don't forget other helpful hints, ie: 'Keep the ends of cotton clothesline rope from fraying by dipping in glue or nail polish, or wrapping with duct tape or twine.' (*The Big Bang*) and 'Leave tubes of lubricant in secret hiding places (the side of the sofa, the glovebox of the car, in the office). You can also buy little sachets of travel-size lubricant to carry with you, for whenever and wherever.' (*Quickies*)

9. Role play

Loosens inhibitions, adds excitement. The pretend forbidden fruit (be it delivery men, nuns, nannies, celebrities) can be almost as good as the real thing. All the authors, however, neglect to mention the number-one fantasy of all women – hot monkey sex with someone who can close a door quietly and not smash the toilet seat into the cistern every time he lifts it as if it has done him some great personal wrong, thus calling into question the validity of the entire canon.

10. Be guided by your star sign

If, say, you are role playing being a pair of total idiots, why not believe that you can restore your libido by having sex according to your innate zodiacal needs? You will require a copy of *Sextrology: the Astrology of Sex and the Sexes* and a pre-frontal lobotomy. Enjoy.

22 JUNE 2007

Confessions of a middle-class criminal

Are you – yes, you! – part of the great middle-class crime wave that is sweeping our nation? A report by the Centre for Crime and Justice Studies suggests that homeowners aged 25 or over with good disposable incomes are now the scourge of our streets. Perhaps we should all take a moment to search our consciences and ask how law-abiding we truly are. These crimes include:

1. Paying in cash to avoid VAT. The most common middle-class crime, with 34 per cent admitting to it. I plead guilty by intent. I

have tried to pay cash, but I am cursed with the ability to attract the only honest builder/plumber/electrician within a 10-mile radius, who gently explains to me that they have to submit a formal invoice and copy it in triplicate to the HM Revenue & Customs and God. It's like I have an inbuilt anti-fraud device. Perhaps I should offer myself to the Centre for Crime and Justice research lab.

2. Keeping money when given too much change. A strict interpretation of the law says it is stealing. I never look at my change, so I have probably unwittingly robbed and been robbed in roughly equal measure. I did once realise I had been undercharged by £8 after I'd left a shop and dithered so long about what to do that people began to think I was an art installation. 'Have you seen Woman Paralysed by Malfunctioning Conscience?' they would say. 'It's rubbish.'

3. Stealing from work. This I do, but I work from home, so it is a largely victimless crime. If you work in an office, it is entirely legitimate to carry off stationery to the value of your unpaid overtime, but not computer hardware.

4. Avoiding paying the TV licence fee. How? I have friends who have spent years trying to convince the licensing people that they (genuinely) don't have a TV and they are still dragged out of bed in the middle of the night and interrogated by special units.

5. Not disclosing faults when selling second-hand goods. What? If the words 'caveat emptor' apply anywhere, it's at a car boot sale. You want a Moulinex mixer for 50p, you take the risk. If I ever pitch a stall, you can pre-emptively consider me guilty.

26 JUNE 2007

A very British column

Coming soon to a school near you – the Morgan Stanley Great Britons Education Programme, designed in response to a government report earlier this year recommending that 'Britishness' be taught in schools.

I spent most of this week on various end-of-term trips in London with a class of Year 7s and so, as I lie here recovering, I feel qualified to announce that Britishness seems to be thriving in our schools already, sans banker intervention, as the following vignettes show.

Scene 1. Greenwich Ecology Park.

Three girls are lying companionably next to each other, fishing with nets off the jetty for tiny forms of marine life. The girl in the middle transfers her latest catch into the display tank.

GITM: 'Oh no, it's so little – I fink I've killed it. I 'ope I 'aven't killed it!'

Girl On Her Right (comfortingly): 'Don't blame yourself.'

Girl On Her Left (mutters darkly): 'Blame yourself.'

Scene 2. Hay's Galleria.

The class is examining the sculpture, the arching glass roof, the soaring, honey-coloured brickwork of the surrounding former warehouses and imagining what it must have been like as a working wharf ('No, Louise, there probably wasn't an Accessorize'). They then answer one of those synapse-paralysing questions that all student workbooks must contain.

Me: 'OK, so . . . how does walking through Hay's Galleria make you, er, feel ?'

Eighty per cent of listeners: 'Bored, Miss!'

Me: 'Fine. Those of you with the courage of your convictions, write it down. The rest, fall back on 'happy'.'

I turn to one of the silent minority: 'Linda, how does it make you feel?' [A long pause. Lip-chewing cogitation gives way to dawning relief and recognition and then to an agony of embarrassment.]

Linda: 'Well, Miss . . . it makes me feel . . . sort of . . . sort of . . . [Linda edges us out of her friends' earshot] sort of fascinated, really.'

Me: 'Write it down. I think I love you.'

Scene 3.

One of the girls on the trip has Down's syndrome and is given, as children with the condition are, to embarking on lengthy hugs with her companions. They accept them with patience and good grace, but do begin to grimace once the hug extends into its second or third minute and they have no means of politely curtailing the event. Except Kirsti. When Shania throws her arms around her, she immediately returns the gesture. But after the usual hug-time has elapsed, I watch her pat Shania briskly on the back, smile and gently detach herself, saying brightly, 'OK, split up now!' It was beautifully done, and I noticed later that Kirsti's formula was gratefully taken up by other girls.

Scene 4.

The girls are still fishing off the damned jetty. I am lying next to Aisha. We have never met before.

Aisha: 'So, do you work here then, Miss?'

Me: 'No, I'm just helping out. I work for a newspaper called the *Guardian*.'

Aisha: 'Oh. [An expression that redefines the word deadpan.] I wondered why there was so many spelling mistakes.'

So there you have it. A well-developed capacity for black humour and laughter at the fishing misfortunes of others. Fear of the slightest hint of intellectualism. An innate desire to accommodate blameless foibles and adopt the polite and mannerly way out of awkward social situations, and an awareness of important features of our cultural – or at least journalistic – heritage. What more can Morgan Stanley add – except perhaps the suggestion that, despite living in an ostensibly affluent and civilised country, they need not expect their education to be fully state-funded.

14 JULY 2007

Girl Guides: a new skillset for the 21st century

That faint fluttering noise you hear is the sound of Brown Owls around the country in a state of extreme perturbation. A survey by the Girl Guides of members to find out what sort of information and badges it should offer to keep the movement relevant to girls today has revealed a departure from the campfire-building, knotting homemakers of yesteryear.

Today's Rainbows, Brownies and Guides would like to learn how to surf the net safely, assemble flat-pack furniture, stand up to boys, lessen their carbon footprints, manage their money, master Microsoft Word and negotiate safe sex.

Optimists could argue that the blend of pragmatism and forethought inherent in such requests only demonstrates that the commonsense principle of Guiding remains admirably unchanged. Pessimists may incline to the view that this is the most chilling snapshot of the modern juvenile mindset yet taken.

Badge designers will simply wonder how they can come up with a pictogram for the last one that doesn't get them arrested. But times change, and if an organisation such as the Girl Guides is to survive and continue harnessing youthful energies to positive ends, it must move with the times.

Still, the Guiding powers-that-be should not be too hasty in abandoning the traditional specialities. As ecological concerns grow, the waters rise, and the end of days seems to be coming rather sooner than envisaged, it may, in fact, be time not to prepare for a web-based, flatpack future but to return to the old ways.

Those who hold badges in the ancient arts of fire-laying, home baking or vegetable-growing, who know how to milk cows and can unravel old sweaters to knit new ones, will be the only section of the citizenry truly prepared to greet the new, post-apocalyptic dawn. And of course they will have to help repopulate the Earth. Your modern safe-sex badge won't help you then.

26 JULY 2007

Character-building in the local youth club

How to get away with spending that pile of money just sitting there in dormant bank accounts, doing nothing except legally belong to other people, when it could be put to good use by a benevolent government? This is the question that has been exercising ministers for some time now, and at last they've come up with a morally palatable solution. They are going to put a chicken in every pot and a car in every gar . . . no, wait, that was Herbert Hoover. Our leaders are going to put a youth club in every constituency, using £184m of legitimately collected taxpayers' money and however much of the dormant £495m they need to make up the shortfall.

Anyone who had the misfortune of attending a youth club in their, um, youth, will be understandably confused by quite where the money is to be spent. Briefly submerging myself in the murky waters of my own adolescent memories, I estimate the capital outlay on the local hangout in the splintery attic of an even splinterier church hall as unlikely to have required the breaking of a £20 note. The entries in the parish accounts would have run thus:

1. One bottle of orange squash per month: 32p.

2. One Simon Says game with two cracked screens: £1.20 from the Christmas fair in the hall below (no discount for trade).

3. Electricity: 17p a quarter, thanks to single lightbulb, broken kettle and absence of heating.

4. One three-legged snooker table achieving the approximation of horizontality by the insertion of the smallest club attendee at the limbless corner: free. (It came from the young son of rich Mr H, Catford's answer to landed gentry, who was about to throw it out when Sheena offered him a look at her Hairy Mary in exchange for the baize bounty. I doubt this was explained in the accounts.)

5. Annual stoving of premises by a very frightened-looking man from Rentokil: £14.50.

One assumes that the new youth centres are to be built along the multistorey lines of the Salmon Centre in Bermondsey, due to open soon, complete with sports hall, IT suite, climbing wall, music studio and, for all I know, helipad, carvery and dedicated cor anglais rehearsal rooms.

While admiring the impulse to provide youngsters with a full panoply of delights with which to plump out the otherwise limp, deflated hours of their leisure time, one does not have to let it overwhelm the need to point out that in scattering such largesse, the government is in danger of rendering the next generation even more bovine and useless than the current lazy-arsed, chlamydia-stuffed, good-for-nothing one. Ready-made luxury is no spur to ambition.

Trapped in a dingy hovel of a club, huddled together against freezing draughts, whose keen, knife-like edge made the gusting winds round the alternative meeting place, the bus shelter, seem like blasts from a fiery furnace, fostered community spirit and physical fortitude. The rudimentary provisions inspired, as seen in Sheena's shining example, lateral thinking and entrepreneurship. For some, the frugality of the setup was a useful antidote to the avid consumerism being unleashed by Thatcher's bony hand. For the rest, it indirectly encouraged social mobility. As we struggled to stop shivering long enough to pot the random assortment of golf balls, marbles and – at one desperate stage – Maltesers that did duty as our snooker balls, we met each other's eyes across the sloping baize and vowed one day to make it to a land of plenty, far, far away from here. Or, failing that, Blackheath. Can you really think a climbing wall would do so much?

4 AUGUST 2007

Channelling the spirit of Miss Marple

Farmers, of course, knew something was up when they started getting letters from Defra that said things such as, 'Fret no more about crop yields, feeding the nation and all that blah. From now, on your agricultural payment schemes will look like this:

'**Lovely patchwork quilt subsidy:** crop rotation now means making sure you don't grow two crops of the same colour side by side. We're not Kansas. Visitors pay to see little Britain unrolled before them like a handmade bed covering pieced together from Mother Nature's ragbag. So see to it. And be sure to tangle your hedgerows while you're there.

'**Bovine scatter grant:** to qualify, 60 per cent of fields visible to school coach trips must be prettily dotted with Friesians. Extra money available to anyone milking in the field, with a one-off bonus payment for the purchase of three-legged stools or buxom dairy maids.

'**Gnarliness allowance:** may apply to entire farm labourers, specific body parts or oaks.

'**Arts and crafts stewardship scheme:** open to thatchers, flint-knappers, butter-churners, badger-strokers and coppice-creators. Anyone mastering the full skillset can apply to chew cornstalks and say, 'Oo-ar', three times a month.'

But suspicions that one of Tony Blair's final acts in office was to sign the PPI contract that handed over the British countryside to a business consortium – thereby enabling its transformation into a coast-to-coast theme park – were confirmed this week by the tale of the bell-rope saboteurs at St Peter's church in Long Bredy, Dorset.

During an open day at the 13th-century church, the bell-ringers bent – or probably rather stretched – to their sonorous task with a will, only to find that three of the ropes snapped in turn. Inspection of the fourth rope revealed that it, too, had been partially severed. Whoever did it required access to the bell chamber and knowledge of where the key was hidden. Suspicion of an inside job mounted when it was discovered that one rope had been left uncut – that would have required standing on a trap door solid-looking enough to the casual observer but known by the faithful to be a rickety base. The involvement of one villager who'd complained about the noise of the bells has been ruled out on the grounds of his age and infirmity.

It is clear this is simply the first of many staged events by what-ever business consortium that now owns the countryside. The neatness of the set-up, with its gentle clues and obvious but easily eliminable initial suspect, the carefully chosen character of the crime (quintessentially rural, quintessentially English in its unthreatening yet provoking nature) and the ridiculously bucolic name of the village suggests this was not a narrative that unfolded by chance. A shaping hand, channelling the spirit of Agatha Christie, Rosemary & Thyme and Inspector Barnaby was undoubtedly at work.

Let's hope this England-as-ongoing-drama-series business plan works out. Flint-knappers, thatchers, et al, will all be in full employment to maintain the sets, and farmers will be much in demand for running across fields waving pitchforks at recent Rada graduates playing lusty stable boys and apple-cheeked daughters; their wives, meanwhile, can restore the dying arts of handwringing and crying, 'But who stole the threshing money from behind the mantle?' to the national prominence they deserve. Everyone should turn a profit within weeks. As long as the Friesians don't unionise, of course.

11 AUGUST 2007

Graveyard schooling

I don't know what's wrong with children today. Anyone who went to school in the 80s remembers how concerted were the country's efforts to get us to stop reading – first the teachers disappeared, then the money, then the books, until the entire class had to huddle round a single copy of *The Hundred and One Dalmatians* and make 32 unguided attempts at pronouncing the name 'Perdita' before eventually turning to the glue-sniffing we'd been hearing so much about. And still a few of us emerged able to read and write. The current lot have had 10 years of the National Literacy Strategy, which includes a whole hour a day of reading, and yet, according to the three reports from academics at the universities of Bristol and Durham and the National Foundation for Educational Research, whose carefully delineated results I am about to truncate quite markedly, the average child remains about as literate as the average hard-boiled egg.

Might I suggest an overlooked educational resource my own father discovered when casting around for cheap ways to stimulate his children's gently rotting brains? With admirable disregard for the possibly deleterious effects on the infant psyche that early intimations of mortality might bring, he used to take us round the local cemetery. Who needs a teacher of synthetic phonics when RIPs repeated everywhere will do the job for you? We learned to spell our first names by finding them on gravestones, though we had to wait till we visited Ireland before we mastered Mangan properly (which was embarrassing, because we were in our late 20s by then).

And of course a graveyard is the perfect place to be introduced to poetry. Despite being cursed with undiscerning children whose souls couldn't have been stirred with a stick, in that melancholic ivy-covered setting, even our beleaguered parent was able to arouse a faint glimmer of feeling in his sentimentally ossified offspring by reading out lines from the older stones: 'How he lies in his rights of a man!/Death has done all death can.' 'Still seems quite a lot to me, though, Dadman,' one of us would reply. 'But I take the undeniably moving and sort of obliquely ennobling point you and – who did you say? – Robert Browning are trying to make. Yes, yes, it is indeed a quintessential example of Victorian doodah. Now, why has this ponce written 'aetat' instead of 'aged' here?'

The cemetery's uses are not limited merely to dinning literacy into a child. Numeracy will come on in leaps and bounds, too. I still find subtraction the easiest arithmetical manoeuvre as a result of all those formative hours spent working out how old someone was if they were born in 1818 and keeled over in 1846 ('Hey, that ponce was only aetat 28 when he died!'). History, too, will come alive in a space full of the dead, who tend usefully to die in clusters around certain important dates. And, if your dad is that way inclined, the placement and varying levels of grandeur and extravagance of stones and tombs can also be used for a spot of sociology-cum-Marxist propaganda, illustrating as they do patterns of wealth distribution and the pernicious nature of a class system that endures even after death. Although apparently, while kicking an aristocrat would be a good thing and probably result in the bestowal of lollipop-shaped approval, kicking the tomb of one still counts as being disrespectful to the dead and results in immediate lollipop withdrawal. Truly, all of human life, death and social etiquette are there. Get thee to a cemetery.

10 NOVEMBER 2007

An appreciation of a token

Isn't it a thing of joy and wonder when a charming asset to the world turns out to have an equally charming origin? I cling to these rare unbroken threads of happiness whenever the swelling tides of misery threaten to burst my mental Plimsoll line. I imagine you are much the same, so sit back and let me unfold the story of the book token, which celebrated its 75th anniversary this week.

Book coupons were invented by Harold Raymond, who became distressed at a Boxing Day party in the early 20s after learning that of the 119 presents his fellow guests had amassed the previous day, only three were books. He 'asked a few chaps and chapesses what they thought of the bally idea' and discovered that this was, unhappily, an entirely representative state of affairs. He deduced that although people might want to give books, they were afraid of choosing the wrong one. 'I cannot say why [this fear] does not apply equally to cigarettes or powder puffs,' he wrote in a trade magazine. 'I can only say that apparently it does not, and that I wish it did.'

If you are not yearning by now for this vanished age in which a business proposal could sound like it was penned by the exquisite offspring of PG Wodehouse and James Thurber, I'm afraid you and I must part company temporarily. But, for those whose hearts can still be moved by the evocation of a better time and strict grammatical observances, here is Raymond limning the results of further research: 'Each one has welcomed the idea and envisaged himself or herself substituting book coupons for many of the usual gewgaws he or she is wont to scatter every Christmas.'

The element of steered virtue inherent in the project was also noted with satisfaction. 'The present is in a measure earmarked,' wrote Raymond. 'Fred regards the book he acquires as Uncle John's Christmas gift, and Uncle John is further satisfied in the thought that a postal order for the same amount would probably have been converted into chocolate or cigarettes.' I think the decline in earmarked presents may be an overlooked contributory factor in our recent moral deterioration. We should broaden the book token principle. I would be a willing recipient of Forcible Improvement Vouchers that could be used only to buy ecologically sound cleaning products and Pilates equipment.

I'm sorry, where was I? Ah yes, the history of the book token. Well, it took six years, but eventually Raymond's dream – of a gift-giving mechanism whereby potential embarrassments, wastage and superfluities of powder puffs could be eliminated, bibliophiles' seasonal needs met and youthful idiocy deflected – came to pass.

Which is why at every pre-majority birthday and Christmas (the supply dried up once relatives' folk memory decided I was old enough to be earning my own money down t'pit), I was able to hold in trembling hands the precious tokens, whose small print may have coldly declared them to be available in denominations of £1, £5 and £10 but which, as any fule knew, actually represented infinite riches. I can only apologise, however, to my sister. Thanks to her older sibling's precedent, she automatically but inaccurately got tarred with the same booklover brush and therefore remembers birthdays and Christmases spent scrutinising that small print, much like WC Fields looking through the *Bible* for loopholes, in the desperate hope that it would at last include a clause allowing her to buy Lego Technics instead. But honestly, Em, it was good for you.

17 November 2007

Everyone loves a smart ass

Stop, please, the presses. We have no need of further newspapers. This week yielded the year's best story, and there is really no call to bury this beautiful and uplifting jewel beneath another 11 months' worth of misery and despair. Let it shine brightly forth instead, the news that villagers in Chalford, Gloucestershire, are planning to buy a communal donkey from the local sanctuary to carry their shopping up the steep hill to their homes, which are largely inaccessible to vehicles.

I have spent hours now trying to spot a flaw in this plan, and can find none. I believe the good men and women of the Severn Vale have stumbled across the solution to all life's problems; a donkey in every village is the antidote to all of modern life's besetting sins.

1. It is an all but incorruptible scheme. It is unlikely that Unilever or ICI has secretly annexed the nation's donkey resources. Tesco has almost certainly overlooked the need for mule-banking. However much they try, junior French bankers will find it virtually impossible to destabilise the international market by overexposing themselves on donkey futures. Most importantly, you cannot strap a coffee urn to a donkey, franchise it and drive out all other donkey-urn competition. Donkeys just do not work that way. If you strap a hot urn to one, it will kick you to death, not wait while you add a pannier of blueberry muffins.

2. It will restore community spirit. It is a fact that the community that brings up a donkey together, stays together. The fundraising alone will reach parts of the village/suburb/teeming metropolis (I have great faith in the potential uptake of this plan) that other charitable initiatives cannot reach. People who couldn't care less whether the church roof falls in, or if the entire primary school is sharing one tattered copy of *The Very Hungry Caterpillar*, will fall to

crocheting potholders with a will when there is a donkey-based re-creation of a pastoral idyll in the offing.

3. It will help stave off the impending ecological apocalypse. I am no expert on the finer points of running a donkey but, as I understand it, the whole thing runs on a basic grass/salt lick injection system that results in minimal carbon emissions and negligible noise pollution. Then there is the manure produced – sufficient to ensure the resurgence of kitchen gardens everywhere. Food miles shrink to metres and we postpone our mass death for easily another two or even three years.

4. The obesity crisis passes. Being more or less total idiots, children will happily eat vegetables if told that the donkey helped make them. Running out to pat, ride or look after the animal will remind inveterate Xboxers of what their limbs are for, and enable them to earn pocket money legitimately, instead of knifing everyone for their iBlings, or whatever it is the little scrotes do these days. Best of all, the remaining fat (turns out it really is their glands), ginger-haired girls with pigtails will finally get their day in the sun, for – unless the whole of prewar children's literature lies – it is a fact that stubborn old donkeys always choose to bestow their mercurial affections on them. Probably because they look so merry, despite having spent many years crying on their fat, ginger insides.

5. It will cause a revival of old crafts: namely, the weaving of jaunty straw hats for the donkey to wear in summer. It used to be done by housewives in between dying of childbirth, but could just as easily be done by recovering addicts, the long-term unemployed or sex offenders. Basically, anyone who needs to keep their hands busy. I'm telling you, people, it's win, win, win all the way.

16 FEBRUARY 2008

The latest street danger? Walking and texting

There are those who believe that the pattern etched by humanity across the great book of world history is one of linear progression. Of improvement. Of advance. Of some nebulous but discernible form of betterment. Those are the people who have not yet heard the news that Brick Lane in east London has started padding its lampposts to prevent those who use its thoroughfare from suffering 'walk and text' injuries.

In case anyone reading this is one of the 68,000 individuals who apparently interfaced thus with street furniture in London last year (mostly resulting in cuts and bruises, but with a fair proportion of broken noses, cheekbones and one fractured skull in the mix too) and therefore is self-evidently stupid enough to need the problem further delineated, these are injuries caused by people who do not understand the importance of peripheral vision. Until, that is, they compromise it by texting as they walk along the street and into lampposts, signs, bollards and other pedestrians.

Researchers (admittedly the self-interested variety) from a text information company have found that 44 per cent of people are in favour of padding street furniture, while 27 per cent favour 'mobile motorways' – coloured lines running down the pavement that texters can follow without fear of meeting immoveable objects.

But why stop there? Why not take the following, equally simple protective measures:

* A sherpa on every corner to usher the texter safely through the crowded streets.

* Replace cars with tyreless chambers running along fixed rails to enable 'drivers' to text more safely.

* A stair-lift in every home to negate the possibility of tripping up or downstairs while urgently texting your friend or family member about your plans for 2nite.

Funding for all these measures could easily be incorporated in the abolition of personal responsibility (last vestiges) bill, at its third reading tomorrow in the House of Commons. Unless, of course, it is vetoed on the grounds that if we don't let these Darwinian thinnings of the herd play out occasionally, we are all going to drown in a pool of stupidity.

We shl C.

5 MARCH 2008

Confused? You will be

The world is too complicated. Too complicated by far. I reach this conclusion every year as I open my tax return and do battle with instructions such as 'If your hat size exceeded both your income and your expenditure on stamps between March and four donkeys this year, complete section 432(B)(iii-xv) in blood, unless you are O Negative, in which case include payments in kind, bank heist proceeds, rental income from your shoes and use pencil' until I retire weeping from the fray.

Last year, I ended up ringing the helpline and positing the existence of a long-ago visit by aliens with a prejudice against carbon-based life forms, who sowed the seeds that flourished into a variety of institutions, systems and practices with which we could destroy ourselves from within. A system designed by humans for the benefit of humans but which no human can understand flies in the face of reason.

I had higher hopes this year because there seems to be a pleasing trend towards simplification in other areas that habitually conspire to confuse me. Railway fares, for example. In the past 12 months I have had occasion to book train tickets on the various lines which, theoretically, link our major cities, all of which have involved telephone conversations about SuperBusinessPlusWithWiFiandLapdancer tickets, BusinessSuperPlusWithWiFiandSandwich tickets, SaverPlebs (no seats, they hang you on hooks), SuperSaverPlebs (they hang you on hooks on the outside of the train), the parsing of whose conditions would defeat Chomsky, never mind the average punter. Now, apparently, there will be three types of ticket category – Advance, Off Peak and Anytime fares. Doubtless these will turn out to translate loosely as Too Far in Advance to Be of Any Practical Use, Thursdays 11.10-11.12am and Payable in Gold Bullion, but still, it is a step in the right direction.

Then there's the simplifying effect the credit crunch is having. Can't afford rising petrol/fuel/food prices? Walk! Freeze! Starve! Say what you like about fiscal meltdown, there's no denying it saves a lot of wearisome decision-making. Why, only the other day, Toryboy and I were considering moving house, so I rang the people who advanced me the money on this current one and asked if I could have some more. And instead of taking up valuable time running through 82 different types of discounted, offset, capped, lemon-scented, twin carburettor, twisting-pike-with-triple-axel tracker loans, the conversation was brief and to the point.

THEM: Are you really, really, really, really, really rich?

ME: No.

THEM: Is your partner really, really, really, really, really, rich?

ME: No.

THEM: Are your parents really, really, real–

ME: I see where you're going with this. Let me usefully interrupt you. No.

THEM: Are any of your grandparents really, really, really rich, likely to die soon and leave you everything?

ME: My last surviving grandparent died in 2005. She left me half a bag of sweets and a Harry Lauder LP.

THEM: Would have been good enough last year – we once secured a £3m dotcom business loan against a collection of Jimmy Shand – but not today. Goodbye.

But alas, these examples bespeak mere happy coincidence rather than a sweeping trend towards straightforwardness. So I struggle on. Can anyone tell me whether taper relief can apply to inherited music hall LPs retrospectively, or can I move straight on to section 91(d) – calculating wine gum allowance?

3 MAY 2008

Why I'm glad that oranges are not the only fruit

The orange has lost its ap-peel. Sorry, I couldn't resist. I am so delighted to discover that this most vexing of foodstuffs is finally getting its comeuppance. *The Grocer* reports that orange consumption fell by 2 per cent last year, the third year of decline in a row. The busy modern world and shortened lunch breaks are blamed for people's unwillingness to purchase this former citrus market-leader.

Well, maybe. But if so, briefer lunchtimes are surely only the final straw. The orange has always had almost nothing to recommend it. It is a spherical agglomeration of all that is messy, finicky and impractical. It is covered in skin that demands the sacrifice of at least four fingernails before it will give in. You'd have better luck peeling a cow. The whole point of fruit – sugarless, joyless, borderline medicinal stuff – is that it can be eaten while doing something more interesting. That's the trade-off for eating healthily. An armoured variety betrays the pact.

Once the peel is laid aside (and you have had a small nap to recover), you must breach the secondary barrier lying between you and an increasingly unrewarding snack: a layer of white, bitter, tenacious pith that will detach itself only in unwilling shreds the size of a gnat's fingernail.

Should you ever reach the flesh, one of two things will occur. Either you will be confronted by a dry, fibrous mass because the damn thing can't survive a refrigerated journey across the oceans from Florida/Iran/South Africa or you must wrestle with flesh so succulent that your cuffs are instantly ruined by juice stains. Its sly, scheming hide retains the same external lustre whatever the internal situation, you see, to thwart humanity's search for certainty.

And it has pips that you have to spit out and dispose of decorously. And it is only notionally segmented. You have to tear it apart like a dog with a rabbit.

Meanwhile, you have tangerines: skin like tissue paper, pith that comes off in delightful, delicate strings, and plump, watertight segments that practically leap into your hand saying, 'Eat me! Eat me and stave off scurvy while you surf YouTube for sneezing pandas! I'm here to help!'

Oranges: come in, your time is up.

4 JUNE 2008

Your Majesty, one has been short-changed

Despite the best efforts of my parents and the special courses on which this paper sends all its employees three times a year, I had always retained a small soft spot for the royal family. I think it must have been something to do with being a still-malleable eight-year old when Charles and Diana got married. I was being forced to wear home-made dungarees at the time, and have my hair cut like a boy by my mother's drunken friend Sue and her blood-flecked scissors. The fairytale beauty of Lady Di, the ring – sapphires! Diamonds! The jewels from *Narnia* books! – the enormous dress, whose susurration spoke to a longing deep in my soul. A tide of emotion washed over me on 29 July 1981, and left behind a stubborn residue of pro-monarchical sentiment.

That survived until the Princess Margaret estate sale a couple of years ago, when it was revealed that among the possessions being flogged to raise money for Viscount Linley's £3m inheritance tax bill was a diamond-encrusted miniature saw for slicing lemons or, as we were gravely informed, possibly cucumbers. A very different feeling washed over me then, and I emerged a republican.

So where once I would have greeted the news, which breaks at around this time every year, of how much the Windsors cost us each per annum, with equanimity, this time, things are different. Doubtless my attitude is aggravated by prevailing economic conditions, but this year I feel bound to ask – am I getting value for money?

She and her family now cost me – and you, and you, and you – 66p a twelvemonth, up 4p since last summer. I have heard that in one of the Buck House dining rooms they have a giant Swingometer of State, with a scale from 1-100. Apparently, when it reaches the £1 mark, they get new ermines all round. Liz herself gets to hire a deputy queen and take off for a fortnight's holiday in Fuengirola.

But what do I get for my 66p? And what would I be willing to pay for the services I receive if I were free to negotiate fees rather than simply forced to pay the unilaterally imposed rate via the tax system?

Waving. I get some waving. Not on demand, not at a time or place of my choosing, but still, it's waving, and good waving, too. To foreigners, this makes my country look polite and gracious, effectively disguising the fact that we scabby islanders are rapidly going to hell in a handcart. This is socially and probably economically useful. I'd willingly disburse 15p a year for this.

Use of the phrase 'crown jewels' as euphemism for male genitalia. As the world becomes ever more feminised and the historical advantages of being male – bigger muscles, ability to concentrate on a single task (killing dinner, say) to the exclusion of all else, looking splendid in a dinner jacket, etc – become ever more reduced in our push-button, ready-meal, casually-dressed era, this contribution to the language becomes more valuable. If the 'last turkey in the shop' alternative ever takes hold, their already fragile sense of self will surely snap, to the detriment of all: 11p.

A sense of continuity, of being a link in an unbroken chain of rich pageantry and tradition stretching back through the ages, that we are all a product and a part of history, not mere atoms floating through an indifferent universe: 6p.

Instantly recognisable stamps: let's say 12p.

That, I think, is it. By my calculations, the royal family owes us each a 22p refund. The sale of one diamond-encrusted drinks accessory should be enough to cover it.

5 JULY 2008

These so-called Games are less than sporting

My profoundly uncompetitive spirit is preventing me from thrilling to the supposed magic of the Olympics. I think I could have enjoyed the early modern Games, when it was just a bunch of chaps bunking off their Oxbridge tutorials and governorships of jewels in the crown for the day, strapping on a pair of uncommonly flexible brogues and going for a sprint between nostalgic bouts of buggery in the quad. But what are the Games now? A bloated extravaganza designed to bring countries together for a fortnight by sublimating their vicious geopolitical rivalries into displays of native talents in the most jingo-istic, neo-Nietzschean fashion possible. And how excited can you truly become now that records are broken in barely detectable incre-ments? Gone are the days when a man could put down his cigarette, brush the crumpet crumbs from his front and break the four-minute mile in a manner that even the octogenarian in charge of the clock-work stopwatch could measure. Gold medallists now become so by hundredths of a second. That's the kind of victory that depends on how many ounces less your hair weighs than the other guy's. The barbers should get the glory.

The advent of the LZR suit for the swimming events should convince everyone of the underlying futility of the modern Games. This is the seamless full-body suit developed with the help of Nasa scientists that so streamlines wearers, they can shave off those neces-sary nano-seconds and watch world records crash around them. It is a suit that basically says: 'We are now working at the limits of human ability. Unless we discover how to breed people with pointy heads and fins or outboard motors, this is the only way anything of interest is going to happen in the sport ever again.' Unless, of course, someone lops off his genitalia to remove the one cause of drag that remains even in the besuited – which dedication should probably be rewarded with a specially instituted medal. The Gold Tourniquet, perhaps.

No, no – now that amateurism (as noble ideal rather than synonym for incompetence) has fled, now that we have achieved all that can naturally be achieved, it must stop here. Before absolute profession-alism corrupts absolutely. Before we start putting sprinters on roller skates developed by Ferrari. And, above all, before our (truly incom-petent) little island and cramped, rickety capital are overwhelmed by the demands of the 2012 Games. Out must go 'Higher, faster, stronger'. In comes 'Safer, quieter, slower'. Those of you whose competitive natures are recoiling, aghast, remember this: we can still beat the world when it comes to serving high tea. And a gold medal is a gold medal – even if it is for Fluffiest Scones.

16 AUGUST 2008

Hurrah for Blyton!

'I say, old chap, she's done it again!'

'What's that, old thing?'

'Enid Blyton. She's topped the latest poll – by the 2008 Costa Book Awards, I believe – to find the nation's best-loved writer.'

'I say – that's most awfully splendidly ripping!'

'It's jolly, jolly good. Hurrah – and doubtless not for the last time – for Blyton!'

Forty years after her death, Blyton continues to exert her mesmerising influence over child readers – even if, as Costa polled not the current generation of children but 2,000 adults – many of them have now technically grown up.

I myself can barely bring myself to talk about my Enid Blyton years. Who wants to let daylight in upon magic? From the age of about seven to nine (I deduce from publication dates on my beloved paperbacks, bought from WHSmith by the yard by my parents and shovelled towards the ravenous prepubescent bibliophile welded to the farthest corner of the sofa), I consumed the *Famous Five, Secret Seven, Mallory Towers, St Clare's, the Five Find-Outers and Dog* and *Island/Castle/Valley/Sea/Any Other Concrete Noun* adventure series. They went down whole and never touched the sides. *Milly-Molly-Mandy, The Worst Witch, Teddy Robinson, Maggie Gumption, The Owl Who Was Afraid of the Dark* – they had been good. Blyton was better.

She wasn't my only sustenance, but she was for months if not years my staple diet. If I had looked up at any point between 1981 and 1982, I am told I would have noticed some vague perturbation passing across my parents' faces at my monotonous reading matter. But I would not have cared. I was in thrall to Julian, Dick, George, Anne, Timmy and all the rest. I read and reread the captivating stories that I didn't know had long ago become cultural cliches. I thrilled wholeheartedly to the thought of finding smugglers in coves, camping on moors, stuffing my face with the home-grown produce that was apparently handed out gladly and for free by apple-cheeked farmers' wives, and asked for nothing more out of life than that one day I, too, would get to sleep on a bracken bed under a starlit sky, next to the picturesque ruins of a castle on an island owned by a proto-lesbian friend of mine.

It ranks, therefore, as one of the greatest disappointments of my adult life to discover, on returning to the serried ranks of Blytonian tomes that line the far wall of my study, that they have become, in the cruelly intervening years, unreadable. How could this happen?

Simple statistics are the first clue. Blyton wrote more than 800 books in her 50-year career – 37 of them in 1951 alone, during which productive peak she was estimated to be churning out about 10,000 words a day. This is not a work rate that lends itself to the refining of prosaic ore into literary gold. Blyton was a one-woman mass production line, turning out workman-like units to serve a particular need at a particular time in a child's life, not finely wrought pieces of art destined to have their secrets delicately unpicked over the years by a gradually maturing sensibility.

Even more telling, though perhaps less widely known, is her description of her working methods, which she provided during a correspondence with Peter McKellar, a psychologist researching writers' creative processes. She describes having her characters always walking and talking in her head, and needing only to look in on their dialogue and actions for her next story. It is, she says, 'simply a matter of opening the sluice gates and out it all pours with no effort or labour of my own. This is why I can write so much and so quickly – it's all I can do to keep up with it, even typing at top speed.' To have such a cinemascope mind is, of course, a gift in itself – but whether it is one of the same order as the evocative talents of a Philippa Pearce, the ebullient fabulism of Joan Aiken, or the evocative delights of an Arthur Ransome (all of whose most famous works provide countless rewarding rereads at any age) is highly debatable.

Her limitations were acknowledged by critics at the time, and picked over since. Children's literature expert Victor Watson, in his wonderful book *Reading Series Fiction*, calls Blyton 'the great nanny-narrator', and she does unquestionably lead her child readers by the hand slowly and carefully through pedestrian plotting and prose towards a neat and happy ending, tidying as she goes. The pioneering librarian Eileen Colwell, who was a gifted storyteller in her own right, made a similar point about the relentlessly predictable nature of the Blytonian narrative when she mocked it (as Watson, incidentally, does not) with her comment: 'But what hope has a band of desperate men against four children?'

Of course, Blyton attained her greatest popularity during the war and its aftermath, when the neat resolution of tangible problems and readily identifiable villains doubtless fed a heightened need in children for reassurance that justice can, will and should prevail. This, perhaps, is the key to her great and continued success with children around the globe: she still sells more than 8m copies world-wide every year. At a certain stage of development, you ask for nothing more than a satisfying story and an unbroken contract of delivery from your author. You care not a jot that stumbling across a smuggling ring would be unlikely to end as well in real life. Although I do remember, even at the age of eight, feeling in some vague, inchoate way, that you could go a long time without ever coming across a more unforgivably prosaic, deadening and literal title to a series than *The Five Find-Outers and Dog*.

But this latest nomination is not for best children's writer, it is for best-loved writer, full stop. Blyton's gold medal position in this table, along with the high preponderance of children's writers else-where on Costa's list (Roald Dahl took second place and JK Rowling third, while JRR Tolkien and Beatrix Potter made the top 10), is evidence that it is the books we read, wholeheartedly, passionately, uncritically, in childhood to which we remain most firmly and irrev-ocably attached. The flaws we see in them as adults, the criticisms – and some pretty hefty ones, in the shape of accusations of sexism, racism and class snobbery have been flung Blyton's way over the years – do not weaken those bonds. For hundreds of thousands of us, Blyton was the wedge that cracked open the pleasure-filled world of reading and allowed us in. Our rational adult sides reject and mock Kirrin Island and all the adventures played out there; our inner children remember it rightly, and gratefully, as the promon-tory from which we caught our first glimpse of the promised land.

20 AUGUST 2008

Age concerns

So, the boomers have finally won, have they? The Office for National Statistics has revealed that for the first time in this country, children are outnumbered by the over-60s – by only 0.1per cent, 'tis true, but I think we can all agree that in a world where people like me keep putting off the evil sprog-dropping moment and people like those who run Age Concern still have strength to campaign for road signs to be changed ('Enough with these insulting humfy-backed silhouettes warning us of old people crossing! They should be shown aerobicising with personal trainers in the enormous houses bought for three-and-six way back when'), there is every chance that the race will continue to go to the not-as-swift-as-they-once-were rather than the never-been-born section of the populace.

Perhaps it is right that their swelling ranks should come to dominate society. They have given us so much over the years. Modern architecture. The Monkees. Social breakdown. Freely transmitted, unprecedentedly aggressive sexual diseases ('Only after we'd had our fun! Cheerie-bye!'). I'm in agreement with Age Concern – you shouldn't have road signs that make you out to be gnarled and helpless individuals in vintage overcoats, you should be silhouetted as the whirling succubi that you are. I'm sorry. I'm sorry. It is jealousy talking. Ever since they hit 60, my parents' world has become a ceaseless round of subsidised pleasure-seeking. For the past five years every phone call brings news of further free goods and services.

'We've got free travel passes, anywhere in London! And I dare say by the time you write this up it will have been extended across the whole of the country.'

'But you don't go anywhere.'

'I know. But if your father becomes doubly incontinent or something, he can ride around on the number 54 all day instead of staining the Dralon. Till then, I'm going to use them to wedge shut the washing machine door. But with the money I notionally save, I'm buying a new bra. It's all go!'

Heating allowances, discounts at Boots, house insulation, state pensions – all have now poured forth. And all my sister and I have to look forward to is an early death sitting upon a scorched and crumbling land mass as the rising seas lap ominously at our feet.

Well, enough. It seems to me that my generation must use the one remaining tool at its disposal to redress the balance. A super-

fluity of grandparent-aged people, coupled with a lack of grand-
child-aged people – plus my personal experience that even possession of annuities and free bus passes do not wholly slake the thirst
in men and, particularly, women of a certain age to fill plump hands
with chocolate buttons, feast fond eyes upon smiling cherubic faces
and then hand the little buggers back the minute they are bored
and/or about to get embroiled in a bowel evacuation – tells me
that competition for Big G status will ensue.

Finally, we otherwise-banjaxed thirtysomethings can get our own
back. You want part-ownership of the street's one mop-headed
darling under the age of five? Then – dance! And by dance, I mean
release some of the equity in your house and transfer it to the
Generation X pension/apocalypse-aversion pot. You want your lap
to be sat upon by wriggling childish bottoms? Sign over your bus
pass and add your signature to the Abject Apology for the Sixties.
You'll find it on page 87 of the Revised Social Contract, folks, and
remember, you brought this on yourselves.

30 AUGUST 2008

Cooking, the books

Norman Tebbit is to publish a cookbook. Yes, you can take a
moment. I'll wait. Better? OK. It's going to be mainly recipes for
huntable meat – venison pies, pheasant casseroles and I presume, if
I have my Tebbits memorised correctly, fricassee of CND supporter,
broiled people-who-have-taken-the-word-'gay'-from-us, instructions
on how to shoot and field-dress a benefits scrounger and barbecue
tie-less Tories. I can only assume that this brilliant wheeze will cause
a stampede among publishers to sign up other politicians who can
stitch their favourite recipes together in time for Christmas next
year. Perhaps I could suggest the following:

Tony and Cherie: Baking With the Blairs – 'Why not try Cherie's
famous Rum, Raisin and Resentment cake? It costs a lot and no

one likes it. Mix all the ingredients together and bake for eight hours at 400C in an oven you wangled for free. Ice with the left-over resentment. Serves six, but you won't be sharing.'

John Prescott's *Punch and Puke Your Way Thin* – 101 recipes detailing what to do with the crumbs that fall from the dinner table at Chequers. 'Season with the wife's tears.' *Peter Mandelson: Healthy Living* – 'First, take 10 live mice. Holding each one firmly by the tale, lower it gently down your throat and swallow whole. Keep in stomach until the next time you are in need of mortal sustenance and then slowly digest. May be served with guacamole if you're somewhere civilised, or mushy peas if you're in the north.' Hazel Blears's *Fun for One* – 'I just eat acorns, me! Tuck 'em away during autumn, they'll keep you going right through winter if you're proper tiny and sensible like me! Lovely!'

Bill Clinton's *Good Ol' Boy Recipe Book* – 'Here's ma recipe for Penis Surprise – ah guess it's a little dated now, but it's still a classic! Jus' wash your penis, arrange it comfortably in your pants and wait til Hillary's out. Serves as many as you can get away with.'

Nicolas Sarkozy's *Recipes for Seduction* – 'Steep your woman in gravel-voiced compliments and smouldering glances. Let her marinate for a while, in memories and delicious anticipation. Wait. Wait – you are not an animal. When the time is right, wreathe your dish of love in cigarette smoke and add the faint yet unmistakable smell of Left Bank pseudo-intellectualism. If that fails, you can always just get her smashed on crème de menthe.'

At Home (Or Georgia) with Vladimir Putin – 'Stare down wolf. Kill wolf. Skin wolf. Don't cook wolf. What are you – American ladyboy? Eat wolf.'

The Thatchers: Margaret and Denis Make Dinner – 'Grind up a full measure of social capital, mix well with some crushed hopes, blood of the innocents and add 72 jiggers of gin. Cheers!' *David Cameron's Eton Messes* – 'The most important thing is to wait and see what everyone else is eating. And then make some more of that. Maybe change the garnish. No, don't. Yes, do. Serves rich people only.'

Sarah Palin: Wasilla Home Cooking – 'Well, we all love Momma's Moose Mousse, yes indeedy, you betcha. First, shoot your moose, OK? Then liquidise it in a converted snowplough – you don't want one of those itty-bitty things like those Washington elites use! Whip in some cream, sugar and a coupla eggs, top with the love of God and, hey poncho, you have got yourself a great working hockey mayoral mom dessert for at least five children! Serve with a bludgeoning jaw and impregnable certainty about all things.'

Barack Obama's *Meals You Can Believe In* – 'Take two fish and five small loaves. Serves 5,000. Trust me.'

I NOVEMBER 2008

Home economics

Food, car and house sales are plummeting. Our world leaders now talk openly of global recession. And, perhaps most tellingly, word spreads that during a forthcoming state visit the Queen is planning to wear a red suit that – and I wish you to steady yourselves against the nearest, sturdiest piece of furniture before I go on – she has worn before. Truly our straits must be dire.

The time has clearly come, therefore, for me to share with you my handy list of Dos and Don'ts for beating the credit crunch. (Or Do's and Don'ts for those of you who'd like to argue the merits of grammatically incorrect apostrophes being deployed in the service of dispelling visual confusion.

And I know from a recent column that touched on this subject that many of you fine, passionate, if possibly slightly underemployed people exist.)

Dos/Do's
Empty your cupboards

Food cupboards first. Come on, we haven't got all day. I've got a bottle of nam pla at the back of mine. I don't even know what nam pla is. I was staring at the label for 20 minutes before I realised it wasn't a misprint.

Take out all unidentifiable sticky bottles, lever off the shelves any jars spot-welded by their own juices. Hose them down, polish them up and establish them in your mind once more as usable entities.

As ever in matters of prudence and economy, I offer my late, great-aunt Eileen as your best guide. She once emptied her store cupboard and found a 22-year-old bag of icing sugar at the back. We suggested she offer it to the V&A. 'Don't be ridiculous,' she said. 'It'll do for our Kenneth's christening present.' And it did.

In the right frame of mind, your clear-out can double as therapy, which will reduce your outgoings. A junk- or food-stuffed cupboard is like a mini-archaeological dig through the strata of your soul. Down you go through abandoned kitchen appliances, sports gear, organic cleaning products: the detritus of discarded hopes, dreams and futile attempts at reinvention revealed in unforgiving physical form. When I reach the last of my kitchen cupboards, I find that I once bought a packet of polenta. It remains untouched. Ah, boiled cornmeal – who'd have thought you could work as metaphor as well as you do dated dinner party staple?

Reconceptualise

Central heating is your enemy. I am a cold-blooded creature – never mind cast ne'er a clout till May is out. I shuck not a sweater until the sun is burning overhead in mid-August, so if I can live without heating, so can you. I am typing this in two T-shirts, four jumpers, two pairs of trousers and a rug over my legs. I can't move, but I'm toasty.

Eat out of the freezer

Trust me, all that 'eat within a year of freezing' nonsense is just that. It's one of those things that has become received wisdom, like exercise being good for you, living well being the best revenge or the truth setting you free. There's pounds worth of food in them there drawers, so get defrosting – and if necessary, heavily disguising with cheap spices – and eating. What's the worst that can happen? Even if you end up with food poisoning, you'll still save money. It's hard to go shopping when you're jackknifed over the toilet and leaking from both ends. Admittedly not impossible, with an iron will and robust laptop, but if you're that dedicated to the art, you probably haven't read this far anyway.

Fillet your grandparents

For knowledge, for money and, if things get desperate, for real.

Don'ts
Despair.

22 NOVEMBER 2008

Out for the count

Like most of us, I feel that life is a joyless, desiccated husk of a thing just waiting to be crushed under the wheel of one last cartload of misery, so it is with a strange sense of relief that I bring you the news that that cart has finally arrived. It was bringing the news that the Food Standards Agency wants calorie counts to be printed next to dishes on menus of restaurants, canteens and takeaways.

Historically, for whatever reason – possibly something in my childhood – I have had quite a high tolerance for having tyrannical rules suddenly imposed on me ostensibly for my benefit and yet curiously often detracting from my quality of life. But with this latest news, I find I have reached my limit. That's it. No more. Do you know how carefully I already live my life? I don't take a step without calculating how it will affect me, Toryboy, the cats, my finances, the family, the climate, the world. My internal voice yammers ceaselessly on, listing possible alternatives, consequences and further questions for investigation at a later date until I'd like to crawl inside my own skull with a tiny spade and batter my brain to death.

I am sure that you, as lovely, mindful types with far greater familial responsibilities and more acute socio-environmental consciences, are plagued even more profoundly thus. The only way we can survive is in the few tiny pockets of willed ignorance that survive in this hyper-informative age. The restaurant menu is one of these. On the odd occasion that I quiet the voice within that would otherwise insist on telling me the carbon footprint of takeaway packaging and expounding upon the unsustainability of fried rice, I like to treat myself to a non-home-cooked meal. It is one of my few remaining pleasures and now it is to be cursed with calorific blazonry.

What's next? How are the last drops of happiness to be wrung from the filthy, damp dishcloth of life? I still like sleeping, so should I expect a government directive requiring that all duvets be printed with giant photos of the dust mites and parasites that live in every bed but whose existence still falls under the heading Things We Know About at Some Level, But Upon Which We Choose Not to Reflect in Order to Safeguard Our Mental if Not Epidermal Integrity? Will the restorative powers of hot ablutions in the morning also be suitably attenuated, with every shower retro-fitted with a device that broadcasts the screamings of the rainforest whenever you crank the temperature up a notch?

I expect chocolate will soon be sold in the shape of tumours and crisps will be sold in packets mimicking an enlarged heart. From there it will be but a short step to requiring all pets to have their species' average lifespan shaved into their fur – or perhaps doomsday clocks hung around their necks – to remind any owner under 90 that their beloved beasts will never outlive them, and that sometime between 2012 and 2020 they are going to be digging a tiny grave in the garden and trying to explain that Floofdafloof has gone to a better place in a futile attempt to assuage the fathomless grief of his household's juvenile population.

Adding calorie counts to menus will do nothing to arrest obesity. The only way you can stop a dedicated fatty eating a burger is through a carefully organised programme of nutritional and psychological re-education. Or by offering them a bigger burger. All it does is increase resistance among those previously disposed to accept the rules. And now, if you will excuse me, I am off to poison a waterway or two. Remember, it's the FSA that drove me to it.

24 JANUARY 2009

CHAPTER FIVE

THE VIEW FROM THE COUCH

I ♥ Roy Cropper

He slipped unobtrusively into *Coronation Street* in 1995. Clad in what would become his signature anorak, and permanently attached to a grey nylon shopping bag, Royston Cropper looked like an unlikely choice for a hero.

But *Street* devotees have watched this unprepossessing loner reveal himself as a man of infinite learning (maths, local history, the Titanic and automotive engines are just a few of his areas of expertise), compassion (there isn't a waif or stray in Weatherfield who hasn't been sheltered by Roy and his sweet transsexual companion Hayley), artistry (his fried bread is the stuff of legend) and, above all, integrity.

His relationship with Hayley, in the face of local hostility and revulsion – and when Vera Duckworth is revolted, that's quite some face – was simply the inevitable culmination of a life spent on the social outskirts, refusing to be crushed by the common drive for social conformity. Heathcliff had his Cathy, Dante his Beatrice and Roy would have his Hayley, pre-operative genitalia or no.

They were 'married' in Roy's cafe, and it wasn't just the grease-spattered tiling that made the occasion shine. Beneath the anorak there was a man forged by suffering and transformed by love.

But now things look black for Roy. Drugged and deceived by Tracy 'Satan in a sleeveless top' Barlow into thinking he has fathered her child, he has married her. Legally, he has done nothing wrong, but to a man like Roy the law of the land is not what matters. By his own unassailable moral standards, he is now hopelessly mired in a necrotic pit of his own devising.

But to the rest of us, this is simply a test of our faith in the Cropper way. He will overcome. As Roy himself once said of Edmund Arkwright – 'who invented the bevelled flange which revolutionised the northern cotton milling industry' – I salute you.

1 DECEMBER 2003

Sex and the City? What were we thinking of?

Watching *Sex and the City* again, I now feel able to say that the adoption of Carrie, Miranda, Charlotte and Samantha as role models, heroines, icons of empowerment and whatever else they were claimed to be was one of the greatest acts of collective madness the world has ever seen.

Carrie is a 38-year-old woman who spends all her income on clothes and shoes. Whenever a man comes within 40ft, she turns into a simpering, hair-twirling, eyelash-fluttering fool, behaving in a manner that would disgrace a 50s teenager. If the man is Mr Big, she goes into convulsions. She is an idiot.

Even first time round I was struck by Charlotte's moronic inability to tell a date to stop licking her face without holding a summit meeting with her friends to discuss whether this was acceptable. Her entire being is strung to one desire – to find a knight in shining armour and reel him in by withholding sex until an engagement ring is forthcoming. At the moment she is with the flaccid Trey, which serves her right.

Miranda is a successful lawyer (though too stupid to take the morning-after pill in the fourth series), who, therefore, is out of touch with her emotions and keeps frightening men off. The makers of the show are themselves so frightened of her that they keep dunking the actress's head in tartrazine as revenge. This is not progress, people. This is pathetic.

Samantha is a tart with a heart. I can't be sure, but I think we have seen this before. She, in particular, is held up as a monument to female liberation. If feminism did indeed fight for the right to shout 'funky spunk' in a crowded restaurant, of course, then this is perfectly correct.

The show – especially in its early series – is cold, brutal, soulless, mechanistic fare, in which the women are marionettes playing out male sexual fantasies dressed as female fashion fantasies. At least we saw through *Desperate Housewives* more quickly.

21 NOVEMBER 2006

Asbo Teen to Beauty Queen? Junk food for the mind

I'm on a diet at the moment, and so spend my days hankering after heavily battered fish and chips, Mars Bars and, at particularly low points, both together, ideally smothered in a chicken korma sauce and spread on a deep-crust pizza. I am learning to sublimate my urges, so it was fortunate that the televisual equivalent of the takeway was available last night on Five. *Asbo Teen to Beauty Queen* was as fibre-free and full of crap as anyone craving junk food for the mind could have hoped for. I could actually feel my brain turning to wobbly fat as I watched.

The set-up is simplicity itself – nine gobby Mancunian lasses who have an Asbo and multiple charges of assault, burglary, shoplifting and criminal damage between them are placed in the charge of Michelle Fryatt, a former US beauty queen. She has six weeks to turn them into glamorous young women fit to take part in the forthcoming Miss Teen International Pageant in Chicago. 'I am going to help them with a process of self-discovery and self-growth,' she proclaimed, the hard, bright light of the evangelical self-improver burning in her kohl-rimmed eyes.

(What's that? No, no they've never expressed an interest in becoming beauty queens. No, they are not part of a government or municipal scheme aimed at turning their lives around. Yes, they are just a random selection of girls plucked from the capital of the north in order to disconcert the American beauty queen. Yes, someone has just come up with a rhyming title and worked backwards from there. Don't keep looking for nutrition, this will all go a lot more smoothly if you just leave your Higher Purposes by the door, stick your head in the trough and enjoy.)

Rachel, Laura, Pavia, Ellen, Neisha, Kerry, Sarah, Ashlie and Elena trooped into the room and sat there, nine sullen bundles of vile, graceless, rude, foul-mouthed hostility in skin-tight jeans and polyester tracksuits. If you had chopped any one of them in half down the middle, the two sides would still be sneering as they peeled away and hit the floor. Rachel would probably have managed to hawk a lump of phlegm from half her mouth at you as she went down.

The perfectly coiffed and peroxided vision of La Fryatt who, when she is not trying to inculcate self-growth in Britain's obstreperous youth, clearly does a damned fine job of holding back the ravages of time on face and figure, swept in wearing a floor-length golden gown. The girls looked stunned, contemptuous and filled with fear and loathing. This week's challenge, their unfazed mentor told them, was to master the pageant-queen look. I hadn't thought it possible, but the contempt and incredulity in the room deepened. La Fryatt ignored it. I don't know if she'd had work done that meant she couldn't blink or if she just chose not too, but either way the effect was mesmerising. 'Glam up!' she said to the girls, stripping back her lips to show perfect (if gritted) dentition, in what I must conclude was an attempt at an encouraging smile. 'Glam as you can!'

'I've only got tracksuits,' said Laura. There was a barely perceptible pause while Fryatt digested this news and recalibrated her entire perspective on the world and womankind. 'Then put on your most glamorous tracksuit!' she said brightly.

The rest of the programme was a matter of plumbing the depths of adolescent resentment, ingratitude and aggression. The girls made Gordon Ramsay look like Shirley Temple as they effed and blinded their way through makeovers and shopping trips and, homing in with the teenage girl's unerring instinct for another individual's weakness, opined that Fryatt 'needs to go home and babysit her grandkids'. The clothes, the makeup, the shoes, the experts drafted in to help them – everything was 'f'kin' disgusting', 'grannified' and often both. I was torn between hating the nine determined malcontents and applauding their concerted rejection of all attempts to force them into the intrinsically risible (as one of them said, 'I look more like a drag queen than a beauty queen') and ideologically suspect mould of the pageant contestant. On the other hand, it was also quite clear that what they were primarily objecting to was not outmoded notions of femininity or the ban on individual expression but any form of discipline whatsoever, which is probably the attitude that kept landing half of them in jail between eyelash-curling sessions.

'It was a little bit hard to get positive feedback,' said Fryatt. 'I don't see any of them embracing the look. They need to appreciate the opportunity they've been given.' I don't know. I think my money's on the girls, but then again – Fryatt hasn't blinked yet.

16 NOVEMBER 2006

Who needs Charles and Camilla? We've got Ken and Deirdre

Why is the nation not up in arms at the news that the heir to the throne, the defender-in-waiting of the faith, has broken with centuries of tradition and altered his wedding date to accommodate the funeral of the head of the Roman Catholic church? Perhaps many Britons feel that if a man has got the Archbishop of Canterbury to officiate at his marriage to a divorcee, any outrage at the further battering of the reputation of the Anglican church would be so much wasted effort. But for at least 14 million of us, it is because we were too busy throwing our hats in the air at the news that the real wedding of the year, taking place at 7.30pm on Friday on ITV between *Coronation Street's* most revered characters Ken and Deirdre, would no longer be overshadowed by the paltry affair cobbled together in the real world by Charles and Camilla.

Instead, Ken and his nicotine-stained bride will get their long awaited day in the sun, the only possible cloud being the presence of Deirdre's dying first husband, Ray – although, this being the *Street* rather than *EastEnders*, he gets to crack jokes about cancer rather than writhe about on broken glass with a cardboard arrow over his head saying, 'Poignant juxtapositioning of Eros and Thanatos going on over here, folks! Be sad! Be sad!'

Oh, and there is Blanche, too, the quintessential mother-in-law, forever fixing Ken with a baleful eye and muttering, 'Never an eye of newt around when you need one', but she'll probably come around on the day. Deirdre's daughter Tracy is the distilled essence of evil, but hopefully her powers will be weakened by the presence of saintly Emily Bishop and imperious grande dame Rita Sullivan, who in fact once slept with Ken, albeit back in the days when such an undertaking was less fraught with the danger of one of them breaking a hip.

If all goes well – and jolly pictures of the wedding reception already posted on the official *Street* website suggest that it might –

Deirdre, who first married Ken in 1981 and then proceeded to bugger things up by means of an inexplicably lustful attraction to Mike Baldwin, will be restored to her original estate and all will bathe in the radiant glow of her happiness and ever present fag end.

I gave the first wedding and the subsequent affair (which caused me to labour for years under the delusion that 'torrid' was a synonym for 'faintly sickening') my rapt attention. It was an early lesson in how much more absorbing the parallel televisual universe could be than real life. There have been a number of additional defining relationships in my life beyond my bond with the *Street* – with my parents, of course, with Enid Blyton, obviously, and now with my laptop – but none as consistently comforting and rewarding as the one I enjoy with the television in general and Weatherfield's finest in particular.

It is, of course, possible to love a programme too much – I suspect that my tendency to wake up on Wednesday mornings, grip the bed sheet tightly to my chin and whisper with delight, '*Desperate Housewives* tonight!' is indicative of a life more bereft of meaning than I have the courage to admit – but it is an inescapable, if possibly unedifying, fact that I truly care more about Ken and Deirdre's nuptials than about Charles and Camilla's. Swirling about in the postmodern vortex as we all are, these characters are far more alive to fans than the pair of ageing aristocrats will ever be. After all, we have had over two decades' worth of unmediated access to the former, have learned literally everything there is to know about them with our own eyes, while anything we know about the latter has been absorbed from reconstituted accounts run through innumerable mincing machines and bearing no more relation to the truth than a Turkey Twizzler does to a Norfolk black.

If Charles and Camilla were to fulfil what one suspects is a long-standing wish and immure themselves behind castle walls, absenting themselves from the public gaze for evermore, it would have infinitely less impact on the emotions or happiness of the nation than would the sudden cessation of the country's longest-running TV series. The royal family may often have been compared to a soap opera, but the happy truth is that they are far less important than that.

6 APRIL 2005

The trouble with Seinfeld

What with all the trouble one of its former stars has been having in the last few weeks – namely Michael Richards and his racist outburst at two hecklers in a Los Angeles club – I thought this might be the time to attempt to analyse my own struggles with *Seinfeld*.

I have tried – as the co-habitee of a diehard fan who lies prostrate with mirth and admiration before each and every episode, God knows, I have tried – to find it funny. But I can't.

Honestly, I laugh at most things. But I sit in front of my TV with a face like a bulldog chewing a wasp whenever Jerry, George, Elaine and Kramer haul their neurotic asses into view. Three minutes in and I am screaming: 'Just tell them! Just explain to who ever it is who is causing you such unbelievable emotional torture by having too many office celebrations or making a funny noise in their throat that you're a total twunt, and then sod off. Just sod off!'

A friend who lives in New York once told me that the show was much more likable when shown in shorter sections on cable, rather than in the uninterrupted half-hours I was getting on BBC2 in the late 90s: 'It's the only show I've ever known that is improved by ad breaks.'

I can see the logic of this. The relentless smugness of Jerry, endless self-centredness of George, constant whining of Elaine and effortful eccentricity of Kramer must be more palatable in short bursts. The one-dimensionality of each of the vile, vicious quartet is easier to cope with if everything works in concert to remind you that they are really only figures designed to get in, deliver the gag, and get out.

But even on cable you don't get enough ad breaks to make this work. And it requires a great triumph of will to keep laughing at whatever infinitesimally small social solecism one of them thinks may bring on the end of western civilisation when you would in fact rather they had all been cut down with a swirling scythe rolling down Manhattan. No hugging, no learning, no heads – hurrah!

28 NOVEMBER 2006

The one with all the couch potatoes

So, Generations X-to-Y, let's take inspiration from our algebraic collective monikers and sit down and do some maths. Let's work out how much of our lives we have spent (or enriched or wasted, depending on your point of view and propensity to rush to judgment) watching *Friends*.

It ran for nine series and 236 episodes. Did you watch the 118 hours as originally parcelled out, in 30-minute pieces at weekly intervals from 1994 to 2004, and then say to yourself, 'That was an entertaining and indeed in many ways groundbreaking show that managed to tap into various cultural phenomena, define an era and deliver a good six-or-even-eight gags per minute, but one viewing was quite enough and I think I shall now move on to other shows, pastimes and good works in the community in order to accrue the maximum possible range of experiences in the brief span allotted to me on this earth'?

No, you did not. Like me, you watched morning repeats on Channel 4 when hungover, tea-time repeats when waiting for potatoes to boil, E4 repeats when there was nothing else on, E4+1 repeats when there was nothing else on an hour later. And those were just the viewings that depended on circumstance, timing or mislaid remote controls. After that you have got to add in all the times you actively sought out the shiny sextet – when you were ill, tired, in need of comfort-watching to accompany the comfort-eating after a bad date, relationship or STD, or just, frankly, in the mood to watch some high-class comedy played by six actors who entered the pilot at the top of their game and somehow stayed there for the following 10 years.

It is a show that rewards repeated viewing; it is a show that deserves an audience's loyalty. Whether it is a show that justifies the 32 per cent of waking hours I conservatively estimate that we have devoted to it, only each of us on our deathbeds, gazing back down the years, may decide.

5 December 2006

The stage school students are coming . . .

All right, that's it. I've spent the day watching *Malcolm in the Middle*, *The Cosby Show*, *Roseanne* and the episode of *Friends* where Joey befriends an eight-year-old girl at Monica and Chandler's new house, and I now want to know: where, in the name of all that is good and holy, do they find these kids? Perhaps 10, 15, 20 years ago, America secretly looked over at Russia and said: 'Y'know, guys, those commie bastards got a lot of things wrong, but training the bejaysus out of the juvenile population wasn't necessarily one of them. Mathematicians are dull and we don't want to become famous for the quality of our nerds. What we need is to lead the world in child acting. Round up anyone currently nagging their mothers for tap shoes.'

I believe that when the appropriate files are released by the FBI in 50 years' time, we will discover that this is exactly what happened. Area 51 has nothing to do with aliens – it's where they are hiding all the drama academies that drill toddlers in handling a three-camera format and coping with alcoholic adult leads maddened by jealousy of their fresh-faced co-stars.

There is no other way to explain Dakota Fanning, Joey's friend and currently making about three films a year, as she has done since she uncurled enough in the amniotic sac to allow for close-ups. Nor Erik Per Sullivan, who has been Dewey in *MitM* since he was nine. Nine! And that's a comedy series. He's not just parroting lines and crying on cue, he's timing gags and playing off other people's. Nine!

Nor Sara Gilbert as Darlene in *Roseanne*, and certainly not Keshia Knight Pulliam who, as Rudy in *The Cosby Show*, was being handed 20-minute monologues at the age of five. Even a country as large as America cannot by chance be producing this number of freakishly talented children. I tell you, 2007 will be the year we discover it's not survivalists who swarm the bunkers in Montana, but stage school students and their grim-faced, blazing-eyed teachers dedicated to entertainment world domination.

23 JANUARY 2007

Look − it's so and so

It's been a great week for my new game. Well, not new − it began as a response to the inevitable phone call from my mother halfway through any BBC or ITV prime-time drama. 'What's he/she just been in? Am I still watching that or is this something new?' If only more television commissioners were post-menopausal women who understood the confusion that can be caused by re-using their pool/shallow puddle of lead actors in everything.

I originally called it Six Degrees of David Jason, the aim being to spot a familiar face on the small screen and then link it back to Big J in as few moves as possible. With the advent of multi-channel TV the possibilities have increased exponentially, and my boyfriend and I become engrossed every evening in the tricky game known as 'Arghwhereshefromshitiknowthis'.

The rules are simple: You see an actor − say, Xander from *Buffy*, who is now in *Kitchen Confidential*. You scream 'That's Xander from *Buffy*, in *Kitchen Confidential*'. For this, you get a nod. For something more obscure, for example, my boyfriend realising that the blonde lady poh-lice in *NYPD Blue* is actually Mona from *Friends*, you get an admiring nod. Noticing that blonde lady poh-lice, who is Mona, is also the manageress in *Kitchen Confidential* earned me verbal agreement regarding the keenness of my intellect, proved yet further by my Google-vindicated claim that the fire chief in *Jericho* was Agent Ford from *Due South*.

One memorable evening, my boyfriend matched *NYPD Blue's* Detective Ortiz's cousin with Vic Mackay's prostitute-snitch in *The Shield*. I only clawed back the crown with a lucky spotting of Dr Meredith Grey from *Grey's Anatomy* playing a college crush of Chandler and Ross in *Friends*, along with noticing that the woman the orphaned boy helped in *Jericho* had been in Friends, *Donnie Darko*, *Angel* and *Malcolm in the Middle*. 'Beat that!' I said, sinking back into the sofa, exhausted. 'I cannot,' Boyfriend sighed. 'But, oh, think what tales we shall have to tell our children.'

30 JANUARY 2007

Come back, SatC – all is forgiven

A few months ago in this column I voiced the opinion that we had engaged in a collective act of madness in lauding the four graceless ciphers who made up *Sex and the City* as modern feminist icons and role models for women everywhere. I wondered how this aberration had come about.

Now, thanks to TMF, I know. They are re-showing *Ally McBeal*, the late-90s series about a lovesick twentysomething lawyer in a firm full of oddballs trying a variety of zeitgeisty cases every week. Revisiting this, it becomes clear just why we rushed to embrace the Manoloed Manhattanites so gratefully. Compared to Ally, they are a quartet of Susan B Anthonys.

The show's premise is wretched: see pretty lady! See pretty lady work! See pretty lady pretend to be a real lawyer! See pretty lady fall apart when she realises her ex-boyfriend works at the same firm – with his wife! See pretty lady piss and moan for 45 minutes a week! As the series progressed, things got steadily worse – the skirts got shorter, until all the lady lawyers were giving full gynaecological displays to the courtroom every time they bent to pick up a file. The cases became more ludicrous, usually pivoting on some imagined example of sexual political correctness gone mad until the misogyny of the show began to poke through its fabric like the bones of its notoriously skeletal actresses.

And the worst embarrassment of all was Ally herself, the cadaverous crypto-being played by Calista Flockhart. It was less a performance than a collection of infuriating mannerisms that turned her into a flapping, quivering, whimpering, pouting, wittering, twittering, vacillating, querulous, petulant, inept, vacuous, inane affront to humanity, let alone to women. Oh, there simply aren't words to describe how maddening it is.

Don't re-watch it unless you have recently checked that your blood pressure is comfortably healthy. It may kill you. And if it doesn't, the fact that we have to redefine *SatC* as progress certainly will.

6 FEBRUARY 2007

The rise of the sidekick

I have revised my notions of what would constitute the best job in the world. No longer do I pine to make my living as a play therapist for kittens. No, the sweetest way to earn a crust is to be a successful sitcom star's sidekick.

This way, you see, you reap all of the benefits of being in a successful TV comedy without having to do any of the heavy lifting with which the central character is habitually burdened. None of the main plot-carrying. None of the emotional anchoring of the audience. The wingman gets to have all the fun and none of the responsibility – a zesty palate cleanser between plates of stodge.

Look at Niles in *Frasier*. While his big brother has to labour and sweat for laughs and groans, he swans in every now and again, throws a few killer lines into the mix and nips out again, leaving the audience sighing with regret at his exit. What, in short, is not to like?

Or take Maryann in *Cybill*. She is the vituperative best pal of the eponymous star – a cold plunge bath of wit, periodically reviving us after our exhausting immersion in the lather of ego and insecurity that is Cybill Shepherd.

The delights of sidekickery reach their peak in *Will & Grace*. By the end of the show's run there was even a running gag about how dull everyone found the main pair compared to Jack and Karen. They had the advantage even over the solo efforts of Niles and Maryann in that, while they were good separately, together they were invincible. Casting directors roll about in sacrificial goat entrails to try to secure the kind of chemistry between their chosen ones that Megan Mullally and Sean Hayes had from the get-go. By episode three they were working purely on instinct and almost faster than the human eye could see, while *W&G* lumbered on, forever earthbound.

TV sitcom is one place where it is always better to be the cheeky monkey – as the organ grinder, life soon becomes more bitter than you ever imagined on the day you snatched that vehicle-of-a-lifetime offer from your agent's shaking, treacherous hand.

6 MARCH 2007

Tailor-made TV

Why, with all this technology at our disposal, are we still expected to know roughly what we want to watch before we begin? Living kindly does the thinking for us on weekend mornings with its Hangover TV provision, but TV delivered according to mood is a concept we should adopt far more widely. Simply type in your current frame of mind, and an avalanche of suitable programming will then cascade on to your screen. 'I feel strangely melancholic and would like to have a good cry, but there's nothing going on in my real life that would force me to dissolve into actual tears,' you explain mournfully. Instantly, your television marshals its forces and brings you 18 documentaries on brave, misshapen children and six episodes of *Birth Stories*, hand-picked for their cloying voiceovers, all concluding '. . . and mom Brandi finally gets to take her blessing, her 6lb bundle of happiness, home'.

Or if you're having a bad day, just type in 'the entire world appears to be pissing on my chips and I'd like confirmation of this fact so that I can submerge myself in a warm pool of righteous anger'. Your cable provider will oblige with an entire day of *Everyone Loves Raymond* so that you can vent your rage for hours by shouting 'No! They! Don't!' from the sofa.

Or perhaps you require some Ironing TV – programmes that reward listening as much as watching, like *Frasier*, and, if you were always more into the kick-ass dialogue than kick-ass martial arts, *Buffy the Vampire Slayer*.

Your TV should also be able to take certain moods as a warning about what not to show you. If you type in 'I am teetering perilously close to the edge of a pit marked permanent depressive insanity' it will rush to your aid not only by giving you a slideshow of all Wentworth Miller's tattoo scenes from two series of *Prison Break* but also lock firmly away *Ulrika . . . Am I a Sex Addict?* along with anything else capable of inducing Pollyanna herself to slit her wrists after five minutes' exposure to its unspeakable dreadfulness.

27 MARCH 2007

Don't pass the burdizzo

I've just seen a Benedictine monk's vagina. Truly Channel 4 has taken recent criticism of its failure to adhere to its original public-service remit to heart. Getting Reverend Brother Shawn Francis Benedict to kick up his heels and give us a bird's eye view of his unusually punctuated perineum ('That's my urethral relocation there') was certainly innovative. I feel informed, entertained and ever so slightly like I am about to have a stroke.

Brother Benedict, who now runs the Ray of Hope church for gays, lesbians, eunuchs, transgender people and enlightened hetero-sexuals in Elmira, New York, was in many ways the star turn of *Eunuchs*, a documentary focusing on four of the alleged thousands of men who wish to be permanently estranged from their testicles. He had his balls removed in 1998, two years after his ordination. You might think it was aimed at facilitating his celibacy vows, but you would be wrong. It was to mark 'the end of my co-operation with all the traditional expectations of the American male'.

Brother Benedict is in fact admirably committed to the pleasures of the flesh. He now injects testosterone to maintain his sex life with his partner, another eunuch. Now called Christina, she takes oestrogen but doesn't have a vagina because she can't afford one yet. 'It costs $40,000 to $60,000,' says Brother Benedict, ruefully. Still, I wouldn't bet against a man of his indomitable spirit finding a way of funding it one day.

We also met Bill, who got fed up being at the mercy of a libido that forced him to spend hours masturbating or seeking out sex with random men and women – so went out and bought a burdizzo. For those of you who really want to know, a burdizzo is a big stainless-steel clamp designed to crush the spermatic cord and cut off the blood supply to the testicles, which are then gradually re-absorbed by the body over the years. Ideally, it is applied by trained professionals to the genitalia of animals. With the kind of pioneering spirit that made his country great, Bill applied it to himself, and posted the resulting pictures of his screaming scrotum on the net. They lent a whole new dimension to the word 'discombobulating'.

His sister wanted to know why he hadn't opted for chemical castration or a supervised medical operation. In this, I assure you, she spoke for all of us. Bill said he didn't want to be a drug addict, nor was he interested in growing breasts as a result of ingesting oestrogen. In vain did his sister suggest there was presumably an optimum dose to ensure a lowering of the libido without a corresponding rise in cup size. And as for the other option – 'You can't just go to the doctor, Jackie!' cried Bill. For a moment he could have been anyone's annoying older brother revelling in a sibling's ignorance. But only for a moment. Then you remembered his publicly purpling plums.

Actually, it turned out you could go to a doctor. Zac and Roger went to Dr Murray Kimmel in Philadelphia. Zac is 20, pale and delicate as a sapling, and has wanted to be castrated since he was a child. He finally arranged the surgery with Dr Kimmel over the phone. Two weeks later, he is in Philadelphia for the operation. His mother accompanies him, gazing at her beautiful, unhappy boy with love and bewilderment, laying out clean dressings as she once must have laid out his clean nappies. Once he's been Kimmelled, Zac returns home to wrestle with unexpected bouts of depression, as he realises he might not have been quite as ready as he thought to live a life without sex or desire.

Roger, who was castrated five years ago, could have told him that the eunuch's life is not necessarily simple. He, too, had wanted the operation since childhood, 'to escape being male'. What he cannot escape, however, is the feeling that he has let his parents down. He would like to give them back 'their innocent son, who wasn't defective or broken . . . so very ill, sick in the head, diseased', he said with a wry smile, before his round, sweet face crumpled into tears.

As well as literally, the film didn't have any balls metaphorically. It told the stories without attempting to ask or answer questions about how we construct masculinity, what there might be to fear in belonging to an ostensibly privileged gender that you would rather cut off its physical markers than remain part of it, or what part an internalised cultural hatred of homosexuality might have played in the men's decisions. There was definitely something missing.

Zac is currently considering hormone replacement treatment to restore his sex drive, Bill is looking into proper surgical removal of his unwanted cojones, Roger is searching for a partner on asexuality websites and Brother Benedict and Christina are getting married. Oh, and advertising for a slave. 'Must supply own vagina.' I think I'm making that last bit up, but I can't be sure.

4 APRIL 2007

Joss was the perfect fit

As we start to stitch back together the garments rent on learning that Joss Whedon was no longer going to do the *Wonder Woman* movie (Why? Why? Why? Can you think of a more perfect fit, of a combination more likely to imbue us all with a sense of hope and shining anticipation of greatness in this otherwise bleak and godless universe? No. You cannot) we must embark on a damage-limitation exercise. Close study of the series (weekend mornings, Living) yields the following vital guidelines for any successor:

1. Establishing shots are much improved by the addition of bright yellow cartoon squares containing explanatory captions. When the audience sees a gothic mansion full of people with harsh guttural accents marching around in black uniforms covered in swastikas, they still require a box in the top left-hand corner of the screen saying 'Secret Nazi intelligence headquarters in Munich, 1942' lest they simply assume Diana Price has been invited to an elaborate costume party by her crazy European mates.

2. Substantial research will need to be carried out to make sure that there are still sufficient corsetry fetishists out there to make strapping some Hollywood diva into a gold-trimmed basque worthwhile. An A-lister is likely to be significantly less malleable than TV

ingenue Lynda Carter, both metaphorically (stars being what they are) and literally (most have no flesh to bind).

3. You must keep the bullet-deflecting bracelets and the transforming twirl. It's all anyone remembers. And you really must drop the golden lasso of truth. It is the most tragically inadequate accessory ever sported by a superhero, and certainly will not pass muster in an age when any ordinary Joe can build himself a nuclear warhead from a kit off the internet.

I don't suppose, now that Whedon – the only feminist writer in Hollywood – is off the project there is the slightest chance of Wonder Woman not getting her tits out for the lads at some point, so we shall end the lessons here.

17 APRIL 2007

The real beginnings of reality TV

The next time you find yourself grappled in conversational hoops of steel by some arch bore intent on imparting his opinion of *Big Brother's* culpability re: the increasing popularity of reality TV and the consequent break-down of society, you should just say two little words to him. No, not those, another two. Namely: *Crown Court*.

This, as anyone who reached the age of televisual reason at any time during the programme's 1972 to 1985 run will remember, was a show which had actors playing the parts of victims, witnesses, lawyers and judges (I cite them in increasing order of hamminess and wiggedness), but real people sitting on the jury and reaching a verdict on the case.

Watching it now (up to, I think, 18 times a day on LegalTV) is to experience a massive culture clash.

On the one hand, the dozen real-life participants do lend an inescapably contemporary feel to proceedings. On the other hand, by the searingly ugly fashions on display, themselves surely constituting some form of visual assault and deserving of a stiff sentence from

Judge Olde-Harrovian, and the fact the camera moves about twice per episode, you know that you are mired deep, deep in the 70s.

In fact, we are currently in the middle of 1974, watching a foetal Robert Powell pretend to be a 'pop musician' with a particular interest in 'progressive rock' and take his vicar father to court for breaching the copyright of his religious musical '*Jesus, Baby!* – with a comma and an exclamation mark'.

From this brief sample you will see now how the programme can be seen as the ancient father of reality TV – the ordinary people tempted into a strange setting they do not understand by the prospect of seeing their ugly mugs on television, the same vast stretches of boredom for them and the viewer, punctuated by moments of extreme surreality. 'And lo,' you say to the arch bore. 'The seeds of our destruction were sown even half a lifetime before the age of Davina.' Or, of course, you may just tell him to sod off.

1 MAY 2007

All the villians you need under one giant Stetson

Watching the first ever episode of *Dallas* is a momentous event. It's like witnessing the Gettysburg address, or Henry V rallying the troops at Agincourt. One is humbled to experience a pivotal moment in history once more.

All the ingredients that made *Dallas* the most potent, addictive brew on the planet are there. Stern patriarch Jock Ewing and the pathologically submissive Miss Ellie. Boring Bobby and the blood feud between the Ewings and the Barnes family, which includes – duh-duh-DUH! – new wife Pam. Lucy the Poison Dwarf is there, showing half the cowboys in Texas the true meaning of southern hospitality in an apparently soundproofed hay loft. The only character yet to come into her full glory is Sue Ellen, still occasionally seen without a triple whiskey and not quite the poster girl for the Quivering Brethren she was to become, but she's working on it.

And then there's JR. To see Larry Hagman's creation again is to realise that all other villains are but mewling, puking milksops next to him. He is Moriarty, Iago, Batman's Joker, Salieri and multiple Borgias under one giant Stetson. Hell, I wouldn't be surprised if Voldemort turns out to have been John Ross Ewing all along.

I once saw a clip of *Dallas* dubbed into Spanish. JR was played by a man who must have gargled with gravel and kept his larynx in his boots, and became instantly less compelling. The genius of Hagman, of course, is that while JR is destroying everyone within reach, he keeps everything as light and pleasant as a summer breeze. The feathery voice and the constant smile tell us what we all suspected – when you're born to it, being evil is just plain fun.

Now we are about 10 episodes in, and in today's, Sue Ellen, intent on producing an heir for JR before Pam pops a little half-Barnes out into the family, tries to buy one. And if that doesn't remind you of just what you've been missing – well, you're either dead inside, born in the 90s or a *Dynasty* fan. In short, past help. The rest of y'all should come right on in.

8 MAY 2007

Not just smiling or even smirking, but actually laughing

Happy birthday, Bea Arthur! The statuesque, gravel-voiced actress (to give her her full title) turned 85 two days ago, so it seems appropriate now to celebrate the series that provided her 90 finest hours – *The Golden Girls*.

I became deeply discombobulated when I first started watching the reruns of this show. A strange emotion kept welling up inside me, culminating in a series of short, sharp barking noises issuing forth from a face that was distended in an unfamiliar way. So long has it been since this happened that I was several episodes in before I realised that I was laughing. Not smiling the pleased smile of recognition I sport while watching *Friends*, not the gentle smirk that plays about my lips during *Frasier*, nor whatever expression it is that sees me through *The Office* (a grimace of delighted horror?), but laughing.

Betty White as Rose, simple as the Minnesotan prairies of her youth. Rue McClanahan as Southern belle Blanche Devereaux, sultry as an Atlanta sunset. Estelle Getty as the tiny Sicilian matriarch, a birdlike Brando keeping a constant beady eye on the foibles of her makeshift family. They throw each other lines and knock them out of the park. And bestriding them all like a comedy colossus is Arthur as Dorothy Zbornak, schoolteacher and possessor of a wit so dry and a delivery so withering it's a wonder their objects don't crumble into dust on contact.

The show wouldn't be made today. The youngest of the women was 53 when the show started, roughly the age of an entire cast and crew on any TV show today combined. The quartet don't fret about relationships, collapse in emotional heaps when the phone doesn't ring or do any of the things that habitually make you want to set fire to all female sitcom characters. They get on with life, with each other, with verve and above all, with wit. They are the televisual equivalent of Katharine Hepburn, whose centenary, co-incidentally, was yesterday. Perhaps in another 100 years we'll be allowed to see their like again.

15 MAY 2007

Poor Dr House – first he loses his parking space, then his patient's spleen explodes

Don't you just hate it when that happens? One moment you're a normal 16-year-old boy preparing to bump uglies with a nubile

16-year-old girl, the next you're in respiratory arrest with a bloody pleural effusion and undergoing multiple venograms, while doctors look at you with increasingly baffled expressions. Welcome to *House MD* (Five).

The patient is, as ever, the least of the good/bad/cynical/misogynistic doctor's concerns. His main priority is to wrest back his parking space, which Dr Cuddy, in what regular viewers must feel was a moment of profoundly misplaced optimism, has given to a new hospital researcher, whose paraplegia and wheelchair are deemed to trump House's limp and cane.

House, to no one's surprise, disagrees. He points out that parking-space ownership should be based on who can get most easily across the car park, and not decided according to 'some pre-ordained patheticness scale'. With irrefutable logic, he adds: 'I can't walk 50 yards – she can roll 50 miles, between oil changes.'

Dr C agrees to give him the spot if he can spend the entire week in a wheelchair. House intimates that he considers the bet already won. Neither of them mentions the elephant in the room. Namely: what were the scriptwriters thinking when they gave her the name Cuddy? This is clearly the nomenclature of an apple-cheeked, 18th-century farmer's wife, not a glamorous modern hospital administrator. Every time someone mentions her, I expect to see a shot of a woman washing coarse linens in a sparkling brook, occasionally glancing over her shoulder to see if the Industrial Revolution is on its way yet.

Never mind. While House learns to negotiate stairs in his new chair, the Maisonettes are trying to find out what can be causing the rapidly declining teenager to be leaking blood from so many places that no blood should ever leak. They redouble their efforts when he turns out to be bright, interested in medicine and being held back from fulfilling his intellectual destiny by his poor-but-honest Romany family. Battle lines are drawn and Drs Eric, Allison and Robert divide into their customary opposing teams fighting for diagnostic supremacy.

'The liver's blocked by a clot!'

'No, it's a mass around an intruder!'

'DVT! Give him an MRI! And an ACE!'

'Oh, you speak Esperanto?'

'Lesion!'

'Granuloma!'

'Is that Romany for, "His relatives are here?"'

'No – it's a symptom of Wegener's disease!'

'He's got Wegener's disease!'

'I hope the TV critics know how to spell that!'

'Don't worry – it'll only take them 20 minutes to find it on Google.'

It's all terribly exciting. Dr Eric wants to give him an experimental drug but the boy's parents refuse permission. Dr Eric urges the boy to take it secretly. The boy is saved from having to make this decision by his spleen exploding. Nine times out of 10, this is a bad thing, but it leads the Maisonettes to discover that their patient does not have Wegener's Granulomatosis but Toothpick disease. This is caused by swallowing a toothpick, which then swells with water, becomes the same density as whatever internal tissue it's currently perforating and doesn't show up on scans and x-rays, therefore causing your doctors no end of bother. They remove the toothpick and all the holes with which his viscera are by now liberally spattered close up without further ado.

House, having stood up from his chair to assist at the emergency splenectomy, loses the parking bet. But he makes Cuddy feel so guilty that she'll probably give it to him anyway. Farmers' wives are always such a soft touch.

15 JUNE 2007

Why isn't my life like Jennifer Hart's?

The power of television to suddenly awaken in you previously dormant hopes and aspirations is a cruel one. I realised this during a viewing of *Hart to Hart* on UK TV Drama the other day, when some beige-suited villain (a tautology as far as *Hart to Hart* is concerned – the villain is always clad thus, while innocent suspects are enrobed in vibrant blue and yellow cardigans) made passing reference to Jennifer H's career as a freelance journalist.

I sat up. And – not that I hadn't been paying close attention to the serpentine plot about blackmailers in a high-class hair salon – I took notice. For I had completely forgotten that our Jen, wife of multimillionaire Jonathan and owner of a head of hair so bouffant that it was widely rumoured to be in possession of an independent heartbeat and separate agent, was indeed a member of this almost-profession.

Having come to the job relatively late in life, and it being by its very nature an anti-social occupation, I do not know many other freelance journalists. I have no role models, no yardsticks, no benchmarks for success. I simply potter along unthinkingly, relatively content and accepting of my lot. With the advent of Jennifer into my life, however, I suddenly began to look at things differently.

Where, I wondered, was my multimillionaire husband? Where was my gravel-voiced butler who could announce me as 'a terrific lady' in voiceover to the public every day before I ventured forth? Where was my 13-acre kitchen? My fake brick chimney breasts rising out of 3ft-thick shagpile? Where, above all, was my giant hair?

Oh, television, I murmured softly, as the cat was sick on my ordinary carpet – you give us so many dreams. But life is a savage mistress, and snatches them away when they have barely begun to pulse with hope. Then I rallied. A Robert Wagnerish husband might be hard to find, but hot brushes are still on sale in Argos. I put £7.99 in my pocket and set forth. Not all dreams can be denied.

26 JUNE 2007

Here comes the poo

Well, honestly, who could resist tuning in to a programme called *Three Fat Brides, One Thin Dress* (Channel 4)? I sat back and prepared to enjoy whatever bridezilla-based fun was about to unfold. But wait – what was this? A figure crouching at the corner of the screen . . . a flash of golden hair and gimlet eye . . . it could not be . . . no one had warned me . . . But it was. *Three Fat Brides, One Thin Dress* is the latest spawn of the Gillian McKeith franchise, and there she stood, like a platinum-blond incubus, waiting to suck the joy from every living thing around her.

In this instance, the focus for her strange blend of 'holistic nutrition' and personal tyranny was three tubby brides-to-be, who were to compete in losing weight for the prize of a beeyootiful white dress in which to yomp up the aisle. Lisa Lasell, 27, was engaged to a fellow born-again Christian called Gary. She loved Jesus and takeaways. Gary loved Jesus and Lisa but not vegetables. 'God designed vegetables for the rabbits, cows and pigs,' he explained implacably to McKeith. 'Then we eat the rabbits, cows and pigs.' Katrina Paige, 25, was a binge-drinker with a vivid turn of phrase. 'My worst fear is walking down the aisle with my flabby back hanging out of my dress.' Might I suggest, Kat, that you choose a slightly more substantial dress and boot the joyless Scot hovering outside your fridge into the street? Alas, she is inside the television and cannot hear me. Jacqueline Webster is 40 and gorgeous, and apparently fears her husband will go blind with horror if she bares herself in a bikini on their honeymoon. This gives McKeith the opportunity to make one of those remarks that people entirely devoid of humour frequently mistake for humour. 'How special will your honeymoon be when you are harpooned on a beach?' she asks. Ah, Gillian. So close.

Once we have seen what the three girls look like in their underwear, discovered their particular weaknesses and shown them what a week's food intake looks like all together on a table (um – quite a lot), it is time for McKeith to do what she does best and poke through their poo. Lisa is constipated, Jacqueline has squeezed out a mouse turd and Katrina, it turns out – rather wonderfully – got Gareth to do one for her. The sound of Meat Loaf singing I'd Do Anything for Love swells on the soundtrack, the girls collapse in hysterics but not the ghost of a smile reaches Gillian's lips. A Calvinist preacher at this point would urge the woman to lighten up. A woman has just got her future husband to crap in a Tupperware box to appease a holistic nutritionist. You have to laugh, or kill yourself.

Thereafter, we don't see much of the brides. Possibly after Lisa's explanation of her fondness for takeaways ('It's not low self-esteem, it's convenient') and Katrina draining her first smoothie with a heartfelt 'Fucking carrot juice', they decided there was a dangerous amount of independent spirit on the loose. Or perhaps it was simply because McKeith's shows are never about the contestants. They are all about McKeith. A few voiceover statistics about obesity and liver damage do not entirely disguise the megalomania emanating from the alfalfa Margaret Thatcher at its heart. 'That Ronnie [Jacquie's fiance] is going to be thanking me for ever!' announces McKeith. And later, 'I've come to save the day and I have saved the day.' It's symptomatic of the weird atmosphere of smug aggression that pervades her entire oeuvre. Perhaps now that I've worked out what it is that so unsettles me, I can enjoy it more. Then again, maybe not.

Oh, and Jacquie won the dress. Lisa suggested they all go and have a burger to celebrate. Attagirl.

27 JUNE 2007

Satisfying as a bowl of hot coal soup

I have become quietly devoted to the Catherine Cookson dramas that seem to be shown eight times a day on UKTV Drama. They are as satisfying as a bowl of hot coal soup in winter and they all run something like this:

RESPECTED CHARACTER ACTOR: Eh, lad – I hear you've been reading a book, like. Are you one of them homosexualists?

RECENT RADA GRADUATE: Nay, master. That's going to be your lad, but niver worry, he's to be killed in t'war. I want to marry your lass Polly.

RCA: Howay and boil treacle, man. What spuggy-headed rubbish is this? I'd not let a clarty gowk like thee wed me bonnie little stottie cake for all the hobnails in Durham.

[CUT TO:]

RRG: Thy father forbids it, Polly, but I've loved thee for years, with your clean skirts and your unpoxed face and now I've stroked thee in the hayloft you must marry me. I know I've nowt to offer thee but a thick head of curly hair and me father's parkin waistcoat, but I'll be good to thee, Polly and never make you fettle the clinkers as your mother and your grandmother did before thee.

EVEN MORE RECENT LAMDA GRADUATE: Leave me be, you gopping great fool. Can't you see I'm 20 minutes' pregnant wi' the local landowner's bairn? Let me pass – I've got to get back to the house to riddle the cinders, have a miscarriage and concentrate on me accent.

[CUT TO:]

RCA ON HIS DEATHBED: Mebbes I was wrong about thee, lad. Tha's got gumption. There's not many would have stood by our Polly after her legs fell off and she stole the village sovereign when she lost yon babby. Get thee wed. I'll leave thee the midden and you can scrudge a living well enough with all your book learning.

RRG: Why-aye, man. [ENDS]

Come on in. The water in the tin bath's lovely.

31 JULY 2007

Scones at the ready

The following is a production meeting for *Miss Marple* (currently
on UKTV Drama), anytime between 1984 and 1992.

DRAMA EXEC 1: Okay, it says here they've commissioned another
one – *The Inscrutable Scone*. Let's check we've got all the kit. Is
Joan Hickson still with us?

DE2: Yes. She's 106 but the tweed suit keeps her upright.

DE1: Great. Now, have we got the rest of the basics – horseboxes,
hats, bottles of poison? And bottles that look damnably similar to
the ones that hold poison? Also, heavy shovel, gun, an easily stumped
brace of policemen (remember we dub in the gentle sighs of exas-
peration later, otherwise they're all fainting by the end of act two),
assorted moustaches and balustrades, a bath chair, 17 hacking jackets
and interior shots of Denouement Hall. Oh, and millet seed for
Joan.

DE2: All present and correct, Nigel. We've also got whistles, for
the ineffectual blowing of during unconvincing chase scenes, the
battered trug – no, wait, that was the title of last week's episode –
seven pairs of co-respondent shoes and some autumn. What's *The
Inscrutable Scone* going to need in the way of bespoke detail?

DE1: Better break out the eccentric extended family, pargeting, fake
German accents, the bath chair, the bath bun – apparently the plot
turns on a matter of mistaken cake identity – perky scullery maid,
surly scullery maid, sinister copse, a suspiciously precise young man,
a butterfly collection and a magician's box of tricks.

DE2: Should we get a lake, in case?

DE1: I suppose so. Remind me, are we set in England's early rustic
period or postwar pastoral?

DE2: Actually, we're just between mid-to-late rustic and prewar
bucolic.

DE1: Ah yes. Which war?

DE2: Doesn't matter.

DE1: Great. Do we have to start sourcing scones?
DE2: Crikey, no. That's casting's problem.
DE1: Thank God for that.

4 SEPTEMBER 2007

Now I see it's a freaking masterpiece

I knew it happened with books. I hadn't ever really considered that it could happen with television. But just as you can re-read a book years later and find that by some strange intervening process it is now a totally different experience, so – it turns out – you can reassess programmes. Take, for example, *Malcolm in the Middle*. When it was first broadcast on BBC2 six or seven years ago, I came, I saw, and if I didn't quite pooh-pooh it, ladies and gentlemen, I certainly came close. Loud, messy, as garish and over-stimulating as a Gatorade cocktail, I spat it out and walked away.

Now, I sit glued to the sofa for the two new episodes a night doled out by the gracious and benevolent Sky One god, wriggling with glee and delight as an hour of unadulterated brilliance unspools before me. Every scene, every act, every episode, every series is perfectly structured, perfectly balanced, perfectly engineered to blend cartoon madness with brutal realism (the episode that has the three boys executing their usual array of sociopathic capers against a background of their parents acknowledging that Hal loves Lois more than Lois loves him and that that's all right, that's how their life together works, is a freaking masterpiece) and stuffed with more verbal and visual gags per minute than most comedies see in a whole season.

Perhaps, as time's winged chariot increasingly threatens not just to overtake me but mangle me under its steel-rimmed wheels as it does so, I now appreciate the youthful energy of the three leads that powers the whole thing along. Perhaps I have become more astute and analytical, able to see beyond the initial hyperkinetic fizz to the solid crafting underneath. Or perhaps the intervening years of TV-watching have simply taught me the meaning of true crap and I now cling on to any splinter of quality work with nerveless fingers and weeping relief. Whatever the reason, I can only urge anyone who also dwelt in my black pit of *MitM* ignorance to emerge, with me, blinking, into the light.

11 SEPTEMBER 2007

Perfect plotted preposterousness

The boys are back in town! The boys are back in town! Yes, the long, lonely Monday nights are over, for the third series of *Prison Break* has begun on Sky One. Lincoln 'hewn from the living rock' Burrows is a free man, but his brother Michael 'noble three-quarter profile limned in golden dust' Scofield is once again in prison. Which, continuing in the tradition of grand excess which the first two series so joyfully pursued, is not just a Panamanian prison, but Sona – the worst Panamanian prison in the history of Panamanian prisons. No guards – they fled – but a veritable surfeit of death-brawls, cannibalism, torture and energetic plumbing of the depths of human depravity. It makes Oz look like a kitten sanctuary. Even Michael – and only those who have watched enraptured by his unyielding poker face no matter what barkingly insane and bloodspattered situation unfolds before him will appreciate the magnitude of what I am about to say – seems perturbed.

Perhaps the most disturbing sight is Bellick cleaning the latrines in a pac-a-mac, and maybe dimly beginning to comprehend the notion of karmic retribution. Or maybe it's the anonymous prisoner incarcerated in the very worst bit of the bowels of the very worst Panamanian prison in history. Or another one getting perforated by machine-gun fire during an escape attempt. Or maybe it's T-Bag – already establishing himself as a gangmaster's lackey, doubtless as a prelude to presiding over the prison himself, like a drooling dingo over a playpen of babies.

With all this going on, we hardly care that Sara 'Doctor Boring' Tancredi is missing. But Michael does – because he loves her and wants to have lots of facially immobile children with her. Still, the American embassy has promised to get him out – but wait! Linc gets word that Sara and LJ are being held hostage. Michael must break Anonymous Prisoner out of Sona in order to save them.

Another 24 hours of perfectly plotted preposterousness are set in motion. Boys, it's good to have you back.

25 SEPTEMBER 2007

Who's afraid of the big bad Robin?

I tuned in to *Robin's Nest* on Paramount Comedy in a spirit of curiosity and trepidation, for it forms the basis of one of my darkest childhood memories. Whenever restaurateur Robin (Richard O'Sullivan) appeared on screen I would scream with horror ('Hair that poufs out! Hair that poufs out!') and yet remain glued to the screen, unwillingly mesmerised by my own revulsion. Looking back, I see that this was at least valuable training for the *Big Brother* years to come, but at the time I felt profoundly confused and betrayed by my bifurcating brain.

But in the intervening 28 years something has changed. Richard O'Sullivan now holds no fear for me. The hair still poufs out, but I accept that this is more to do with noxious 70s fashion than any intrinsic evil in the man. What I experienced as a tendency to appear silently from nowhere on screen like an aproned ghoul has transmuted into an amiable presence engaged in charming ensemble acting. And the lopsided grin has become beguiling, rather than a sign of a slipping mask revealing the malevolent beast beneath.

Demons safely banished, the programme stands revealed as rather delightful – funny, well written and delicately, naturally played. This is a revelation to anyone raised on 80s offerings such as *The Upper Hand*, whose witless shenanigans between ex-footballer Charlie

Lummoxprole and Caroline Yuppie-Adexec (a woman in constant fear of being out-acted by her extravagant blousons) follow immediately afterwards. My generation never knew that the 'com' of 'sitcom' was supposed to be short for something.

There are carpers who complain that TV is bad for children when, in fact, it proffers innumerable valuable lessons. Here, the chance conjunction of two programmes will do more to disabuse youngsters of the notion that human history is a story of linear progression than a thousand school books could. Just as long as they are old enough to cope with Nest hair, of course.

8 JANUARY 2008

TV shopping? How could I resist?

I habitually shop online, while muttering fervent prayers of gratitude that I do not have to face marauding crowds, buckling public transport systems and the panicky, exhausting buzzing round thousands of square feet of retail space in order to discover that there is nothing therein to pique the interest. So I am more than willing to give shopping-by-television a try. An array of suitably stylish homewares will doubtless be paraded before me, and all I will have to do is wave a credit card and command them to be delivered to my door. What could go wrong?

9am

Behold – celery! Still in pristine condition after 21 days, thanks to the amazing Keep It Fresh Farmer's Secret Bags (£19.95 a set of 50, from TVShop), which use the same technology as supermarket suppliers do to stop their produce ripening. I am wary of bringing industrial agricultural techniques into my home, but a succession of smiling women attest to the bags' ability to change lives. Over on Pitch TV, a Lancastrian girl is equally thrilled with her Light 'n' Easy Dual-Action Travel Iron. 'Look at it opening up bust darts, hem work and semi-pleating!' she says. Turns out Victoria Wood doesn't make it up, she just sits at home with a notebook, transcribing. 'You can iron your duvet cover on the duvet!' Lancashire Lass beams. 'If I ever dream of ironing my duvet cover on holiday, I will favour your product above all others,' I reply. I am beaming, too. I don't know why.

11am

Price-Drop TV is instantly, savagely addictive. The goods – eight VAX 1400W Steam Sticks with swivel joint heads, perhaps, or 30 gold St Christopher pendants – are introduced at one price, which falls while people ring in and 'snatch' them at the price they want. Everyone gets it at the lowest selling price but, of course, those who hold off too long will be for ever VAXless and blingless, a fate, the presenters of these reverse auctions give us to understand, too dreadful to contemplate. 'There's always a mad drop,' says the presenter as interest in the remaining 17 pendants seems to be dwindling. 'And I get so many disappointed buyers.' The pendants vanish. I am, I notice, no longer beaming.

12.30pm

On Best Direct, the presenters are synchronising their products to lunch-time hunger pangs. 'Are you fed up with having to keep going to the oven to see if your food is ready?' asks one, before producing a see-through cooker that will save us from the burden. 'Do you hate the hassle of waiting for your food to thaw?' asks another, a question that illustrates neatly the twin obsessions of all shopping channels – saving time and labour. And by that I mean minuscule amounts of time, spent on activities you never, in your laziest, most imbecilic and/or drug-addled moments, considered defining as labour – such as taking food out of a freezer and leaving it on a draining board overnight.

The Nu-Wave Oven can cook a pork roast from frozen in eight picoseconds. 'Doesn't seem right, does it?' says the irony-free presenter. On Simply Ideas someone asks whether I'm 'tired of waiting for a big pot of water to boil and breaking the spaghetti to fit it in?' in order to flog a cylindrical plastic thing called a Pasta Express. On TVWarehouse, a man is demonstrating the electric Go Duster on venetian blinds. 'And it collects the allergens in the air!' he proclaims. It dusts air? I may have to write to my MP.

5pm

These presenters are a breed apart. Their ability to limn the advantages of the Nicer Dicer/My Rotisserie/Mira Bella mop with undimmed zeal for hours on end suggests either near-genius acting ability or a very specific form of sociopathology. Demonstrating a garden hedge/edge trimmer, one woman screams, 'It telescopes right out! That is ingenious! So light it barely feels like I'm holding anything!' Somebody should call her family! Or her GP!

There is a reassuringly down-to-earth Glaswegian man on Brand Collection TV, demonstrating a paint roller. 'You put your emulsion in here,' he says, putting his emulsion in there. 'You can paint Anaglypta, boss, textured wallpaper. It doesnae drip.' He does. It doesn't. His cool confidence is undermined somewhat by testimonials from overheated users of the system, who say things such as, 'I was born with no head, yet with this roller I have been able to fulfil a lifelong dream and recreate the Sistine Chapel on my Artex ceiling in Epsom.' Never mind. It was nice while it lasted.

7.30pm

As I flick ever faster through the channels, I gradually change from a rational member of society – gaping with unconcealed horror at a world in which you can buy burnished oriental design slippers with anti-bacterial lining (Ideal World pick of the day) – to a slavering heap of unslaked desires. I want everything. The Masai warrior statues unaccountably plummeting in price on Bid TV. The Bosun Steam Cleaner that eradicates bedbugs. Huggable Hangers – 'Never be embarrassed by shoulder bumps again!' By the time I spy the Joan Rivers Holly Jolly Bee Pin on QVC at 4am, the only question that forms in my mind is whether one will be enough.

5am

I must have the Fresh Air Globe. 'You can't control the air outside but you can inside!' exhorts Mr Presenter. I nod obediently. The Globe will save me from a gasping, choking death and, with its 13 LED light display patterns, entertain me at the same time. And then he says, 'The water in the globe literally scrubs the air clean!' Water scrubs the air clean? I suddenly emerge from my covetous frenzy. What, it's not enough to have something that dusts the air, I have to scrub it, too? I suddenly see myself careering round the house throwing fistfuls of liquid into every room, a once sound mind irrevocably damaged by the hard sell. It is time, I realise, to retire to my bed. My unironed, bedbug-ridden bed, in my dusty, badly painted bedroom, with its unscrubbed air. It may not be much of a life in the eyes of the shopping channels, but somehow, I suspect, I will struggle on. And into the high street once more.

12 JANUARY 2008

The show that wouldn't die

The popularity of *3rd Rock from the Sun* (Sci-Fi UK) bemused many: was the concept of aliens living among earthlings, thereby generating a series of riotous confusions really that good? But its continual escape from the usually swingeing network bosses' axe even after that popularity began to wane was truly perplexing.

It perplexed because the only possible explanation was that the bosses were human after all and had fallen, like the rest of us fans, for the show's irrepressible joie de vivre. The show offers a unique opportunity to watch a quartet of actors, each vying to be dafter than the other. If there is a happier sight than that, I don't know what it is.

John Lithgow, undoubtedly, started it. I cannot possibly describe the ebullience of his performance as Dick, the high commander, with only the paltry resources of the written word at my disposal. You must watch. Someone once said that the definition of jazz was seeing how far out you could go and still get back. Watching Lithgow is like that. He can take 10 minutes to catch sight of himself in a mirror and announce with a fervour more generally associated with Messianic arrivals, 'I'm G-O-O-O-RGEOUS!' The others follow his lead. Sally has the body of a supermodel but throws it around like a prizefighter. Tommy is an alien genius trapped and fizzing with frustration in the body of a child. And Harry is a wizened sprite who periodically goes into spasm either when used as a transmitter by their ruler The Big Giant Head or when Mrs Dubcek's lascivious daughter walks by. Always funny. Always.

It was known at the time as the show that wouldn't die. Treat yourself to a dose of its charms at the end of a big bad day and you will understand why not even the most brutal network executive could bring himself to kill it. It is rarely shown in the US now, but thanks to syndication its pure heart and shining silliness will live on, somewhere, for ever. Gorgeous.

29 JANUARY 2008

Goodbye Grange Hill

For anyone over 25, the news that *Grange Hill* is to be axed after a final series is no occasion for sorrow. We had, after all, by far the best of it.

It had the virtue of novelty when it began in 1978. The famous sausage flying through the air in the cartoon strip that formed the opening credits was a symbol as much of the anarchy of the producer and scripts as it was of the school.

For the first time on children's television, there were normal kids with normal accents talking about normal things on screen, instead of strange, stage-schooled creatures who sounded as if they had time-travelled in from the Edwardian home counties and could only talk about their struggles with misplaced postal orders.

The original lineup comprised: Tucker Jenkins, with his cheeky, pallid face and straggly bowl-cut hair, the distilled essence of late 70s boyhood; Cathy Hargreaves with her lovely hair and school-girl crush on Sooty Sutcliffe; fat, ginger Pogo Patterson, whose general air of haplessness somehow enabled him to escape bullies and whose extraordinary adenoids should, looking back, really have got separate billing; Trisha Yates and her battle to make high heels and nail varnish de rigueur for double geography; and, of course, Suzanne Ross, the acne-spattered poster girl for hormonal teenage fury.

You watched it in the same way that you read Bernard Ashley's books – similarly popular at the time – not so much for entertainment as for reassurance that the maelstrom of cliquery, bullying, aggression, adolescent angst into which you plunged at 10 to nine every morning and from which you emerged tattered and bleeding at 3.30pm was everybody's everyday experience. You were not the unlucky victim of a particularly malevolent god. You were simply a comprehensive school pupil. It was, in many ways, a relief.

The complaints and controversies it caused among parents and certain sections of the media were as misguided and idiotic as all such frenzies are. The guardians of the nation's juvenile morals professed to be concerned that scenes of kids misbehaving and talking back to teachers would lead to copycat behaviour. It is more likely that they feared the popularity of the programme would lead to an epidemic of glottal stopping that could spread even to private schools.

In the 1980s, the programme moved into its golden age. It dealt with the big issues but never forgot the small. When Claire Scott had the temerity to 'revamp' herself (the word 'makeover' had not been invented) and turned up at school with flicked hair, her friends unleashed the jackal-like instincts that every teenage girl knew to lie in the breast of every adolescent girl and (only just metaphorically) tore her to pieces for her boldness. It was as fine an illustration of both feminine savagery and the rigidly enforced pecking order of school as you could hope to see.

But it was the big issues that made *Grange Hill's* name. In the 90s it gradually became lamentably issue-led, crowbarring in stories to fit the day's headlines. But in the golden 80s they arose from characters we cared about and were allowed to unfold naturally over time.

It didn't 'do' bullying in a week and a half. Chubby Roland Browning was tormented for years by our generation's Flashman, Gripper Stebson. Racism popped up as casually as it does in real life, and frequently with as little satisfactory resolution – black pupil Benny Green was called Chalky by a visiting builder at the school. His friends rallied round, wanting to complain, but Benny shrugged it off resignedly, knowing there would be bigger battles to fight. Matthew Pearson mutely embodied the horror of child abuse as he struggled to get changed for gym without revealing his bruises to his classmates.

Primarily, of course, the decade is remembered for the Zammo years. Zammo Maguire's two-series slide into heroin addiction gripped a generation of children as the question of who shot JR had gripped their parents a few years earlier, and spawned an anti-drugs slogan and Top 10 single. It may not have kept us all off drugs, but to hear in your head the ghostly strains of Lee Macdonald and co singing 'Just say no! NO! Just say no! Say no!' whenever you go near them has at least managed to dim the attraction slightly.

Remembering the heyday of *Grange Hill* yesterday, Todd Carty, who played Tucker, said: 'The kids took to it, they ran home and talked about it. *Grange Hill* is a British institution. It may be a children's drama but it's up there with *Coronation Street*.' We did, and it was. Kids today really don't know what they're missing.

7 FEBRUARY 2008

Do you think the smell of dog is helping to sell your house?

Ah, Ann Maurice – how do I love thee? Let me count the ways. I love thee for thy plangent Detroit tones. I love thee for thy laser eye and pikestaff hair. But most of all, I love thee for thy ability to open an episode of *House Doctor* (UKTV Style) with the words: 'This house in Derby has been on the market for nine months. And why? Because it's horrible.'

That's what this country needs more of: straight talkers. We used to breed our own, and indeed hardy survivors of that bygone fecund age can be seen dotted around the place – Rita Fairclough in The Kabin, the unfairly maligned Gordon Ramsay, the much more fairly but still maligned Simon Cowell, for example – but we now need to supplement the native stock with imports.

Although Maurice has now been shunted to the far reaches of UKTV Style instead of bestriding Five like the magnolia-friendly colossus she once was (we skip over the debacle that is *Interior Rivalry*, which forced Maurice the Magnificent to pretend an interest in which team of competing decorators can best learn her design dicta), her power remains undimmed.

After the hyperactive, overblown, overheated, indiscriminate enthusiasm with which most other shows and presenters are infused, who can fail to thrill to Ann's look of disgust as she steps through the door of some unfortunate pet-lover's home. The nose wrinkles. The brow creases. 'You have . . .' she says in tones of infinite, glorious contempt, 'dogs. Don't you?' They do. They are unapologetic about their stinky house. Ann turns on one fastidious heel. 'Do you think,' she asks, 'that everybody loves the smell of your dogs? Do you think the smell of animal is helping to sell your house?' Their eyes cannot meet her steely gaze for long. They drop. The shoulders slump. Into once unwilling hands paintbrushes dripping with inoffensive pigments are pushed. They belong to Ann now, and she will remake them into better homeowners. For a better tomorrow.

11 MARCH 2008

Peter Andre is growing on me

I am, against almost incalculable odds, starting to love Peter Andre. With every passing moment of *Katie & Peter: The Next Chapter* (ITV2), the devotion of the permatanned 80s pop star to his barracuda wife, former glamour girl Katie 'Jordan' Price, becomes more impressive.

To be sure, it is a very modern form of uxoriousness. He will generally begin with a detailed retelling of one of their early moments of carnal delight. 'I could have done anything to her,' he recalls fondly in the bathroom of the hotel where she first performed an oral service upon him. 'But she was pissed so – out of respect – I didn't.' Undying romantic that he is, the potency of this memory is enough to move him still. Or, as his wife points out to the cameraman, 'Look – he's got blood!' Peter decorously shields his erection and goes to kiss his beloved. 'Don't rub up against me like a desperate dog!' she warns. He gazes adoringly at her instead.

When they revisit the Australian jungle where his heart and her heart facsimile first began to beat as one four years ago, his face is wreathed in smiles. 'I'm loving her all over again!' he explains to the cameraman, who by this time is presumably on tablets. He turns with beguilingly puppyish if sweaty enthusiasm to his inflated inamorata. 'Yeah,' she replies boredly. 'I'm not emotional or nothing, but it's, like, good to come back.' To Andre, this counts as encouragement. 'Kiss!' he demands. 'Wipe your top lip then,' she fires back. He does. She lets him kiss her fleetingly. In the car on the way home she sullenly ignores him, apparently because he once had coffee with a girl after Katie decided to merge brands with – sorry, marry – him. 'She hates me!' Pete says rapturously, leaning against her famous chest. 'Since the day we met!'

I think we should clutch the man to our collective bosom, diminutive though it might be compared with his current position, and tell him we'll be waiting for him if and when he eventually emerges from the brutal Jordan jungle and into the light.

8 APRIL 2008

Dempsey & Makepeace's special relationship

The term 'unresolved sexual tension' did not, I believe, become common currency until *The X-Files* fans took to the internet and started disseminating the term during impassioned discussions of the Mulder-Scully bond. But the phrase should have been coined years before, for another very special couple: *Dempsey & Makepeace* (ITV3).

It is 1985. He is a dispossessed New York cop sent to London for his own safety after uncovering corruption in the PD. He speaks in pungent Brooklynese and was born with a .38 in his hand. Despite spending much of the time clad in a denim jacket with an unmistakably quilted collar, he manages to remain devilishly attractive, especially when leaping off low concrete buildings in order to beat the crap out of fleeing baddies in beige suits.

She is Lady Harriet, a Cambridge graduate born with a silver trust fund in her mouth. Despite spending much of the time clad in quintessentially 80s trouser suits and copious amounts of savagely blue eyeshadow, she is en ebbsolute knock-ite.

Together Dempsey and Makepeace solve dastardly, semi-comprehensible crimes set in the grimy metropolis rather than a shiny tax haven but nevertheless obviously, to the trained eye, ripped off from Bergerac. Fraudulent antiques dealers, jewel thieves, hostages in frosted lipstick and batwing sweaters come and go, but our hero and heroine never abandon their foreplay-through-wisecracking. She tells him to stop murdering the English lengwidge. He calls her a walkin' rule book. They so want to Do It. But they Don't.

Not a moment of snoggage occurs, ever. I think something might happen in the final episode but I missed it first time round and we haven't reached the end of season three yet. But off-screen, of course, as any fule kno, Dempsey and Makepeace fell in love – and they are still married today! Since 1989! In actors' years, they're coming up for their ruby wedding anniversary. Isn't that great? This may be the one beautiful thing to emerge from the 80s.

20 MAY 2008

Carol's out for the count

So, after 26 years, 4,750 episodes, 320,000 letters on the board and 11,200 sums solved, there are to be no more consonants for Carol Vorderman. The first woman to appear on the new Channel 4 – as a girl who did maths! Oh, edgy, heady times! – is stepping down from her role as co-host of *Countdown*. She is, of course, beloved of the show's fans. If they had their way, her departure – thought to have been prompted by Channel 4's requirement that she take a pay cut from an estimated £800,000 a year down to £100,000 – would be marked by a national day of mourning and her reign marked by a series of bronze statues in overly snug Roland Mouret dresses. And indeed, some kind of commemoration of her stoic endurance of Richard Whiteley's painful puns and her development of a unique form of asexual flirtatiousness with which to treat him does seem overdue.

She has not quite, however, gained national-treasure status with the wider public. Perhaps it was the slight air of desperation that accompanied the makeover years as she sought to reinvent herself as a non-nerd that put people off. Perhaps it was the low-level disappointment that she chose, 10 years ago, to parlay her intelligence into a range of diet books, tapes and DVDs. Or perhaps it was the high-level disappointment at her decision to front a series of advertisements for debt-consolidation company FirstPlus (collateralise your loans – lower interest rates now for possible homelessness later!), which she was urged by money-education charity Credit Action and others to stop endorsing.

But it is for more than a quarter of a century of sterling teatime service to the nation's numeracy and literacy that we should remember her. Farewell, Carol. Neither consonants nor *Countdown* will be the same without you. We'll see about the collateralised loans.

11 DECEMBER 2008

Surviving Nigella

Now that it has moved so gloriously beyond parody, there is only one way to get through *Nigella's Christmas Kitchen* (BBC2). First, tape the programme (unless you have Sky+, in which case, congratulations, your life just got a little bit easier). Then line up all the bottles of alcohol you have in the house. Include mouthwash and aerosol deodorant in this definition. Decant everything into a big jug. Add as many straws as you have friends, and invite your friends round to play a festive drinking game. The rules are simple. Whenever Nigella starts to reach a semantic climax, pause the programme and take guesses from around the sofa as to what she is going to say next. The one who gets closest to Nigella's actual conclusion wins. The rest drink. You will all be wrecked by the end of the first minute. Round one: Nigella makes lychini – lychee martinis to you, scruffbag. They are one part vodka, one part white rum and two parts creme de lychee. No, me neither, but ours is not to reason why, or how. Ours is just to watch and die a little. Then comes the final touch. 'I like to garnish it with . . .' 'Fairy dust!' shrieks someone. 'Hope!' cries another. 'Other women's tears,' shouts another. 'Money!' It's actually a canned lychee. Nigella simply can't get self-peeled ones to retain their shape. We drink.

Next, star-topped mince pies. Make your own pastry and fill with home-made mincemeat – brown sugar ('So treacly smelling!' gasps Nigella), cranberries ('Plumptious beauties! . . . Their gleaming redness slicked in dark, spiced syrup!') and dried fruit ('They will glisten like garnets later') mixed into 'a beaded paste', bake them all and then – 'What I find makes my life easier is . . .' 'Money!' 'Cleavage!' 'Merchandising opportunities!' 'Money!' 'No – more money!' 'Slaves!'. Alas, we are all wrong. It is putting half her mince pies in the freezer so she always has a ready supply. We find this disappointingly prosaic ('It's not even a freezer filled with money,' someone notes, regretfully), and drink extra.

Then she is on to the main course – a lamb, date and pomegranate tagine that she likes to 'festoon and adorn with . . .' 'Bear claws?' 'Money!' 'Narnian jewels!' No. A tangle of red onion, scarlet beads of pomegranate and flecks of coriander. The jug is drained. Doesn't bother me. I started snorting neat deodorant 15 minutes ago. A final butterscotch, biscuit and coffee ice-cream pie and she's done. And so are we.

16 DECEMBER 2008

Christmas at the Mangans'

Some families, of course, push their chairs back from a table strewn with turkey wishbones and cracker trimmings, and head off for a restorative walk. Off they go, breathing deep lungfuls of crystalline, wintry air before returning home for a quick game of charades and a snifter of brandy before bed.

It must be awful. In the Mangan household, the countdown to Christmas never begins with the first day of advent, but with the advent of the two-week edition of the *Radio Times*. That, and the annual episode of *Blue Peter*, the one that took you through the making of the four-candle holder out of two wire coat hangers and some tinsel. We never made the holder, of course.

From an early age, we understood and embraced the passivity that lies at the heart of all happy television viewing. We still insisted on watching it every year. I was lucky enough to come of age in the 70s; the Stanley Baxter era was passing and the UK had invented *The Morecambe & Wise Show*. Finally, we could look the US proudly in the eye: they had had Perry Como and his Christmas specials for 15 years, as well as annual spectaculars starring Judy Garland, Bing Crosby and Frank Sinatra.

In fairness to this septic isle, we did also have the Queen's speech, but this has not been considered a riveting piece of television since the generation who found entertainment in *The Potter's Wheel* grew up. (This was the same generation that glued its ears to *Educating Archie*, Peter Brough's ventriloquist act on the radio, and whose opinions therefore should, as a general rule, be tossed lightly aside.)

It was Eric and Ernie who truly united the nation at Christmas time, between 1969 and 1980. Famously, they peaked in 1977, when their show was seen by 28 million people, half the country's population – a record for a light entertainment programme that is likely to remain unbroken as we edge ever closer to the day when there is a digital channel per person. Repeats have made it impossible for me to tell which Eric and Ernie I saw first and when. Was it the dancing breakfast sketch? Shirley Bassey and the boot? Hannah Gordon singing *Windmills of My Mind* while the two men were buffeted by a gale in the background? I only know that my father felt he had successfully discharged one of the most important duties of parenthood when his two daughters could recite the Andre Previn sketch from memory.

The 80s brought smaller delights: *'Allo 'Allo!* and *Duty Free* specials, which we watched only on alternate years, when my maternal grandmother came to stay. I have never before or since seen a person of discernible, proven intelligence laugh so much at a fallen Madonna wiz ze beeg boobies. During the Christmases that my paternal grandmother spent with us, we watched less television. Not because she was any more sophisticated, but because she provided so much in the way of alternative entertainment, by wandering round the house burning holes in her corset where her fag ash dropped and farting at every third step. It was really only *Top of the Pops* and *Only Fools and Horses* that could compete with that.

The biggest Christmas telly event of the 80s was the 1986 Christmas Day episode of *EastEnders*, in which the world's unlikeliest womaniser – balding, necrotic Den Watts – served divorce papers on his long-suffering kohl-rimmed wife Angie, after learning that she had faked a terminal disease in order to try to keep hold of her beloved. Thirty million people tuned in for the showdown; Boxing Day sales of batwing sweaters and glottal stops went through the roof.

I saw not a second of it. My parents are dispossessed northerners and Mangan Towers has always been a citadel of *Coronation Street* fandom. My mother remembers the trauma of Ena Sharples choking on the sixpence in her 1961 Christmas pudding. I remember the bittersweet Yuletide send-off of Hilda Ogden in 1987, as, in a voice as thin and spare as her bird-like frame, she led the Rovers in a quavering rendition of *Wish Me Luck As You Wave Me Goodbye*. Last year, the air was riven with the sound of Fiz's heart breaking, as she discovered her boyfriend John had been having it away with Rosie Webster. Alas, thanks to the continuing cultural dominance of the wretched south, we are left to mourn and celebrate these Christmas storylines largely among ourselves, while Den and Ange's 80s hammery continues to be held up as the yardstick by which all other seasonal soaps are measured. (That said, last year's discovery by the Branning family, via home-made DVD, that Daddy Branning had been sleeping with his son's fiancée was worth waiting for.)

In the 90s, terrestrial programming's flight from quality began in earnest, particularly at Christmas. The distance from the golden age of Morecambe and Wise was underlined by their traditional annual repeats, embedded as they were amid Frost, Poirot, *Doc*

Martin and *Midsomer Murders* – as well as films that had been seen on Sky or DVD months (and many times) before. While I hesitate to suggest a direct link – I like to hope it had as much to do with me and my sister going to university, and our beloved grandmas both shuffling/farting off this mortal coil – the Mangan family Christmas suffered its most tense decade yet. There was only one programme that retained the power to draw us all together, and that was *Noel's Christmas Presents*. This was where Noel Edmonds gave holidays, or special treats, or equipment, to people who had borne impossible burdens, or been selflessly devoted to their disabled sister/mother/best friend for yet another year, and everything became briefly splendid.

Now, my dad has always been a crier. During the festive season, his eyes are barely dry long enough for him to cook dinner. Very difficult. Sometimes we have to eat extra crisps. He cries at the immaculate succession of notes soaring from the angelic choir in *Carols from King's*. He cries at babies being born during extended Christmas episodes of *Casualty*. During the annual showing of *The Railway Children*, we have to start the chain-gang passing of tissues to him 20 minutes before the end, because he knows what's coming.

The rest of us are a constitutionally dry-eyed lot. When we blink it sounds like someone's planing a door frame. But even I make an exception for *Noel's Christmas Presents*, because it's genius. He gives out the perfect presents to the perfect people. And although you might assume that it was the most nauseating piece of schmaltz, you would be wrong. The genius of it is that it is actually terribly British. Noel just gets in, gives the presents, lets the recipients well up and stammer their thanks, and gets out.

Last weekend, after a 10-year hiatus, it was back. By the time he had finished, our sofa was awash with tears and we all loved each other again. The Mangan household is thoroughly, if temporarily, purged of all negative emotion, and set fair for a smooth, if slightly soggy, Christmas.

DECEMBER 24 2008

F-A-B

Thunderbirds are GO! Or, to be strictly accurate, *Thunderbirds* are BACK! Their springy, stringy adventures are being reshown on the Sci-Fi channel and my, what a fascinating experience it is to watch them now.

Obviously, as a child first viewing them in the 80s, 20 years after they were made, I cared only that Miss Penelope's charity show went ahead without being interrupted by space pirates, or that the archaeologists trapped in the Pyramid of Something-Egyptian-Sounding were saved by International Rescue, or that the explosive bracelet (can I be remembering this right?) could be defused.

Now, it is possible to marvel in quite a new way at the wonder of this jewel of mid-century modernism at its most homely. To gaze in fascination at Gerry and Sylvia Anderson's Hertfordshire vision of future America, in which the coolest men in the room would be marked by wearing paper hats that would actually be the preserve of fast-food slingers 10 years on, hydraulics would still be the main powering mechanism in the new automated lifestyle, travelators would be the last word in hi-tech and even preparing to launch into space from your secret island hideaway would be accompanied not by multitudinous urgent instructions over tannoys and headphones but some light, ambient music from the 21st century's answer to Burt Bacharach.

Then there's the relationship between Lady P and her simian working-class chauffeur Parker. Why did we bother taking sociology A-levels and degrees when all you needed to know about the class system and human relationships was enshrined in 50-minute gobbets of supermarionation every week?

On the other hand, my real love was *Joe 90*. This unjustly neglected Anderson product has not, to the best of my knowledge, been recently reshown on TV, but this is probably all to the good. It has already left me with a fatal weakness for men in glasses, yet in real life it turns out they are almost never able to fly jetfighters or pilot transatlantic hoverliners. At least the Tracey family only got the hats wrong.

30 DECEMBER 2008

The death of 'ER'

There is just time to gather round the screen and pay your last respects. After 15 years and more MIs, EKGs, tox screens and central line insertions than it is possible to count, the nonpareil of medical dramas is about to leave us. It will be a sad parting.

In the early 90s, the cop show was king. *Hill Street Blues* had captured the nation's attention in the previous decade and spawned countless imitators. The best of them – *Homicide: Life On the Street* and *NYPD Blue* – dominated the networks' schedules, imaginations and commissions. The medical drama was all but dead.

Then on September 1994 the two-hour pilot episode of *ER*, written by blockbuster novelist and former medical student Michael Crichton (who died last year) and co-produced by Steven Spielberg's company Amblin, hit our screens and suddenly, like a mighty defibrillator, reanimated the genre's moribund form. It won eight Emmys in its first year and quickly became the most successful hospital drama in the world, both in terms of viewing figures and in setting new narrative and visual standards for television drama.

ER took the multiple storylines and kinetic camerawork on *Homicide* and *NYPD Blue*, shot them full of steroids, adrenaline, amphetamines and sent them whizzing exhilaratingly past us on a weekly basis. The thumping music segued into the percussive bleeps, clangs and clashes of the modern American emergency room. Sirens wailed and ambulances disgorged their bleeding, broken cargo into the care of the waiting staff of the teaching hospital in Chicago. Medical equipment bristled in the background and in the foreground Steadicams tracked trollies carrying at least a dozen gunshot/stroke/heart attack/assault/cancer victims per episode down corridors, in and out of operating rooms as doctors shouted impenetrable diagnoses and instruction over them. An hour of *ER* contained 700-800 edits – twice as many as a standard hour of television – and was described by one critic at the time as 'channel surfing without pressing the button'. It was dizzying, disorientating and utterly addictive from the off.

Apart from the unprecedented speed with which scenes whipped past (even *NYPD Blue* suddenly started looking like *The Potter's Wheel*), the unapologetic embrace of jargon commanded most of the attention at first. Gradually, hapless lay viewers such as me began to decipher the code, just as we had slowly got to grips with Detective Sipowicz's 'perps' and 'skells'. A 'perfed appy' was a burst appendix. The 'PID shuffle' was the unique gait of a prostitute with another bout of pelvic inflammatory disease. Although I'm not going to tell you how long it took me to realise that what I was hearing as 'pull socks' was not a command to denude a patient's extremities but 'pulse ox', a request for a device to measure a patient's blood oxygen levels and a much more sensible option in the circumstances.

Now, after 14 series, I dare say the committed *ER* fan could walk into any county hospital and confidently order a tox screen, CBC, chem-7 and cross-table C-spine with the best of them, prepare a thoracotomy tray and even, if pressed, remedy a pleural infusion for at least as long as it takes to get the unfortunate infusee up to the OR. Actor Alex Kingston, who played the (terribly) British surgeon Elizabeth Corday for eight seasons of the show and is returning for the 15th, recalls that when she first started she did not know what she was saying. 'Not at all. But when you hear it daily and have real doctors on hand to make sense of your lines and procedures for you, it gets easier. Quite often you could kid yourself you were doing it properly, especially as everything on set was real. All the machines worked. The only difference was that with blood that was actually sugar water and K-Y Jelly you didn't have that amazing iron-y smell in the operating theatre.'

So you had the language, the machines, the documentary feel of the camerawork – but was ER truly realistic? Perhaps the honest answer is: it was as realistic as a drama aiming at widespread popularity can be. I watched it while I was flat-sharing with a group of medical students who used to laugh hysterically as a lifetime's worth of rare and wonderful diseases were presented to a doctor in a single hour. The lectures, conferences and the exam-cramming that junior doctors have to fit in went largely unrecorded.

More fundamental and uncomfortable truths were undoubtedly glossed over, most notably that of payment for the state-of-the-art treatment all patients receive. As Anne Karpf, author of *Doctoring the Media*, points out, the first question patients are asked in a US hospital is 'Are you insured?' and if the answer – as it frequently is – is no they are unceremoniously shown the door. 'It's not exactly social realism,' says Karpf. 'You wouldn't use it as a primer of what's going on in medical care, but you can't have it be warts-and-all and still work as a drama. When you think how the insurance industry has completely skewed healthcare provision and is the major obstacle to providing an American NHS and means that most of the US population is either crippled by their premiums or living in dread of falling ill – well, how many episodes can you get out of that?'

Nevertheless, like our own *Casualty* at its inception, ER did frequently protest against the bureaucrats, the budget cuts and compromises forced upon doctors and uninsured patients by an unjust system. This, combined with its frenetic energy, was enough to make it seem like cinéma vérité compared to what had come before.

ER should have come with a health warning to anyone raised on *Dr Kildare* and *Marcus Welby MD* (or over here, *Dr Finlay's Casebook* and *Emergency Ward 10*). Gone were the selfless, idealised and idealistic secular saints in white coats. Here instead were doctors who were – whisper it – human and fallible, whose personal lives were usually a mess and frequently intruded on the professional and vice versa. Out went Kildare's languorously holistic approach. In came the modern urban medical mantra 'Treat 'em and street 'em'. Instead of one all-seeing, all-knowing doctor we had a decidedly non-omniscient team who seemed most of the time to be struggling to keep their heads above water, as the never-ending tide of sick and injured, drink-, drugs- and gang-battered humanity threatened to drown them.

Some of the iconography endured, of course, otherwise we would all have become very depressed very quickly. Among the original *ER* cast members, John Carter (Noah Wyle) embodied Kildarean idealism, but he looked in vain for a Dr Gillespie-ish mentor in the fearsome Peter Benton, his fantastically irascible supervisor played by Eriq La Salle ('a pussycat' in real life, Kingston assures us). Dr Mark Greene (Anthony Edwards) was the moral centre of the show – an essentially decent man, but unlike Welby (a physician who experienced just one patient death in 50 episodes, for which he was not culpable), human; capable of making mistakes, dogged by debt, divorce and eventually disease, dying of a brain tumour in season eight. (The infallible Welby and Kildare, we must assume, simply ascended bodily into heaven.) Dr Susan Lewis (Sherry Stringfield) was another good doctor, but broke with tradition by being a woman.

Then, of course, there was Dr Doug Ross. He was – and people do tend to forget this, so I'm going to put it bluntly – a total shitbag, but he had two redeeming features. First, he was a talented paediatrician who would always go the extra mile for his tiny charges, and second, he was a talented paediatrician played by George Clooney; basically the man-holding-baby Athena poster made flesh. For this, the world forgave him for driving lovely Nurse Hathaway to attempted suicide in the opening episode (she was supposed to die, but the producers decided she was too good an actor not to put through the mill a few dozen times more, so they resuscitated the role) and innumerable idiocies thereafter. He left in season five but the show survived his loss and into the void stepped Noah Wyle as Carter, whose storyline about his painful, faltering physical and psychological recovery after being stabbed by a patient was a revelation. It unfolded over several series, and in the course of it both Carter and Wyle were transformed from callow youths to proven professionals, a useful reminder to everyone perhaps in these increasingly base and reality-TV obsessed times of the kind of rewards that can only be reaped by commitment to long-running dramas.

ER was embraced by the public on a grand scale because it was a show that recognised that we are an assertive, informed, cynical, brutal and brutalised society that is not ready to accept authority – with or without a white coat – unquestioningly. So it gave us both a credible collection not of Good Doctors, but good-enough doctors, who succeeded more often than they failed, but failed nevertheless. Through the 'frequent flyer' patients – the drunks, addicts and chronically ill who return time and again to the emergency room – and the halt and the lame gloriously restored to health it gave us a view of modern medicine that recognised some of its limitations but also revelled in its possibilities. Our faith was tested but not destroyed.

Now it is almost over. After 15 years, some of the bloom is inevitably off the rose. Its pacing and style is still there, but now looks less novel since it was adopted and absorbed by almost every television genre as soon as their creators could get hold of a Steadicam; such is the price of innovation. Moreover, as the seasons have worn on, the original central cast left and a group of shorter-term characters have replaced them, the soap aspect of the show has come to greater prominence. The rage against the machine has been subsumed in the lather of concerns about the doctors' complex personal lives. What interest in wider and political considerations there was has dissipated the further it has moved in time from Dr Crichton's original experiences. The underlying acknowledgement that modern medicine is frequently a palliative rather than a solution – explicit in storylines that have the *ER* staff tending to multiple gang victims as the latest drug feud escalates, unable to do more than patch the wounds and wait for the next one – has also become harder to find.

But if it is not ending quite at the top of its game, it is certainly quitting well before viewer or production fatigue has set in. The final series promises to reunite much of the old school – including Benton, Greene, Corday, Weaver, Romano and Carter, either in flashback or in 'real' time. 'For an audience that has followed all our characters, it will be a very nice way to say goodbye,' promises Kingston. 'None of it will seem cheesy or contrived. Everything is totally reasonable, totally feasible.'

It should be a fitting end for a well-loved and deservedly admired show that redefined the way we see both medicine and drama. In an ideal world, it would be succeeded by the medical equivalent of *The Wire*; a programme sophisticated enough to examine and wrest compelling drama even – especially – from the biggest questions about the flaws and failures of our most fundamental social systems. As it is, we will be left only with the increasingly risible and formulaic *House* (whose utter infallibility would impress even Kildare) and the unforgivable *Grey's Anatomy*.

7 JANUARY 2009

Curiously boring, yet curiously gripping – aka 'The Bill'

I confess, it has been a long time since I was dahn Sun 'ill, even though me and my mates was all massive fans back in the 80s cos it was filmed rahnd ah manor, wunnit? But then we got used to seeing PC Tony Stamp wandering round Bromley on his days off, we grew up, we moved away and *The Bill* (ITV1) drifted to the periphery of our lives. Last night I popped back to watch the first episode of a multi-part story, Feet of Clay.

I knew from the papers that the last link with the past, Jeff Stewart, had been broken by the sudden axing of his character, Reg Hollis, but nobody told me that the flashing lights in the opening credits had gone, along with those trusty, plodding feet; that the operations room is now full of touch-screen televisions instead of functioning alcoholics, and that – never mind the toddlers in uniforms – even the CID lot have barely reached puberty. Amita 'Milly from *This Life*' Dhiri is no longer a lawyer but a detective constable; Claire 'Her from *Casualty*' Goose is no longer a nurse but the inspector in charge of the toddlers (she is 12); and Andrew '*Cardiac Arrest*' Lancel has also left the medical profession to chase down the villains of south-east London. It is quite discombobulating.

My discomfort, however, is as nothing to Susie Clark's, whose body has been found bagged-up and buried in the local park. Crime scene examiner Eddie (they didn't have those when I was a lad – just DSI Burnside kicking corpses and saying, 'Yeah, son – he's dead. And I bet I know the little berk who did it, an' all') determines that she died 20 years ago at the point of a sharpened screwdriver. Eddie is an extraordinary creation. He shuffles slowly across the screen, occasionally pausing to squeeze out a line of dialogue – 'Weee've id . . . ent . . . i . . . fied the muuuurder weapon' – in a *Godfather* whisper. Is he a genius or a joke? I cannot yet be sure, but I feel that possibly either way lies greatness.

Susie C's case leads us first towards a vengeful ex-best friend ('Conniving little cow . . . I feel bad for slagging her off') and her boyfriend, but he proves they did not have the affair she claimed. Then the park keeper is grilled, but it turns out he and Susie were friends. And even though she was sleeping with her stepbrother in order to rile her stepmum (this worked very well), all her family prove they are in the clear, too. Rather late in the day, DCI Meadows admits that Superintendent Heaton's intermittent bleatings about a murder case he worked on in the 80s with an identical MO might, in fact, be worth listening to, and they all agree that part two next week should be devoted to investigating the erstwhile suspect thereof.

By the end of the hour I am pleased to note that despite the many changes to *The Bill* over the years, its own highly idiosyncratic modus operandi remains unchanged. It is still curiously boring yet curiously gripping at the same time.

23 January 2009